DIGGING FOR LOST AFRICAN GODS

The Record of Five Years
Archaeological Excavation
in North Africa

By

Byron Khun de Prorok, F.R.G.S.

Officier d'Academie. Officier de
l'Instruction publique.

THE NARRATIVE PRESS
TRUE FIRST PERSON ACCOUNTS OF HIGH ADVENTURE

With Notes and Translations by
EDGAR FLETCHER ALLEN

The Narrative Press
P.O. Box 2487, Santa Barbara, California 93120 U.S.A.
Telephone: (805) 884-0160 Web: www.narrativepress.com

ISBN 1-58976-030-1 (Paperback)
ISBN 1-58976-031-X (eBook)

Produced in the United States of America

TABLE OF CONTENTS

INTRODUCTION

From the very beginning there has been a great charm for me in the old stones of dead civilisations, whether they be in the New or the Old World, and exploration always reached a beckoning hand.

Perhaps my friendship with Sir Ernest Shackleton did much to turn my mind in the direction of work similar to the one which ultimately seemed to be the task allotted to me. His personality, and the story of his wanderings, were inspiring, and clothed the skeleton of science with warm and living flesh. Before I had passed the quarter of a century mark, I had been a wanderer among the castles of the Rhine and the Carpathian mountains, the ruins of Mexico and the Everglades of Florida. I had tried my amateur observation in the sites of the prehistoric cave-dwellers of Switzerland, the dolmens and megalithic remains of Cornwall and Brittany. Then followed the new excavations of Rome and Pompeii and, for the last five years, I have been digging into the sand and silt that has covered the ancient cities of Africa.

My first travels were with note-book, palette and brush, but the pick-axe has long supplanted these gentler tools, and now the germ of digging has laid hold on me, I think it will last to the end of my journeying. The fascination and romance of excavation grows; archaeology is not an over-populated field, but there is no end in sight to the work to be done. North Africa, the Sahara, Syria, the mountains of Peru and the jungles of Yucatan hide lost empires.

There are many problems to be solved, and youth is well served by the new field of science. There is room for all the fire and enthusiasm that go with early years.

This book is an attempt to put on record in simple language, these efforts of the last few years, and to tell the tale of the real thrill of excavation undertaken in collaboration with great archaeologists and scientists, of whom I am only a pupil.

My deep gratitude goes out to those who encouraged me in my undertakings; to the venerable Père Delattre, to the Abbé Chabot, both constant companions in the work; to the Abbé Moulard and M. Merlin; to Professor Henry Fairfield Osborn and the late Mitchell Carroll, and to Professor Kelsey and Professor Washington. Without their help I should have failed, and, without their scientific qualifications, excavation would have been impossible. My enthusiasm in the early days would not have been enough, but these great men, who knew their field so minutely, made exploration into archaeology, and as treasure was recovered from the earth, so they put my feet on to the solid foundation of their great learning, and taught me something of the subject.

Concerning all who helped so freely and so generously I would say much, but I am restricted by the number of the pages at my disposal, and if it should seem that there is distinction among the great number of people, may I say that it is not so. Everywhere and by many people, I have been aided, sometimes almost miraculously; always generously, and wholeheartedly. It is they who stood by me, corrected my faults, accepted my enthusiasm and sometimes checked my impetuosity, who have really done the work that has been accomplished on the plains of Africa. I was fortunately the instrument in their hands.

I am glad of this opportunity to express my thanks to one whom I call "the incognito gentleman" who has steadfastly refused to have direct reference made to the great help he has given me, and with him, in gratitude as sincere and appreciative, to couple the names of many others.

When discouragement has faced me, and the work has been threatened, counsel and practical aid has come from Mr. W. F. Kenny, from Robert Lansing, Professor Robinson, Professor

MacLean; I have fallen back on them, knowing their tolerance of my hopes, sure of their sympathy.

The field is so varied. I went from continent to continent, and everywhere there was a friend who both could and would give of his best for the sake of the work.

In Africa, M. Maurice Reygasse opened the whole field of prehistoric man to me, and in that field and others gave me the benefit of his great knowledge. At Utica Count Chabannes la Palice gave the expedition magnificent assistance, record of which will be found in the chapters dealing with the work there.

At Carthage, we were greatly helped by M. Louis Poinssot, in addition to the members of the scientific side of the expedition, who have already been mentioned, and by Mgr. Lemaitre.

In Paris there are many people who have borne with me, and have given me invaluable help and friendship. My mother and Mme. Rouvier have ever been staunch friends and allies, and I should like to pay tribute to the cordial companionship of M. Stephane Gsell, M. Louis Bertrand, and a group who include Mr. Fred Singer, M. Michel Veber, M. Widor, Colonel the Prince de Waldeck, and Baron d'Erlanger.

Crossing the Atlantic once more, I would say another word of thanks to Dr. Maloney, Mr. G. P. Putnam and Mr. Lee Keedick, while over the border in Canada Major Shorey, and the Hon. Charles Murphy have completed the chain of people who surrounded me with friendship.

My thanks are due also, and very greatly, to Mr. C. Streit of the New York *Times* and Mr. Kellerman of Pathé Frères, who did so well for the expedition in regard to news and pictures, which made the people of the United States aware of the work that was being done.

In parting, let my final word be to two companions who are now no longer with us.

To Jules Renault, who died a martyr to the subject, and in the place where I have tried to work, I owe more than I can say. It was he who placed my feet on the first step, who pointed me directly to the great opportunity, who inspired me by his own devotion and by his story of the land. Through his tired eyes there yet gleamed the light of vision and inspiration.

And to my friend of many wanderings and many years, Prince Edgard de Waldeck, my thoughts ever return. No man had a finer companion or associate. What was to be done, he did, and always with a great charm and happiness. Whether it were taking the motion pictures on the very early days, before the world really knew what we were trying to do, or laughingly defying the "curse of Scipio," as we dug deeper, he was always ready, the life of many a diversion, and the soul of good humour. He died, not long after the strange coincidences connected with the curse had happened, in consequence of a motor accident on the Riviera.

Our museum at the hill of Juno is named after these two men; their names deserve to be remembered so long as Carthage, either old or new, remains. Finally, it is gratifying to be able to record that the French Government, in recognition of the value of the services rendered to France and French science, bestowed decorations on the principal scientific collaborators of France, the United States and Canada, who were associated with the five different expeditions.

In addition it is proper to say that Professor Francis W. Kelsey, of the University of Michigan, was elected Corresponding Member of the Académie des Inscriptions et Belles Lettres, the highest scientific recognition France can give.

Chapter 1

CARTHAGE: FINDING JULES RENAULT

Carthage represents the buried site of a once great and flourishing city, whose actual foundation is lost in time, but of which we know at least that it reached a population of nearly a million people. In the earth are relics of all the civilisations that have flowed across the isthmus; from the Berbers, and possibly the Egyptians, down to the Barbary Pirates.

Mingled with their bones are the ashes of lost empires.

There is no more challenging field for archaeologists and explorers than this area of North Africa. It is a land full of romance and tradition, whose soil covers the remains of beauty, wealth and mercilessness. The work of great sculptors lies buried deep, and the bones of little children, sacrificed to Tanit, are as plenteous as straw on the threshing floor.

Archaeology need not be nearly so dry as it sounds. Actually it is full of romantic interest. The men who work in distant fields, uncovering ancient civilisations, are the men who are literally digging up history, filling in vacant dates, establishing known facts and as ruthlessly demolishing other theories. There is little argument against the stones of old civilisations.

Interest is varied, in this Cinderella of the sciences, as varied as the colouring of Africa, where sunset and sunrise are sufficient in themselves to arouse enthusiasm even in weary men who have been delving into the earth all day, and have remembered at evening that there are twenty years, and twenty years again, of work to be done before all the excavations are finished in the complete rediscovery of Carthage.

The re-discovery? It would be better, perhaps, to say the re-discoveries, for in the earth on the peninsula that is almost an island, there are many cities and many civilisations.

To be as simple as possible, when speaking of excavation and exploration, let us dismiss the story of these civilisations for a while with a word.

The silted earth of Carthage contains the relics of a dozen different civilisations, each definitely marked, and capable of identification.

To be in Carthage is to become an explorer. To stay for a while is to be inspired to stay for the remainder of one's life. To sit, as I sat one day, high on the steps of the ruined theatre, looking out to sea, across the narrow stretch of land that intervenes, is to realise that the center and soul of Africa's charm and beauty is there, which Tanit ruled and Scipio cursed.

I sat there, staring over the broken stage of the theatre, trying, as I always do, to reconstruct the scene as well as the buildings, wondering what manner of men trod the floor to entertain the millionaires of Carthage, wondering if the urge of natural beauty had interrupted their drama as repeatedly as it interrupted my thoughts.

It was towards evening. I carried under my arm Audollent's *Carthage Romaine,* a book that did much to send me on my way to Africa, but reading came hard. Over the sky spread colour in all shades from faintest lavender to richest purple. The sky and sea threw colour to each other. They were one, welded together in glory that is still too magnificent for description. Over all the land spread a quivering rose-tinted glow that was a thing in itself. It was detached, much as a gauze curtain might be, used on any stage other than the one that stretched before me. The stones took on life, became molten as the light reached round, and almost into them.

I sat there much longer than I realised. In the first place I was a little tired. It had been a day of exploration along Cap Gamart, and rest was welcome.

Across the inner curve of the Gulf of Tunis, Bou-Kornein reared his sacred head to the sunset, catching the changing lights, and adding them to the opalescent wealth of the waters of the gulf.

Almost daily there is the same magnificence of the sky, a grandeur that grows neither stale nor familiar, but that one evening has its own hold on my memory, not untouched by tragedy and adventure, a hold that crystallises at least for me the ultimate romance and value of the work of exploration and the restoration of lost civilisations.

Across the bay, the fishing fleets in regular order and unhurried, were returning to port, and it was not a difficult stretch of the imagination to believe that they were the Vandal fleet of Genseric returning from Rome. Sixteen centuries can fade as quickly as the sunset in Carthage, and the fishing boats were little different, either in size or form, from the terrors of the seas that sailed into Carthage about 300 A.D.

Byron, who has interpreted the spirit of the Mediterranean better than anyone else, caught the meaning of such an hour:

Ave Maria! Blessed be the hour
The Time, the clime, the spot, where I so oft
Have felt that moment in its fullest power
Sink o'er the earth so beautiful and soft
While swung the deep bell in the distant tower
Or the faint dying day-hymn stole aloft
And not a breath crept through the rosy air,
And yet the olive leaves seem'd stirred with prayer.

That hour is specially impressive when one sits alone in a massive ruin of the city of the dead, surrounded by the wondrous basilicas of the days of Augustine and Cyprian, now partially restored.

Opposite where I sat is Cardinal Lavigerie's great cathedral to Saint Louis, whose bells throbbed without effort through the air. Everything conspired to keep me there. Certainly I had no desire

to move, until my eyes were suddenly focussed, and out of rev-
erie I came to attention. A wisp of smoke was rising from a mass
of ruins on the opposite hill.

"Some Arab," I thought, "making his home in an old cistern,"
as they often do.

It refused to be dismissed so easily. The smoke perplexed me,
and I was ultimately compelled to follow it. I climbed down the
ruined steps, and made my way across, to examine the cave of
the fire.

There, a strange spectacle greeted me. An old Roman cistern
had been fitted out as a living room. It was poorly furnished, and
not particularly comfortable. It is, by the way, now the museum
of our expedition, where many people hear the story of the work
and find what literature they need.

An oil lamp gave a slender light, which fell on to a bearded
old man who lay on a camp-bed, reading. Around the walls were
packing cases which served as shelves to carry ancient books
and maps. An Arab servant stood by, arranging pot sherds on a
sheet of paste-board near the old man's bed.

Obviously the man was ill. The least practised eye could read
the pallor on his face, while the fitful light emphasised the trans-
parency of his skin. A light that was certainly not earthly shone
through him. Death, I judged, could not be far away, yet even in
the face of the tragedy of it all, the weird significance of the
scene spoke more than aught else of the inexorable power of the
lure of Carthage. These two silent men, one very close to the
great silence, were working away in a transformed Roman cistern, cataloguing relics of the dead city.

The cave was only partly restored. Pick-axes and trolley rails
were piled around the walls, and water was oozing through,
trickling down behind the sick man's bed.

Perhaps I was diffident, or probably it was the strangeness of
the scene, for it was a moment before I could address the man
who had made his home in a ruin of Carthage.

"You are welcome to my Roman cistern," he said, with a
faint smile. "Visitors are rare here."

The Arab brought me a chair, and I sat by the bed of the dying man. There was no question about his condition. His eyes burned with fever, and his cheeks were pale and hollow. He had a smile for me, however, and noticed the book I had laid down.

"You must be interested in these old stones," he said, "if you are wading through those eight hundred pages."

Then he was silent a while. A light other than fever burned in his eyes.

"For fifteen years," he continued, "I have been digging in this land."

It seemed to me that he had not flourished greatly in those fifteen years.

"You are an archaeologist?" I ventured.

"Yes," he replied. "Once an operatic star, but now I am writing a little about the great field of Carthaginian history and archaeology. I have published several books...assisted by the French Government!"

For hours we talked of the excavations, and that night I fell asleep wondering at the strange encounter.

Early the next morning, I was back again at the ruin, to hear the continuation of the experiences of my new friend.

I stayed by the sick man for days, and we resolved, when he should be better, to join forces in attempting to excavate Carthage. Unfortunately he did not realise how dangerous was his condition, and all my efforts failed to persuade him to leave the unhealthy cistern. A strange, almost fanatical devotion possessed him.

"You have put new life into me," he said, in a burst of enthusiasm. "We shall do great things together."

His knowledge of Carthage was amazing, and coupled with the specialised knowledge of the particular spot, was his long experience of North African exploration. How great a man this was, whom I had discovered living under impossible conditions for the sake of the work to which he had devoted himself, most people will know when I say that that is how I discovered Jules

Renault, who truly laid the foundations of much of the success that has attended later efforts in this field.

Jules Renault had few, and poor, helpers. He dreamed, as we all did, of a skilled body of men, excavating under expert direction. That dream was realised, but not in his lifetime.

During the few weeks I spent with him of that winter, he influenced me to take up the work of excavation, and, being able to pull him round in health a little, we began with his home in the ruins.

Renault was in receipt of a small grant from the "Services des Antiquités," which barely met his expenses. I soon learned that the man was starving himself, was martyring himself in the cause of Archaeology. So, together, we decided that I should return to France and try to raise funds for the excavation of Carthage, and, with the assistance of the Père Delattre, try to locate the Punic (or Phoenician) city.

It was not to be. Just before I was due to leave, my companion and friend had a severe relapse. The damp chill of his habitation crept into his starved body. The hand of death could not long be stayed. He was brought to realise his extremity, and almost he was persuaded to let me take him to more comfortable surroundings, and to proper care. When I thought he was consenting, he turned to me with the smile that was at times heartbreaking, so wan and yet so courageous.

"It's no good," he said. "The 'Curse of Scipio' has got me. I am going to follow Borgia, Falbe and the others who have tried to explore these haunted ruins, and died in the attempt."

Often previously, in a half-joking way, he had told me of old Scipio's curse, but I was to learn later, much to my sorrow, that this local superstition certainly claimed strange coincidences in my experience in Carthage.

When at last I had to leave for home, I could not help feeling that I should see Jules Renault no more on earth.

"Goodbye, and good luck," he said. "You have a great task before you, and perhaps I shall recover enough to help you again when you get back. There are great treasures at Carthage yet to be uncovered. Courage, and patience, and you will make these old stones speak again."

His harsh cough echoed in the damp vault, and his camp bed rattled. It cut deeply into me to leave him there – I had learned to admire him so greatly, but I had arranged for him to be moved in a few days, despite his protests. My fear was that the removal had been too long delayed.

The sun was sinking as I left him. It was just such another spectacle as when I had first seen the smoke from his hermitage climbing up to the purple skies, the smoke that had caught my attention, and had introduced me to a friend, and also to a work that needed to be done.

My last glimpse of him was through a ruined vault. His drawing materials were in his hand, but his head had fallen forward in sheer exhaustion, following the effort of saying farewell. He was asleep.

Kilari, the old Arab, was tending the fire in the garden, cooking the evening meal.

As I looked back on the ruin, I saw the thin trail of smoke rising again above the grey stones, dimly visible against the twilight sky. The bells of the Cathedral were tolling, but at that moment they seemed full of foreboding.

A week later, I heard that Jules Renault had died. He had died in harness, among his books and relics, a true martyr to science if ever there was one.

Chapter 2

CARTHAGE: THE FIELD TO BE EXPLORED

With the passing of Jules Renault I had lost a friend, but his enthusiasm remained with me. Life, more or less, is like that. An avenue opens, which we hope to tread in company. The companion is taken away, but the avenue remains. What I hoped to do *with* Renault, had to be done, for his sake, and for the sake of the great mine of hidden civilisation that is Carthage to-day. Of the certainty of the work, no doubt remained. The germ that held Renault had attacked me, just as violently. Until the excavations were finished, or I was finished, Carthage was my master.

Therefore, since it is of but little service for one man to dig alone, it was essential that a strong organisation, properly financed, should be gathered together, an organisation which should have the benefit of the best brains in the various schools of learning which Archaeology covers.

No one man can contain all the information. Not even Leibniz could have comprehended all the sciences, the intricacies of all the languages and civilisations that are to be met in the richest natural museum on the face of the earth.

That is exactly how to describe Carthage. It is a natural museum, uncharted and uncatalogued. Its treasures are so thick in the earth that not even a spadeful of dust can be thrown away without danger of losing some priceless fragment that may open up a new field of investigation, resolve doubts, or fill in blanks in the historical sequence of man's journeys on the earth.

In Carthage, if it rains (and it can rain), it is quite probable that the flood will wash off the accumulation of centuries from a wonderful mosaic or tiled floor, right in the middle of the street. It has happened before to-day, and it will happen again.

After *any* rain you may walk across the earth and find handfuls of blobs of iridescent glass, thousands of years old, relics of the ancient glass factories. They glisten and gleam on the top of the soil, and the Arabs have called them the "tears of Carthage."

Their legend-loving minds have woven these bits of glass into romance. To them they are nothing less than the tears of the Carthaginians, crystallised and preserved; tears that were shed over the ruin of the wonderful city, now shining again at the feet of prosaic men who are trying to reconstruct the glory that was Carthage.

The earth of the isthmus is so rich that one is driven to haste, ordered haste, always feeling the urge of some stupendous discovery close at hand. Who knows?

It is enough for the seeker after thrills to remember that the Vandals' loot from the pillage of Rome, was carried to Carthage, was buried there, and has never yet been discovered.

Civilisation in those days was a procession of looters, and Carthage received and paid the tribute common to all wealthy centers. Captain Kidd and all the famous pirates who roamed the seas, were tyros, effete, inartistic, and ineffectual in comparison.

Four hundred Vandal ships sailed back to Carthage from the sack of Rome.

Whether that treasure lies at our feet out there or not, treasure even more important is being discovered day by day. Literally, one cannot kick the wall of a shallow pit without bringing a "museum piece" to light. And that piece may belong to any one of a dozen civilisations.

It may, most fascinating of all, to me, belong to the Phoenicians, or it may belong to the early Christian time, or to the Vandals, or even to the ninth crusade. It may carry a cuneiform inscription, or it may be a lamp inscribed with the maker's name, and his pleading advertisement.

They advertised in the Roman period. We discovered a lamp which carries, so far as I know, the earliest recorded advertisement. Translated it reads:

PLEASE BUY OUR LAMPS, ONLY ONE CENT
THEY ARE THE BEST

and it carried the maker's name and address.

Much of the history of the isthmus could, indeed, be written from the lamps. In the museum on the spot, with a little explanation here and there, the casual visitor can get a very sound understanding of the progress of affairs. There are the crude lamps of the early Phoenicians, which later were greatly improved, and there are the lamps of all those who succeeded them, gradually becoming more notable for their workmanship.

In the silted earth of the hollows, we estimate that one yard represents one hundred years. We can dig through the various strata, and go from one period to another, and each period demands specialised knowledge.

Even the "unskilled" departments of excavation are intricate.

To recover the specimens which give the archaeologist the material for his reconstruction of the habits, homes, and public life of the period, modern mechanical science in all its branches has to be invoked. Any department of the practical sciences that contributes to the welfare of a modern city is equally necessary for the restoration of the ancient.

This had been borne in upon me by the sight of Jules Renault trying to pierce the secrets single-handed. If the work were going to be done at all, it needed to be done systematically, and without hindrance.

To do it well needed money, and to obtain money, public interest had first to be aroused. That I took to be my immediate task in the whole scheme.

Yet so little was known about Carthage. Père Delattre had himself been struggling to restore the ruins of the early Christian period, and had done much more, single-handed, than any man might reasonably have been called upon to do, especially when it is known that Père Delattre is a priest, living in the monastery of the White Fathers, and has no outside funds to draw upon.

It is true, of course, that the Institut des Antiquités makes Père Delattre a grant of 1,500 francs a year for his work, to be expended in excavation. Putting that into terms that can really be understood, the money at his disposal amounts to twenty cents a day. But somehow the miracles have happened. The Basilica of St. Cyprian, Damous El-Karita, and the famous "Victory," which was re-assembled from more than 250 fragments, were saved to posterity, among thousands of other important discoveries, by the savant who has a dollar a week grant for the purpose.

Money buys services in geometric proportion in Africa. You can get so far with a hundred dollars: but a thousand dollars represents vastly more than ten times the value of the hundred, in work accomplished. And I believed that, if the world could know more about Carthage and its possibilities, interest and funds would be forthcoming.

My problem was how to make it known, and what to make known. Just to say "Carthage" meant so much that it would mean nothing. Carthage looks like earth. It is principally remembered for its destruction. . . ."Delenda est Carthago," but that was only one Carthage.

Carthage is not earth. It is human earth. To appropriate the famous *bon mot* of a gruff English politician, who was discussing the river Thames with a visitor from another country who knew of bigger rivers, is to sum up the situation. As the Labour Member of Parliament said, "The Thames isn't water, it's liquid 'istory." Just so, every inch deep is solid history on the isthmus.

The date of the first foundation of Carthage is lost. History and legend combine to give an approximate date of the middle of the ninth century B.C. But as yet there is no certainty. Our present work may ultimately decide that point, as well as many others.

Legend and poetry have credited Queen Dido with the foundation of the city. It can do little harm, making due reservations, to leave it at that for the moment.

Certain it is that the city rapidly assumed considerable importance in the economy of the civilised world. Historians rank it fourth. The first settlement on the peninsula of Carthage actually known is Cambe, which probably served as a Phoenician trading station centuries before the arrival of Queen Dido.

Thirty miles north of Carthage is Utica, which, by general consent is conceded to have been founded, about 1200 B.C. by the Phoenicians, who, we know, were building trading stations along all the coasts of the Mediterranean.

To Dido, however, romance brings us again. By virtue of the eternal epic, Virgil has kept the story of the love-sick Queen and Aeneas, fresh. Its charm has persisted for enough centuries to establish Carthage in our imagination, if not the date of its foundation in our accredited histories. And, rightly or wrongly, the story of the land enclosed by the bull's hide, will persist as long as Carthage, even Carthage restored.

Utica was the older settlement, and the Tyrian colonists named the trading station "Kart-Hadach," the *New City*. The Punic name has remained through its many mutations.

As a trading station, Carthage prospered. Its people were merchant adventurers, with the keen commercial sense peculiar to their semitic origin. Not warlike for the sake of warfare, economic reasons alone compelled the Carthaginians to expand their territory. They subjugated first the Berbers, of the interior, who intermingled with their conquerors, and formed the people called the Libyo-phoenicians. In approximately two hundred years from its foundation, the people of Carthage governed Africa from the Pillars of Hercules to Hieropolis.

So much in two hundred years! There are twenty-five hundred years to dig out! And each foot of earth reveals how similar the old Carthaginians were to modern commercial nations. They remind me very much of the English, with a strong dash of North America. Carthage, like England, was only a dot on the

world map, but somehow managed to rule the destinies of mankind for a long time, and she did it in much the same way that
has characterised what might be called the "English period". . .
by colonisation, ships and trade. Her citizens were shop-keepers,
meek in their ways, and, true to the promise, the meek inherited
the earth! – until the Prussians of antiquity came along with the
same need of expansion, and the Romans smote Phoenicia in
envy!

Undoubtedly the Carthaginians had the prototype of Greeley,
and their sons were advised to "Go West, young man!" At least
we can discover that they traded with the Canaries, the West
Coast of Africa, the coasts of England, and probably the Baltic,
too.

Carthage was in turn the London and the New York of the
old world, and, for the sake of understanding, imagine what discoveries future archaeologists might make if either London or
New York had been subjected to successive holocausts and
repeated destruction, each period being safely stowed away
under a little earth while the new civilisation reared itself
proudly, and forgetfully, on the ruins of the old.

Carthage was fabulously rich, the richest city of the old
world. Income tax returns, unfortunately, were not apparently
published, but Flaubert gives what has proven to be a historically accurate description of the parade of wealth among the
Carthaginians in his *Salammbo*. Such a display would discount
Fifth Avenue, or even Hollywood's efforts to show how wealthy
wealth should be.

Little evidence has yet come to light concerning the lot of the
poorer classes in Carthage. There can be shrewd guesses, however. The Magons, Barcas and Hannos of Carthage (people
whose identity is established by inscriptions found recently),
lived at the expense of many a tormented slave, working to
death under lash and torture in the mines of Spain and Numidia.

I said the Carthaginians were not fond of war for war's sake,
but they were clever enough to make a business of war, and to
deal with it as they dealt with most other things. They hired pro-

fessional fighters to carry on their campaigns while they continued to amass the spoils of trade. Mercenaries, among whom
were the Numidian horse and the Balearic slingers, made
Carthage feared and famous. The outer world hated the
Carthaginians, and distrusted them. The creed of a rogue was
"fides Punica"; Punic faith, and their contracts too, were often
"scraps of paper."

Their cruelty was as thoroughgoing as their commerce. For
three years, we unearthed an average of 2,000 human sacrifices
a year in the Temple of Tanit.

The tombs at Carthage and Utica demonstrate their wealth,
their cunning and adroitness, their brains and their vanity, and
the Temple of Tanit, their cruelty and vice. The ruined cities of
the Mediterranean tell of the vastness of their commercial enterprise and business capabilities, and, fortunately, on the right side
of the balance sheet this time, we know that Carthage produced
two of the greatest heroes of all time, Hannibal and Hamilcar.

Yet these people invented business, as it is understood to-
day. It is now beyond doubt that they were the first real explorers, the first to organise overseas trade, and they were the first
bankers. They invented contracts and bills of exchange. Probably they had a stock market, or clearing house! Carthage issued
leather money of representative value, which was currency
through her dependencies, anticipating modern economists in
the matter of paper money.

The shipbuilding firms of Utica made contracts covering
their work. Probably before excavation goes much further; some
other trade convenience, which appears to us of extremely modern origin, will prove to have been in vogue among the Phoenicians.

How long they have had a coinage, I do not know. Coins
have been found buried with the dead, but, strangely enough (or
not so strangely, whichever point of view one takes), the coins
are always out of date. It really seems as though the Carthaginians hated to lose good money, and it is held on quite tenable
grounds that the reason we discover this out-of-date coinage in

the tombs is that the friends of the family took away the currency and put in its place valueless tokens. This idea may be heresy, originating with the envious Romans, who joked at the Carthaginians, as we do, more pleasantly, with the Scots.

Much of our historical information concerning the Carthaginians comes through the Romans, and their point of view was undoubtedly distorted and coloured by prejudice. Anti-Hannibal propaganda could not have been bettered (or worsened) by the most vituperative of the scaremonger press.

Most schoolboys remember the story of the great general in exile, who wanted to escape with his treasure, and did it by a trick, filling his treasure jars with lead, and sticking a layer of cold coins on the top, which he left behind!. . .That is a Roman joke.

To begin to talk about Carthage is to jump ahead. There is always a link between one layer and the next, but there it is; the dust of Carthage is so thick with history that one takes a handful, and it is mixed.

After such a digression, let us pick up the thread again.

Boundary friction...how familiar it sounds...from Africa!...brought Carthage into a struggle with Greece in the sixth century B.C. It arose between the two settlements at Cyrene, and it came to real issue at a time fortunate for Carthage. Nebuchadnezzar had destroyed Tyre, which gave Carthage a fairly free, and little-disputed, command of the Mediterranean. In 550 B.C. the Carthaginian troops under Malchus invaded Sicily, and conquered most of it, driving out the Greeks.

But Malchus had not been entirely successful, which displeased his government, and he was recalled. Being the son of his time, he, in revenge, laid siege to Carthage itself, and in this attempt rather bettered his percentage, for he became master of the city.

The quickest and most popular road to power in that period was assassination. Malchus suffered, and was gathered to his fathers. He was put to death by his own party, and succeeded by Mago, the son of Hanno, who later completed Malchus' efforts, and added Sardinia and the Balearic Islands to the territory of the Carthaginians, forcing commercial treaties with the Greeks of Sicily and Italy.

Shortly thereafter, by agreement, Rome and Carthage created a buffer state of Sicily. In 509 B.C. in the time of Polybius, Italy was assigned to the Romans, and the African waters were allotted to Carthage. Sicily was neutral ground.

The Greeks, however, brought no lasting gifts to the Carthaginians! In 480 B.C. was fought the battle of Himera, and it was a sorry day for Carthage, whose general was Hamilcar, grandson of Mago. Report says that 150,000 Carthaginians were captured. And then followed a period of peace. War ceased for seventy years, but when it broke out again, between the same peoples, the mighty cities of Selinnus, Himera, and Arigentum, with their magnificent temples and innumerable works of art were destroyed.

All this, of course, makes work for the archaeologists. Diodorus says that the marks of the Carthaginian crowbars could be discerned on the gigantic columns of the Temple of Selinnus columns it was believed that only an earthquake could shake. But the Carthaginians were closely akin to the earthquake!

For revenge, the Greeks rallied under the tyrant Dionysius, and the Carthaginian colonists in Sicily were massacred. War succeeded war, with success now on one side, now on the other. Sicily, the cockpit of the ancient world, soaked in blood, saw Hamilcar, Timoleon and Agathocles.

Agathocles penetrated Africa, and Carthage trembled, for though he was not finally successful, he showed the way for a greater and more ruthless warrior, whose people were not slow to follow in the footsteps of the unsuccessful Greeks, this time to succeed, where Agathocles had failed.

Pyrrhus, the last Greek hero to quit the arena, with his last breath cried, half in shame and half in envy "How fair a battlefield we leave for the Romans and the Carthaginians."

War with Rome commenced in 268 B.C. and continued for more than a quarter of a century, generally in favour of the Carthaginians.

During the second Punic War, Hamilcar, accompanied by his nine-year-old son, Hannibal (who had already sworn eternal hatred to the Romans), having first subdued the rebellious tribes along the African coast, crossed to Spain. After many victories he founded Carthagena, which became the emporium of Carthage in Spain. He died gloriously in one of the local battles, and was succeeded by his son-in-law, Hasdrubal, who was governor of Spain for nine years, but was ultimately murdered by a Gallic slave.

Hannibal was leading the army at twenty-four years of age, having already given proof of his prowess. He re-organised and strengthened his armies in Africa and in Spain, and struck at the heart of the power of the Romans. His armies were small, comparatively, not many more than a hundred thousand in all, of whom ninety thousand were infantry, and twelve thousand cavalry. He had, in addition, some forty elephants. But he crossed the Pyrenees, the Rhone and the Alps, and in face of tremendous difficulties, reached the plains of Italy, with half his army in commission, opposed by Roman forces that outnumbered him four to one. His blows, and his victories, were swift. The Romans were wiped out at the battles of Cannae, Allia and Lake Trasimene.

But while Hannibal was fighting in Italy, Scipio had crossed to Africa, and laid siege to Utica, annihilating the forces of Hasdrubal and Syphax, near Testour.

Then Hannibal was recalled, after sixteen years of the most brilliant fighting in history. He landed at Hadrumetum (Sousse) in 203 B.C. and was defeated at the great battle of Zama. The Romans forced their terms on Carthage, which meant ceding Spain, Sicily, and the islands of the Mediterranean. The great Empire was at an end.

The Empire was at an end, but the Carthaginians were not, – neither was their city. Foreign affairs had gone against them, but trade still remained, trade and wealth sufficient to withstand even the strain of Roman extortion. Hannibal confined his attention to local reform, to the establishment of internal peace, law and order. Agriculture was revived, and finances were reorganised.

Mindful of his vow, Hannibal maintained his hatred of the Romans to the end. When things had progressed to a degree at home, he sought foreign alliances, of which the Romans heard, and Hannibal died by his own hand.

For fifty years there was peace, but Cato the elder instigated a campaign of hatred, whose final policy was the utter extermination of Carthage. The campaign culminated in 146 B.C. when the siege of the city, planned and executed by Scipio Æmilianus, wore down the heroic defence, and Carthage fell.

Carthage was wiped out. With deliberate cunning the Romans fired the city. It burned for sixteen days, and the buildings, temples and palaces of a great city and a great civilisation, were left in ruin, soon to be covered and lost.

There are men working among the ruins to-day, hoping that some of the priceless antiquities may still remain.

It would be a miracle, almost, if our pick axes, digging up history, could hit on the lost library of Carthage!

We know, at least, that the Roman Senate gave the libraries to their Numidian allies after the capture of the city in 146 B.C., and a hundred years later Sallust saw the priceless books in the hands of King Hiempsal. He adds, rather dubiously, "I say nothing about Carthage, for I think it better to say nothing about her than to say too little."

But how invaluable even that little would have been to us diggers.

One work escaped, witness in itself to the magnitude and scope of the great library. It was Mago's treatise in twenty-eight volumes, on Agriculture. Mago was a Carthaginian Shofete, or Judge, and in these twenty-eight volumes laid the actual foundation of husbandry as a science. They were translated, by Cassius

Dionysius of Utica, into Greek, and later by command of the Roman Senate into Latin by D. Silanus. *(Columella,* i. 1.13.)

The world will be richer by much more than the mass of the Vandals' loot, if we can discover more of the commercial treatises of Carthage. Science – if ever it can be excited – would find sufficient excitement for a generation if only. . .If only! And that is the urge behind archaeology; that is the germ which reached me through Jules Renault, through Père Delattre. To tell something of the known facts of Carthage, to show what had been done, to fire the imagination of the people who could do much more with the hint of all the buried records that would add to our knowledge, and perhaps to the charm of life.

Perhaps we shall find the lost literature of this great people, some day, in the ruins of the different capitals of the Numidian kings, at Cirta, Bulla-Regia, or Khamissa. There are sacred books buried in the temple of Tanit, at Carthage.

One famous example of the literary possibilities of the lost library is the Periplus of Scylax, the world's first great history of exploration. It deals with an expedition led by Hanno with a two-fold object – exploration and colonisation. Thirty thousand settlers were deposited on the way west, to start colonies.

Hanno was a Carthaginian admiral, and in himself an example to those naval officers whose personal bent has been adventurous exploration. He was the Columbus of Carthage.

The fleet at his disposal on his venture, comprised sixty vessels of fifty oars each, and his voyage was long and significant. The records of his expedition were hung at the temple of Melkart at Carthage, as a thank-offering.

A Greek "reporter," a Herodotus of the day, took down an account of the proceedings, and his report has become world famous. From him we know that Hanno passed the Pillars of Hercules (Gibraltar) and reached the isle of Cerne, 10 degrees north of the Equator. This may be the site of Arquin, since the crews calculated that the Pillars of Hercules represented the half-way line of their journey from Carthage.

Here, Hanno impressed interpreters, and passed the Senegal river – full of crocodiles and hippopotami. For the first time they saw tropical negroes, and heard them playing at night with cymbals and drums, and shouting and singing, much as they do today. It is within the bounds of possibility that even "jazz" was a Punic discovery, twenty-five centuries ago!

The fleet continued, past the volcano of the Cameroons to the land of "hair covered men." It was not an anthropological expedition that discovered the "men" that were first called "gorillas" by the Carthaginians.

Like Will Beebe, they captured a few specimens, and their skins ultimately were placed on exhibition in their home town.

The word "gorilla" was not heard again for many centuries, until Stanley and Livingstone explored darkest Africa afresh. Still, one wonders what feelings of alarm and amazement filled the "publisher" of the Periplus in Carthage when he was presented with a gorilla as an exhibit. . .if publishers in Carthage were given to such window display! Probably they were, being acute business men, and Carthaginians!

Not a fraction of the significance of this Punic civilisation is comprehended by the world. Historians are possessed of certain facts. The records are tucked away in erudite volumes, lying high and dry, and probably dusty, on library shelves. But, even America owes a considerable debt to the Carthaginians. How considerable the debt is, only America can judge, for it was Himilco, the Carthaginian, who discovered Ireland. One would be quite safe, I imagine, in saying that very few Irishmen know that even in the earliest Carthaginian days, the land of Ire was called the "Holy Isle, with abundant *emerald* pastures, and covered with eternal fogs." (See *Ora Marit*, of Festus Aviennus.)

There is no limit to the fascination of Carthage, but we shall meet many of these people again, possibly more intimately, as the story of the excavations is told in greater detail. These, and many others who have carved for themselves a lasting significance, for each period is rich in lore and value.

I have dealt with the Punic era perhaps more at length than is fair to subsequent times, but on the whole it has been possible from exterior sources to gain some general knowledge of the people who came after the Phoenicians. Of the people, and the habits, of the early dwellers on the isthmus, knowledge is not so widely disseminated.

For example, it is not generally known that the Carthaginians invented the "dumb" trade. They told Herodotus of a land called Lybia, where the natives came down from the forests and left gold dust on the shore, for which the Carthaginians exchanged merchandise. The exchange was made in the absence of both parties, and only decided when each side was satisfied with the bargain. One can venture a guess, however, that the civilised Carthaginians held the scales. If the merchants grew tired of the dilatoriness of the Lybians, they simply sailed away, without trading, so to teach the salutary lesson, and since the merchandise was necessary to the people of the forests, the lesson was readily learned. The last word is usually with the higher civilisation.

Some laws of the Carthaginians bore a close resemblance to laws we know. In particular – prohibition. All signs point to the fact that the people of Carthage were inclined to heavy drinking. They were famous for their wine, and even exported it to Rome. From the vast number of amphores and vases discovered at Carthage, Utica, and under the sea at Djerba, it is evident that wine occupied a prominent place both in trade and in the social life of the city. However, the debated amendment was anticipated by a Punic Volstead during a war that antedated the recent world conflict by many centuries. . .(Ref. Arist. Econ., i. 5.)

In the garden of the Monastery of the White Fathers now at Carthage, there is an inscription at the base of a restored monument, dedicated to "the marvellous wine merchants, and the splendid and pure quality of the wine, from the grateful city of Carthage."

So excavation leads us to the past, to tell of people, who centuries ago, were very much of the same nature as we are ourselves, and lived a life not so very different. They were without the modern complications of aerial navigation and wireless telegraphy, but they had their own problems, and life was quite intense enough. In some ways, perhaps, I should have preferred the joys and emotions of Carthage to those of to-day. They were not so crowded as to lose their power, and when they were experienced! But that is imagination after all.

That great civilisation was destroyed, deliberately and of set purpose, destroyed through envy and malice, by the Romans, who, in 116 B.C. attempted to establish a colony there. The effort was still born. Julius Caesar, after his magnificent campaign in Africa, which ended in the defeat of Cato, Varus and Juba, attempted another revival in 46 B.C.

The inception of the scheme again touches a modern note. Rome had its unemployment problem, and it is said that Caesar, dreaming in his camp among the ruins, had a vision of the difficulties at Rome, and like modern statesmen in countries whose industries cannot absorb all the working classes, thought to alleviate the misery by migration. He determined to make Carthage anew, with Roman colonists. This time the venture succeeded. In an incredibly short time, Carthage became the second city of the Roman Empire, and even excelled the glories of the earlier Phoenician city.

Christianity came at the end of the second century, and, in the fourth century, historians mention no less than 580 adherents to the faith. This is another terrible chapter, whose full significance is only slowly appearing. The persecution of Christians in Africa was more merciless than the persecution in Italy. The amphitheatre at Carthage saw the tortured martyrdoms of those noble women St. Perpetua and St. Felicitas. Cyprian, Bishop of Carthage was beheaded, and at Cirta, Lambessa and Utica, hundreds of Christians were burned to death in furnaces.

Dissension and schism added to the troubles of the church. It was at Carthage that the schism of the Donatists arose, as a result of the debate between the Bishops of Numidia and Carthage. The Donatists met their final defeat in the vast baths of Gargilius, which we believe are now being excavated. Here St. Augustine, Bishop of Hippo, at the councils of 311 A.D. by his wonderful oratory and erudition, resolved the heresy.

But schism in defeat was dangerous still. The Donatists, though defeated, persisted, and their antagonism stretched over many years. Ideas last longer than the men who give them birth. In 438 A.D. the fanatical Donatists allied themselves with the forces of Genseric, king of the Vandals, who had been treasonably invited by Boniface, governor of Africa, to invade the country.

The provinces were conquered. Cities and monuments were destroyed, and Carthage was occupied. Genseric died in 477 A.D. and was succeeded by his son Huneric, who inaugurated the most terrible persecutions history knows.

Thereafter the vicissitudes are too numerous to be dealt with in detail, in the compass of this short introduction. The Vandals prospered a little while, and "like snow upon the desert's dusty face" were gone, but not before they had ravaged Rome, and brought the booty back to Carthage in four hundred vessels. Amongst the treasure were the spoils carried to Rome from Jerusalem. History records that the seven-branched candelabra and the gold vessels of the Temple were last seen at Carthage.

Local revolts succeeded, one after another. There were periods when the Berbers were supreme.

St. Louis of France commenced his ill-fated Ninth Crusade and died at Carthage.

There was a Spanish Period, a Turkish Period, marked by one of the most remarkable naval actions in English history, when, in April, 1655, the entire pirate fleet of the Bey of Tunis, was destroyed by Admiral Blake.

And, finally, there is the Husseinist period, when French interests became uppermost. Peace exists now in a land that has seen more bloodshed and horror than almost any other part of the earth. But, the glory has gone out. Civilisations that once were mighty and proud, lie in the dust.

That is what I began to say, that is the thought behind the sketch of the principal movements of the recorded history of Carthage. The germ of enthusiasm is virulent. On the peninsula now are men working almost unceasingly, striving to compel the crowded earth to surrender its secrets, to release the wonders that have been hidden away.

The land is so full of possibility. The actuality of its treasures, scientifically and intrinsically priceless, is unquestionably established.

Jules Renault would have carried on with us, but he died. His enthusiasm still persists. It persists in all of us who have Carthage at heart. On me, as spokesman for the living and the dead, devolved the task of bringing the urgency home to people, to whom a few short years ago, Carthage was only a name. Happily, to many thousands of people whom I have met, and to whom I have spoken, Carthage is now more than a name. It is a challenge, and a heritage.

Chapter 3

ORGANISING EXPEDITIONS
– AND OTHERS

The fact that I felt the tremendous importance of continuing the excavations, and of preserving for posterity the things that have been lost for so many centuries, did not immediately impress other people. My adventures were many, and varied.

Enthusiasm has at least added to my experience, both of life and people.

However, subsequent to that preliminary trip to Carthage in 1920, I returned, as arranged, to France, to begin another kind of excavation! It was necessary for me to excavate a few of the treasures of the present, to be used for the purpose of excavating the treasures of the past.

I contrived a small preliminary committee, which met at my Paris home. Fortunately we were able to obtain the help and enthusiasm of M. Louis Bertrand, the great French writer on matters concerning Africa, and he presided at the first meeting. M. Stephane Gsell, the African historian, gave us his help too, and among others were Mr. Fred Singer and Mr. Stoever, who both accompanied me later to Africa.

The first plan of attack was decided. With a small party we sailed for Africa. We were met at Carthage by Père Delattre and Dr. Carton, and proceeded to call upon the Resident-General, Lucien Saint, who was instantly enthusiastic. The proposal to begin a campaign for the preservation and excavation of Carthage appealed to his imagination.

From the Resident-General we went to Mr. L. Poinssot, Director des Services des Antiquités, and there also we found an encouraging welcome, reinforced by the promise of whole-hearted collaboration and advice.

The official permit to begin work had already been prepared, and was delivered to us on March 12th, 1921.

It was a great moment for me, for in concrete form it meant the fulfillment of my promise to my dead friend, Renault.

Knowing that this was only the beginning, however, we did things that perhaps seemed foolish to other people, but they proved their worth. All the time we had in mind the need for an ever-increasing popular support, a public interest ever widening, reaching to those who hitherto had been content to leave the whole labour of excavation and archaeology to the scientists. We wanted to show that excavation has its importance for the man in the street, that the work belongs to nations, not to a few selected individuals from one or two academic groups.

We took films of what we were doing. It was the first time that archaeological research had been filmed, and the idea did not meet with very great favour at first. Since then, however, the value of the step has been recognised, and it is a common prac-tise in many universities to-day, to use films for instruction. Our photographer was the young Prince Edgard de Waldeck, who had spent a fortnight of intensive training in Paris, preparatory to this task.

Photography helped us on the spot, eventually. We discov-ered many things about the motion picture camera, more than its manufacturers expected.

The camera was our private detective, and it was the means of instilling a greater aptitude for work into the Arabs, who did much of our digging.

Of course, like all groups who are excavating not too far from the tourist routes, we had our casual visitors, and souvenirs were much in demand.

It was impossible to supply the demand, or to comply with every request for trophies, but as far as we could, we tried to make it interesting for the visitors. We arranged such exhibits as were possible, and allowed the tourists to wander around and see what they could. For the most part they were unattended, but all the time the camera man was turning away at the handle, and achieving unexpected results. When we came to develop the films, we had a very moving picture of the acquisitive tendencies of amateur archaeologists! They had been caught in the act.

The pictures showed them glancing carefully around, to see if anyone watched. Reassurance spread over their faces, their eyes brightened, their hands crept to our discoveries, swept over them like devastating locusts, and. . .our trophies were palmed and pocketed.

One can visualise them, at the end of the journey, showing their discoveries to other interested people, and one can hear the truthful and prideful boasts.

"I picked that little thing up myself, in Carthage!"

Well, it advertises Carthage to the world, and ultimately may prove to be seed well sown.

The camera is nearly indispensable to an exploring and excavating party. It is a charm for the native workers.

Foolishly enough, I suppose, I must explain that the reason archaeologists employ workmen is, that they want work done. Ambition rises high in the director of a group when he sees a squad of fairly muscular men with pick-axes and shovels. With such an army, one could conquer the three parts of Gaul! But, for all their stature, they are children, and work they sadly dislike.

Tomorrow, and tomorrow and tomorrow...
Creeps on this petty pace from day to day...
to the last syllable of recorded time...

That might well have been written originally of Arab workmen. Under ordinary circumstances, they will do anything but work; they will evidence an interest more academic than the professors over the minutest fragment of discovery, and will stand around in awe and wonder when the dust is being sieved. They will discuss this or that, or anything. They are the world's best dodgers. Their picks move with a graceful and slow motion, and the tenderest relic is safe from harm, from their blows.

The "movies" changed all that. Under its stimulus, the Arab becomes fired with an enthusiasm that is both baffling and contagious. If he dreams there is hope of a picture, and is warned in time, he will don all his Sunday clothes, dress up the family, and press-gang all his friends, and so long as the crank is turning, he will work. Work – serious, heavy, sustained labour, becomes his passion, if so be that he may later see himself reproduced on the screen.

I am afraid we learned to exploit that tendency a little. There were days when we had an operator with a filmless camera turning away at the crank for dear life. Then we accomplished much. It is a pity that the Carthaginians were deprived of the motion picture camera. Its presence would have made the lot of the slave at least more enjoyable, if no lighter. The work would have been done as expeditiously, and the slave master's arm would not have risen and fallen so frequently, nor would the whip have coiled into living flesh so mercilessly.

Of course, this passion for the films had consequences that could not be foreseen, and having happened were difficult of explanation.

There was generally a camera going, and I remember that one day a group of unsuspecting tourists was passing along through a newly excavated spot, where the men were still at work. On the runway above, three Arabs were pushing a tipcart along the rails to the dump. They mistook the dump, and launched the load on to the heads of the innocent visitors. That accident needed diplomacy of the highest order to explain, particularly in face of the wholehearted and frank laughter of the childlike Arabs, who instantly ceased work in order to the more enjoy the spectacle. And the laughter of Arab workmen is fundamentally sincere! They will laugh at any misfortune to other people, and drive themselves into complete exhaustion, if the joke is on the other fellow. Especially if the other fellow is the foreman.

The foreman got it one day. A crow-bar fell on his foot, and it must have hurt him considerably for he lay on the ground moaning in agony. Did his workmen help him? Hardly. It was too much of a joke, and they laughed themselves into positive fatigue, and lay alongside the victim, too tired to work.

Our cameras and motion picture machine were working steadily. We soon had good records locked up in yards of film, and Dr. Carton took us round many of the dead cities, while Père Delattre devoted many hours of the day explaining to us the field of Carthaginian archaeology.

Père Delattre has passed on to me a priceless boon, the experience and knowledge gained in a life work at Carthage, and of fifty years of digging and study.

With the result of this first year's work, I returned to Paris, where we showed the films at a private view in the home of Mr. and Mrs. Fred Singer.

There our inexperience betrayed us. Full of confidence, we started to show the films ourselves, and before we knew what had happened, we had several hundred feet of film unwound and coiling on the floor. Meanwhile I had to keep on talking, before an empty screen. It might have been a fiasco, but luck was with me, and ultimately we had the whole party at work on the floor putting the film to rights.

That was the beginning of adventures in lecturing that have lasted for five years. But it was a beginning. Soon thereafter I sailed for the United States on my first real lecture tour.

It seemed a dreadful undertaking to lecture before the American public on what is universally considered the driest subject on earth, in the driest country on earth, and to begin before popular imagination had been fired by the discovery of Tut-ankhamen's tomb.

Before commencing the actual tour, I made several visits to "Castle Rock," the beautiful home of Professor Henry Fairfield Osborn, whose daughter Josephine, had been a member of the original Carthage committee. It was due to Professor Osborn that the funds for the first year's work were obtained, and at his home, I met several other people who were instrumental in raising financial support for the campaign.

I remember, though it seemed strange to me at the time, how guests were allowed to sleep on the roof if they wished to watch the stars, and that many hours of an evening, I talked with Langdon Warner about Mongolia and the Sahara.

While I was on the train to Castle Rock, for the first time, my valise was stolen, the valise which held all my records, and a number of "squeezes" and objects that I particularly wished to show to Professor Osborn.

It could not have been the first warning of the curse of Scipio, but it was a disastrous moment for me. On that valise depended much of the possible success of the American tour, and for several days search parties were out, detectives were engaged, and rewards offered. At last, the valise was found in the fork of a tree, and the only things that were missing were my dress suit and Punic jewels.

Castle Rock, and that summer, will be always a happy memory for me. I think of it often, and of the great company of scientists and explorers, Scott, Peary, Shackleton, Amundsen, and scores of others who have enjoyed the hospitality and encouragement of the Professor and Mrs. Osborn.

My first meeting with Lee Keedick was more interesting to me than to him. I knew nothing about lecturing, and less about lecture tours, and I did not so much as guess what was waiting for me! Lee Keedick impressed upon me that it was my only chance of raising funds, and that, incidentally, he had arranged the tours of many of the world's great explorers, including my two friends, Shackleton and Amundsen.

"But," he added, "you must be known. The newspapers must have your story, and they must write it up all the time."

This disheartened me for a while. I had never given an interview, and was not in any hurry to begin. Newspaper men and newspapers, I held in awe. I had seen something of what they could do. But Lee Keedick was adamant.

"Tomorrow," said the manager, "expect the entire New York press to pay you a visit at Castle Rock."

They came while I was at luncheon, and I am afraid I sent them home again. Disaster upon disaster, but I could not help it! Some people called it temperament, others had words not so kind, but I was helpless. They were so many, and I was alone. I felt that I could not possibly be the man they wanted to see.

Of course, I found my lecture manager in a furious mood, and he told me that our contract was useless until I "got Carthage on the map again – Dido's home town!"

So, the next day, being duly chastened, I came to town and called upon the gentlemen. The result was, I fear, what I had dreaded. Several of the more conservative papers carried correct and quite useful articles, but there were one or two which worried me. Not Carthage, but my "long ungraceful legs" made front page articles. They made much of my excitement at digging up Hannibal's bones, though my work is at Carthage, and Hannibal died at Bithynia on the Sea of Marmora!

When Tut-ankh-amen's tomb was cleared, and the reporters were returning home, we were visited by a few at Carthage. They were what are called "sleuths for news," and one man pestered me day after day, day after day, wanting something interesting. It must always be "interesting," something with a "punch" to it, with scope for the imagination.

I had little news just then, but he went round the museum and elsewhere, and at last he came across a huge pile of bones. They were actually camel bones, that one finds in bushels during the course of excavation, but he saw in them the bones of the elephants of Hannibal, and I fear I did not dispel the illusion. At any rate, he went out of our sight like a hare, his feet kicking up little puffs of dust.

By the time he reached the telegraph, those bones had ceased to be dry. He had done what no other archaeologist has so far succeeded in doing. He had re-created the stables of Hannibal, mentally of course, and sent across a message which gave this priceless information to the world. Such are the vicissitudes of reportorial adventures, however, that by the time the news reached the Pacific Coast, it was the veritable teeth of the great Carthaginian, Hannibal himself, that had been restored to the wondering world!

Thereafter I confined myself to speaking to academic and scientific gatherings, which I enjoyed, as much for the peace as for the appreciative people with whom I came into contact. And they kept me very busy.

After a lecture in Washington, and a generous donation from a patron of the work at Carthage, who still insists on being anonymous, I went to Johns Hopkins to lecture for the Archaeological Institute of America.

It seemed, of course, that in throwing up the public lecture tour I had jettisoned a great opportunity, but there must have been a special providence looking after me. I am sure that I deserved all the anger that Mr. Lee Keedick managed to hide, and he did not hide it all, and that I perhaps deserved to be faced by disappointment. But I should like to make it clear, if I can, that I was very jealous for the scientific accuracy of reports concerning Carthage. I was only the pupil of great men, and the reports gave rather a wrong outlook on the work they were doing.

However, I had, more or less, burned my boats, and providence provided another fleet!

When I left my programme high and dry, and took the opportunity offered to lecture at Johns Hopkins, I had the good fortune to be the guest of Professor and Mrs. David Robinson, one of America's leading archaeologists, and I found the lecture was to be given to a very large audience, which, fortunately for me, was very enthusiastic.

It was not actually my first public speech of course, that had been inflicted upon the French Institute at New York, where I was introduced by the Vicomte de la Jarrei, the explorer of the Sahara, who spoke so long and so well that when he had finished

I had no new contribution to make in addition to what he had already said. Incidentally, that was my first attempt to speak with the films, a feat in itself, for the operator was enthusiastic, and more fluent than I was, for many times I found myself centuries behind the picture on the screen.

On that film, for example, the temple of Tanit was excavated in one minute, forty seconds. A world's record in archaeology, for any temple! Hannibal sped over the Alps faster still, and we ourselves sped across Africa in a manner that would have made Barth, Rohlfs and Duveyrier squirm in their graves. It was hopeless to try to signal the operator to slow down. He was deaf and invisible. The lecture was in French, and the audience entirely American, but they listened courteously, without complaining. The film came unstuck about every ten seconds.

That was an hour of exquisite agony, but the audience was kind. I believe they enjoyed as much seeing my face and my efforts to keep calm when the lights went up, as they enjoyed the pictures. Perhaps more. Certainly, they enjoyed it more than I did. I tremble still at the memory of that night.

Following Johns Hopkins came an invitation from the National Geographic Society at Washington. My well-meaning friends had told me that it was a very learned, very cold, and very critical audience, and I was miserable. I was more miserable still when I found that my hip flask...I am doubtful if I should mention this...had been left at the hotel! The lack of that friend, who had warmed my heart before lectures in many a drawing room, nearly broke me. If it had not been for the kindness of Mr. Grosvenor, President of the Society, and his sympathy and encouragement, I think I should have pleaded heart failure. Still, I muddled through. The audience was splendid, and many people sought me out after the lights went up again. They put friendly questions to make me at my ease, and they expressed their thanks, and said that I was "very young"...!

At the meeting of the Archaeological Institute of America, held at Yale University, Professor Robinson and Professor Magoffen told me that the Institute had elected me the Norton

Memorial Lecturer of the Institute. This was a travelling lecture-ship of $2,000, awarded each year to a lecturer on European archaeology. The great honour was bestowed on me on the day that my engagement to Miss Alice Kenny was announced. Miss Kenny was holding a reception at her parents' home on Fifth Avenue, at the very moment that I was delivering the lecture at Yale. Needless to say, my thoughts were far from Hannibal, Tanit and Punic Carthage that day. And on the next I started on the tour as the Norton Lecturer, taking a journey which included the important centres between New York and Toronto.

I had a bad quarter of an hour at Rochester. I had enjoyed the fine American hospitality of my friends at dinner, and we arrived at the lecture hall to find a crowd of several hundreds of people waiting outside, unable to get in. Ultimately we had to break in, and, for certain reasons it took us twenty minutes to get inside, and the lights going. Fortunately the crowd was typically American; it took everything in good part, and we were all soon creeping around with matches and candles, supplemented by a few electric torches.

We could find nothing; lantern, films and motion picture pro-jector were all missing. So was the janitor. But at last we got the lights on. Then we had no screen! One or two, more adventurous than the rest, borrowed a sheet from the house next door, and I fixed it with safety pins to the bottom of the drop curtain. Then we took the basement by storm, hunting for the lantern. It was a great campaign. To several groups were given definite objec-tives, and ultimately we found most of the essentials, excluding the janitor, who was suffering from an overdose of personal lib-erty, exercised contrary to the rules laid down by Mr. Volstead. He didn't revive till morning.

Quite naturally, Professor McLean of Rochester was desper-ate, since the arrangements for the lecture were in his hands, and he had most carefully instructed the janitor. I was terribly sorry for this good friend of mine in his dilemma, who had six hun-dred people waiting and foraging for a couple of hours, in order that they might hear a lecture on archaeology. It was proof, at least, that the subject had caught on.

After endless troubles the lecture started, but the machine refused to function, and being urged, retaliated by ripping up several hundred feet of film. It was a bitter blow, because I had only one print, and this was only the beginning of the tour.

All things must come to an end. The lecture was no exception. Long after midnight we finished, and the good-natured crowd gave us a wonderful ovation. I have a warm heart for Rochester and all those good friends, as well as gratitude for the magnificent help that city had lent to our work in North Africa.

My personal adventures in and about Rochester did not end with the lecture. It was there that I landed in the wrong Pullman car, in full evening dress, tired out after a lecture. Unwonted noises awoke me a little later, and I peered out. My consternation can be imagined. The Pullman was reserved for a woman's club or school, and the rightful occupants of the car were there, getting ready to turn in, blissfully unaware of the man in their midst.

The porter had made a mistake in showing me to my berth. My coach was probably the next one. It was decidedly awkward for me. My valise with my day clothes and my pyjamas was under the lower berth!

In the small hours I caught the Pullman maid, who nearly screamed when she saw me, and that would have been confusion worse confounded, but she simmered down when I told her my sad tale. I asked her to get my valise out and hand it up to me, so that I might change and make my escape before the girls awoke.

The valise was the crux of the whole matter. Three different times during the night I had climbed out to get that bag, nervous and covered with perspiration at the thought of being discovered, but the valise was wedged in. The weight of the lady who lay on it, held it fast.

The maid ultimately secured the bag for me, and now it seems more humorous than it did then; I got away before the ladies awoke.

Another time, I found that my connections would not work out, my second train being snowed up. I began the last sixty miles of the journey in a motor, and that, too, was snowbound. The last four miles I undertook on foot, and got snowed up myself. When I arrived at Mrs. Coonly Ward's home near Rochester, I was carrying my films in a hat box, feeling like Captain Scott.

Once, without money, (the thieves had even taken my cuff links!) when it was too late to wake up the members of the reception committee and I should have been too nervous to try, anyway – I made four trips between my hotel and the station on foot, and in the snow. It was bitterly cold, and the snow was fine dust, which worked into my pumps, for I was still in evening dress. There it froze. There was another lecture ahead, however, and I simply had to make that train. In small consignments I carried everything from the hotel to the train, and piled up the stuff on my bunk; valises, antiques, and films all carried through the streets of the city at two o'clock in the morning.

My last quarter went to the Pullman porter next morning. I had saved that for the purpose, despite the comments of the station porters who thought I was too much of a tightwad to pay for help with my luggage.

It will be long before I forget those six miles, after two lectures.

Chapter 4

THE METHOD OF EXCAVATION

It is a fact of which I am proud to make confession that the wealthy people of the United States do take very much to heart the advancement of science in all its departments. Ultimately, a cause that is established as being of value to the educational development or final well-being of humanity may hope for a reasonable measure of support. And the help is forthcoming in many, and interesting, ways.

Many good friends of our expeditions have been insistent on remaining anonymous. Here I would say that, although one reluctantly respects their wish to be unknown, we in Carthage; Père Delattre, the Abbé Chabot, and a company of distinguished and self-sacrificing men, are duly cognisant of their generosity, and wish that we could make known to the world of science what Carthage owes to them. They are building, I firmly believe, even better than they know. Perhaps the future will permit of my telling the story of the silent people. At any rate, the very stones speak, and I imagine that these donors will not be able to come to Carthage and return without feeling the undisclosed satisfaction evoked by the work they made possible.

It will be a happy day when I can show them what they have done. My Arabs will dress for a gala day. They do that on the least provocation. How much more will they be *en fête* for the founders of their work.

Five years, now, the excavations have been in progress. The first year, really the first two, we were very restricted. I had to appeal to a very limited number of my own personal friends, who saw the possibilities of excavation even before my trips abroad could be undertaken. And the result was more than encouraging. Difficulties abounded, naturally. We were working in a district that, to this day, retains the ineffable impenetrability of the old Carthaginian traders, and to make an inch of progress necessitated a mile of negotiation.

Negotiation indeed. The people who hear about excavations would hardly believe that an exploring party has its own special lawyer, always on the job. It is not exactly an open field for us. The land belongs to someone, and that someone is likely to repent of his bargain in leasing permission to excavate. Especially likely if a "find" of any importance is brought to light.

We once acquired a piece of ground that bore signs of archaeological value, and we entered into a proper and legal contract with the owner for the right to work there. We found something. It wasn't terribly important, as antiquities go, but the former proprietor, who had thought us wrong, and that he was getting good money for bad land, thought that, if the little discovery came so soon, the big discovery would come later. He preferred to dig on his own account, and he drove us out of the excavation at the point of the gun. He would have used it, too, if we had resisted at that moment.

Thanks to the French Government, the law is a real force in Carthage now, and our friend found himself locked up for a while.

There is no sharp practice in the way excavating parties get the right to work. It is all open and above aboard, and the landowner usually gets a very fair deal, whether he gives it or not. But the landowners try all sorts of tricks.

Against these indigenous difficulties we struggled along for two years, and all the time the work tended to increase. Perhaps we got a little more ambitious as the days went by, and wanted to see as much as possible accomplished in our lifetime. We had to go out for help.

For the third year's work we received some assistance from friends who were beginning to wax more enthusiastic; but the fourth year was the *annus mirabilis,* our wonderful year.

That fourth year! That was the year when we had a committee in Washington, with the help of M. Jusserand, and his associates, the year when the American Universities came in. Fifteen thousand dollars from this one, five thousand, five hundred from that, and so on. And not only the money, but their scientists, too. Very soon, we had no fewer than fifteen trained men, and ten students on the field. And how we went to work!

Relatively speaking, it wasn't a lot of money. But, by the time the dollar has reached Paris, it has multiplied itself three times. When it reaches Carthage it has multiplied itself three times again. It is a dollar when it leaves America. It is twenty francs when it reaches Paris. And even an American could live quite nicely on twenty francs a day in Carthage. People say fifty thousand dollars more fluently than they say a million francs, but a million francs goes further.

I have to confess that sometimes we had our own little worries out there. People came to see us, and we weren't properly advised who they were. That is incidental to the work. Publicity did that for us. It is surprising to many people, who get an original brain-wave, and take a run to the excavations at Carthage, to know how many other people have had the same brain-wave, at the same identical moment, and reach the excavations simultaneously. It is a fact that in order that the work may go on, we have had to put Carthage, or at least our little bits of it, in a state of siege. We have barbed-wire entanglements to keep off the invaders. Some of the invaders are marauding Arabs, and some marauding tourists.

I, myself, nearly put my foot into it one day. I should have succeeded if the visitor had been any other than he was, or had not been blessed with a sense of humour. I was up to my eyes in Carthaginian dust, working away, when someone spoke to me. In the heat of the moment I took him for a Cook's tourist, though Cook's tourists are not distinguishable from those pertaining to

other travel bureaux, and I shoo'ed him out. I even detailed an
Arab to show him the way out, so that he might be sure to find
the exit.

You can imagine my terrible consternation when I met him in
New York. He was a very kindly disposed, and a very rich man,
interested in archaeology! And I went to him, most creditably
introduced, to see if he would come over to Carthage and help
us!

He remembered the incident, and he recalled it to me. He told
me how I had packed him off, and had lent him an Arab, "and
your very choicest specimen, too," to see him off the premises.

It seemed for a moment that I had embittered him, but I was
so glad when I caught what must have been a twinkle in his eye,
as he said, "and now you come and affront me with a request for
help!" Do you know, he did help, wonderfully.

I think the most priceless error of that kind, though, belongs
to the Abbé Chabot.

Abbé Chabot is a grand old man, but very abrupt at times.
For purposes of the excavations, he lays aside his usual clerical
dress, and dons khaki. And he carries always a cane, not for
offensive purposes, though it is good propaganda for the Arabs.
He really needs it. The Abbé approaches age, and he loves the
excavations very dearly indeed. They represent a life work for
him.

Can you imagine with what blanched amazement I beheld
him one day driving a most exalted personage out of the ruins?
How exalted that personage is in the service of diplomacy, and
of what country, I ought not to say. Suffice it to say that under
other circumstances, had the chief actors been less human, it
might have been an "incident."

Even now, it is difficult to repress a shudder when I recall the
forbidding figure of the Abbé, expelling that other great man,
and flourishing his cane the while he cried "Allez! Allez!"

A few minutes later the Abbé himself was a little perturbed,
like a naughty child, when he knew what he had done. You may
be sure we told him. The dear old cleric was unaware of the

honour that was being paid to his work, and failed to recognise his own visitor, mistaking him for a tourist who had no business there at all. It ended happily, fortunately, because the two people concerned were. . .well, just those two people.

The support of our work has its own romantic and lovely side. Of course, we are never forgetful of the people who are able and willing to do quite big things for us. They have the great satisfaction, too, of contributing to what many of us think is a universally important work. But what can we say that is fitting, of the efforts of a group of boys and girls, none of whom is probably used to his teens yet, who are sending a donation year by year? The story is worth telling.

There was a boy. A hundred percent American boy. He was promised a Mediterranean tour, and he somehow heard the lecture on Carthage, and then nothing would do but that he should be allowed to take actual part in the excavations. He came, and he had his own particular little spot wherein to work; and he dug up some antiquities. I remember there was a particularly good specimen of a lamp among his finds. Naturally that lamp and those antiquities meant the world to him, as, indeed they ought, for with his own hands he had unearthed something that had lain in the dust, unknown, for many, many centuries. He had a tangible link with Carthage in its greatest days.

When he returned home he carried with him, by permission, a little case containing some of his own discoveries. And he had an imagination, which we could not have given him. When he reached home, he promptly organised a Junior League among his own friends, and they contrive somehow to send us a donation to the work, year by year. When we can, we send back to the group a specimen or two, so that all the young friends may have evidence of what their sacrifices mean in the field of archaeology.

Now we hope to have about a million francs for the work, and that means much to us, for we have several fields of excavation, of which I shall speak more fully in subsequent chapters.

It was at Washington, in a room of the Cosmos Club, that the
Franco-American committee, for the excavation of Carthage,
was formed. The committee consists, on the one side, of His
Excellency M. Jusserand, the then French Ambassador; M. Paul
Leon, Directeur d'Academie des Beaux Arts; Père Delattre;
Stephane Gsell; M. L'Abbé Chabot and M. Merlin. On the other
side, representing America, the Committee included Mr. Robert
Lansing, Mr. Merriam, Colonel Fowler, Mr. Mitchell Carrol,
Mr. Fred Singer, and Professor Washington.

The size of the necessary staff for the actual work of excavation will perhaps convey some idea of the varied interests represented, and the number of departments which must be catered
for, if excavation is to yield the best results.

Our staff was

General Director...	Professor F. W. Kelsey
Associate Director...	De Prorok
Engineer...	Mr. G. Stoever
Scientific Advisor...	Prof. Washington
Cataloguer...	Prof. Petersen
Petrographer...	Mr. Swain
Punic Antiquities...	Abbé Chabot
Christian Antiquities...	Père Delattre
Assistant Surveyor...	Mr. Hayes
Architect...	Mr. Woodbridge
Tanit Area...	Mr. Harden
Motion Pictures...	Mr. Kellerman
Special Correspondent...	Mr. Streit
Motor Transport...	Mr. Swain
Specialists, Urns, etc...	Dr. Orma F. Butler
	Miss N. L. Butler
	Miss Julia E. Brittain
Representing McGill Univ...	Major Shorey
Utica...	Abbé Moulard

Assistants: C. C. Wells, Rey de Villette, Hinton O'Neill,
George French, Mr. Morris and G. Scott.

In all, a staff of twenty-five people, all specialists in their different lines.

Thanks to the effort of the committee, and the support we were successful in obtaining, few expeditions have left for the field with a more complete outfit than we had that year. Most of the party sailed in the S. S. *George Washington,* and spent the trip over discussing plans, and reading up North African archaeology.

With Professor Kelsey, we gathered round the great central table of the Salon, and had most valuable lectures from him, interspersed with accounts of his lifelong and crowded activities. He was the whole spirit of the company, tremendously interesting, and of sound counsel.

Perhaps here, just to conserve the spirit of the voyage, it will not be out of place to speak of the practical side of Archaeological exploration. I trust that it may not prove too dry to be of interest. It is, of course, of first importance to those who take more than a general interest in the subject.

The fact is, that up to the last decade at least, Archaeology has been the Cinderella of the sciences. It has gone forward for many centuries in one form or another, but it has been the pursuit of the very few.

To the best of my knowledge, the first recorded archaeological expedition was organised and prosecuted by Nero. As Auguste Audollent says, in his *Carthage Romaine,* we have to go back to that victorious barbarian for the original effort at excavation, at least semi-archaeological, in Carthage.

In the year 65 a Carthaginian, Caesellius Bassus, suggested to Nero a way in which he could get money for nothing. Nero's coffers were almost exhausted, his manner of living was such as is generally known, and it was urgently necessary to get more funds. Bassus reported that he had found several particles of gold in a cavern at Carthage, and firmly believed that he was on the track of the treasures of Dido. Nero listened eagerly, and fitted out Bassus with an expedition of some three hundred soldiers. When they reached Carthage the soldiers were not enough, and the civil population was drawn upon for extra labour. But Bassus worked in vain.

He returned, so the story runs, to Nero, to report lack of progress, and Nero, enraged at the disappointment, and seriously in need of specie, sent Bassus back to Carthage to try again. With him he sent a number of other soldiers, to watch over Bassus and his men, to keep them at work. Failing success they were to be crucified. Legend credits Bassus with suicide during insanity, and adds that the unsuccessful workers were crucified.

Such was exploration then, and Dido's treasure still remains to be located. (Audollent, *Carthage Romaine,* p. 50.)

In recent history, the real impetus, from a scientific point of view, was given by Napoleon, whose protégé, Champolleon, was interested archaeologically in the civilisations of antiquity. That is to say, it is only during the last century that serious excavation has taken place. With Schliemann and Troy, the imagination was first awakened to the lure of lost cities, and the fascination of digging for them. Scientific exploration properly so called, really dates from our own time, under the leadership of Flinders Petrie, and Sir Arthur Evans.

One thing we have learned, above all others, by scientific approach to the subject. It is not the size of the discovery that determines the magnitude of its importance. If only the old explorers would have preserved the things they threw on to the refuse heaps! A fragment of pottery, a tiny bit of stone, may contain information that can give us more historical knowledge than the discovery of a golden treasury. Some of the "waste" might have supplied missing dates, or have linked two civilisations, hundreds of miles apart.

Consequently, in our work at Carthage, we sieve the earth on a certain site, and examine it minutely before dumping it into the sea. It is utterly impossible to give a faint idea of the work thus involved. But it is work essentially worth while.

So highly catalogued and so thoroughly specialised are the various departments of archaeology that from such a tiny example as a bead, fallen from the necklace of a body found after a lapse of twenty centuries, we can determine the date of the period in which that tomb was made.

As Professor Kelsey was continually emphasising in those round-table conferences as we churned away across the Atlantic, the viewpoint has changed.

Excavation used to be conducted for the collection of specimens, for museums, or for private owners. Now, it is not the thing found that is all-important. It is the environment of the discovery, so that proper consideration by trained men may ultimately result in the complete reconstruction of the civilisation or conditions of life, of which the things unearthed are our tangible evidence.

I remember Professor Kelsey saying with great emphasis that no excavation should be undertaken without a sufficient staff of experts to supervise and record the work. He went so far as to say that where such a staff is not available, the interest of science will be best served by leaving ancient remains protected by the earth.

The Professor is right, as we have discovered by practical experience in conjunction with the submarine work at Carthage. Some of our work there goes below sea level. Now, as soon as an object is uncovered, the water is quickly pumped out, and the sun is allowed to get at the vase, or whatever it may be. The sun rapidly dries the specimen to its original hardness, and so it is saved. Recently, we have saved over two hundred vases from the Temple of Tanit, simply by letting the sun dry them before they were touched. In previous excavations many important vases and urns were lost, because we did not have adequate pumping apparatus.

As a further experiment, we are attempting a thin stone partition between the Temple and the sea, so as to prevent infiltration as we dig deeper.

The Arabs, who are doing the sieving, need careful supervision lest, through ignorance, they should destroy a valuable link with the past. The objects found have to be preserved and photographed and catalogued, and this means considerable time and research. Specialists have to be called in to give their views, and in some cases, it means years of collaboration and collation before the material can be assembled and made ready for scientific publication.

Professor Kelsey, who represents the modern scientific outlook on excavation, rightly insists on a record so carefully made and verified by measurements, photographs, and all possible data, that any object can be put back into its exact place, and the earth restored to its original appearance, should such a replacement for any reason be found necessary. That means work, but significant work, especially in the case of architectural ruins.

When we come across the ruins of buildings, it is necessary for the architect to be advised, and the architect must be one skilled in the technique of buildings of the type discovered. He studies the ground, and the position of the find, and watches closely for any fragments that might otherwise pass unrecognised, and yet would give valuable hints of the disposition and appearance of the building. The way these pieces lie in the earth often indicates both the plan of the building itself and the use of the particular fragment in the building.

In spite of all this (and I suppose that I have given the impression that we go over the ground with magnifying glasses, on our hands and knees, in the interest of science), there is a huge mass of discarded earth to be got rid of somehow. We don't exactly go over the earth grain by grain, but we do go through it like people hunting for a needle in a haystack; and we go through quantities of sand that would have delighted even the walrus and the carpenter, immortalised by Lewis Carroll. This earth used to be moved away by mules under the charge of Arabs; one mule to two Arabs. Now it is carted off by trucks, carrying a ton each, and the dumping is done by the driver.

Even in so prosaic a matter as dumping refuse, scientific application is essential. At Carthage it is positive that there is no spot in a reasonable radius that does not hide some buried ruins, and therefore we were faced with the question of covering a ruin still more deeply, or of excavating a site and then refilling it with the surplus soil. We were actually like the Irishman who had more earth than he knew what to do with, and proposed digging a hole to bury it!

Science showed us how to use the earth to good advantage. It is dumped into the sea after a thorough sieving, and in this way we are slowly gaining on the sea, which is valuable progress, for in a few years we shall have reached the submerged walls of Carthage, which lie a hundred yards from the shore.

The alluvial deposits at Carthage are enormous. In the hollows between the hills we have calculated that as much as a yard a century is deposited. That means there are twenty yards of sand and earth between the surface and the Phoenician city. On the way through that, we pass the débris and ruins of Byzantine, Vandal, Roman, and other civilisations. And of course, it is the Phoenician ruins that are our goal.

In the five years of our work, we have taken care to measure the speed of the earth deposits. The method is simple, but accurate. Iron measuring rods are sunk to rock bottom in several of the hollows, and records are carefully kept of the changes. The deposit is due, of course, to the action of wind and rain. Each year we find a few inches of sand and earth on the roof of the home of the Expedition.

One other factor of difficulty is the great Medjerda river, which, in antiquity flowed by the city walls. The Romans, so thorough in their frenzy of destruction, tore down the walls, and the river ran uncontrolled for centuries. The natural result was a considerable addition to the weight of earth above the Punic city.

Free to flow where it would, the river changed its course. The mouth is now thirty miles away, silting up the ruins of Utica, where we are conducting another field of excavation that should prove of the utmost importance.

Utica was a great seaport in Phoenician times, but the Medjerda has left such a great deposit that the harbour is silted up, and the coast line is actually twenty miles away. So, at Carthage we have to fight the sea, which is now higher than the ruins of the Phoenician city, and at Utica we shall have to change the course of the river to prevent the ruins being covered up again.

These are the things we talked about on the voyage, because we were all keyed up by the prospect of a great advance. We talked about what we had done, and what we were going to do. Of all our future plans, perhaps two stood out most vividly.

The first was the use of the Aeroplane in archaeology. That venture, as an experiment, materialised three years ago, and since then we have continued, year by year, our prospecting from the air.

In 1922, we took our first films and photographs from different heights, which resulted in our being able to trace the great submerged walls of ancient Carthage. Flying above the Gulf of Tunis, we were able to film clearly six miles of submerged wall, showing constructions a hundred and fifty yards from the present shore. I can still remember the interest with which the news was received by the Royal Geographical Society, when I lectured to them on the subject in London.

The aeroplane was piloted by Captain Peletier d'Oisy, the famous French ace, who recently made the phenomenal flight from Paris to Tokyo.

Our use of the aeroplane this year is to be more varied. At the moment we are using it to film the whole coast line, especially at a spot where we have located a sunken galley – a stupendous find, of which I shall say more later – and at the legendary island of Djerba, where we have located a city under the sea.

Through photographic exploration from the air, and with the use of a new type of rock drill, we hope very shortly to answer the important question of whether the whole Tunisian coast has settled since those old days, or whether the Mediterranean has risen in the last three thousand years.

The aeroplane will be used further afield, in exploring the Sahara. We have found that the outline of cities and walls are far more easily discerned from the air than from the ground level of those great spaces across Africa.

Always further afield! We thought we had done much, with the aeroplane, and it seemed, as we talked on the ship, that we should have to wait for mechanical science to give us something new before we could proceed on any but the lines we have already adopted. But just there, as though to give a greater thrill to an already thrilling event, we discussed another proposal, which is now on the eve of being launched.

Almost at once, even before I finish writing this, I shall be starting forward with a picked body of adventurous souls, varying in age but not in enthusiasm, across the Sahara. It will be a scientific expedition in miniature, and we are promised a few external thrills, en route.

We are motoring to the Hoggar, a thousand miles south of Carthage, travelling in specially designed six-wheeled Renault cars, and we hope to do in ten days what it took weeks to do on camels. We shall be linked with the outside world by wireless telegraphy. Messages will be relayed to Paris, and from there, in turn, news will be transmitted to America, of the discoveries we may make on our journey.

We hope to establish one or two things on this journey, the first, some details of the trade the Carthaginians did with the desert. We know they got much of their gold from that source. And it may be that there is some real foundation in fact for the presence of the Emerald mountain, which figures so much in matters concerning Carthage. There are lost cities in the desert, of whose existence we are assured, but whose site is uncertain.

Along the way there are sad reminders of the price paid by some of those who blazed the trail. On our route are the graves of the Flatters, Palat, and De Foucauld expeditions, whose members lost their lives because of the fearful hardships, the lack of water, and the unceasing attacks of the murderous Sahara tribes. We shall pass their last resting-places, lonely spots in the desolate wastes. We shall pass, with motor car, wireless, and a mounted machine gun. How different the lot of succeeding generations! But in passing we shall remember them, the pioneers, the real explorers.

Chapter 5

PÈRE DELATTRE

The object of excavation needs to be kept in mind. It is easy to lose the broad and scientific view in the excitement of the moment of a new discovery. Very often things of rare beauty appear, which would be ornaments to houses or museums in other countries, and occasionally cupidity is aroused.

If the specimens are several times duplicated, there is naturally no reason why they should not be allowed to leave the country. If they are unique, as is often the case, and essential to the restoration of a site, then they must remain, despite the pleading and scheming of collectors.

We have, therefore, to be very alert, much more alert than is generally realised. I remember a very illuminating incident in this connection.

We had all turned out to help Père Delattre in the recovery of further portions of the Basilica of St. Cyprian, one day, and we were hot and tired and a little dirty. I say a little, because there have been times when we were dirtier, but not much. We had worked all day, and were on the point of finishing. Scattered around, but in their places, were bits of marble, parts of columns, plinths and pediments, which gave promise of very considerable advance in the restoration of the basilica.

Scattered around also were visitors. It was before our introduction of barbed wire entanglements. I had finished, and was walking back to headquarters. As I went along I was met by a most excited tourist, who perhaps took me for one of his party. He was too excited, I suppose, to think. In high feather he ran to meet me, to tell me of his wonderful find. He had been souvenir hunting, and, reposing in the tonneau of his motor car was one of our precious pieces.

Very confidentially he told me about it.

"I am going to take that back home with me," he said. "I'm building a new house, and this will be rather a surprise for my neighbours, don't you think? I'll be the only one to incorporate part of the basilica of St. Cyprian in a modern house. That capital will make a wonderful tea-table."

I was too amazed to speak for a moment, but I could feel the blood stretching the veins of my face. This well-intentioned Vandal was very much barking up the wrong tree. I could not have felt much more amazed if a burglar had told me in confidence that he had just robbed my house. But he was absolutely not to be repressed. I must also listen to the tale of his mechanical genius.

"It was a bit of a job," he boasted, "but we got it into the car. Just four of us. Myself and my chauffeur, and two Arab fellows who were lying about. It looked as though we wouldn't get away with it, but we did. Just look at it. And now I'm going, while the going's good."

I found my voice.

"The devil you are," I stormed. "Do you know what you are going to do? You are going to take that stone and put it back exactly where you found it, you and your chauffeur, and *my* Arabs!"

He did.

It is the most astonishing thing in the world how little thought people can give to the question of whether they should or should not take specimens when they find them. Probably it is because the stones are lying on the surface of the earth, apparently ignored, looking as though they belonged to nobody. These people, or at least most of them, would never dream of stealing the same specimen from the British Museum or the Metropolitan. One has, at times, to drive that home, in Carthage.

That same basilica of St. Cyprian probably is the most illustrative and interpretative example of our work at Carthage. First
the stones were discovered, and with them other details that
helped us to get an idea of the habits and customs of the time.
They were then mounted in the places they had occupied when
the basilica was first built, and now it is intended to restore the
surrounding land to a condition as nearly like the original as possible. It is already quite easy to imagine what the early Christians saw, and how the place looked to them.

Looking down the avenue of pillars, one sees the sea. It is
best in the sunrise or the sunset, for then the grandeur of the isthmus is at its greatest. Such colours fill the sky, and are reflected
in the sea, as Turner dreamed of, but hardly dared depict. The
sun rises across the Gulf of Tunis, and the mountains are
wrapped in a purple haze which is reflected in the bluest of blue
seas. On the shores the waves are gentle, of clearest emerald.

Beyond the columns of the basilica can be recognised the
ruins under the sea. There is a deeper blue, and a deeper green
outlining the walls.

The columns St. Cyprian knew are always rich. Their colour
without the sun is of old ivory tinged with gold, but when the
sun reaches them they are shrouded in a soft mist of red. Imagine these, with the purple and mauve of the mountains and the
blue and emerald of the Gulf.

On the earth is a gorgeous carpet of North African flowers,
interspersed with mosaics, the eternal pictures in stone. In the
sky the birds sing. We have larks and nightingales in Carthage,
and the nightingale sings in the mornings, too.

The basilicas stand almost on the very edge of precipices,
positively blood-red in colour at all times, but intensified a thousand times at sunset and sunrise. The red rocks are pinnacled,
and jut out to sea, as though they were a file of sentinels guarding the entrance to the Gulf of Tunis. Cape Carthage towers
above the basilica, and on its garden-covered summit are the
white buildings with blue windows, and a slender minaret
pierces the sky, above all else. The village spreads out like two

wings of the symbolical dove which was sacred to the Carthaginians; the same symbol that is found in the hand of Tanit.

Sidi-Bou-Said they call the sacred city, and Mahomedans claim that St. Louis is buried there. They too have made him a saint, "The Marabout," asserting that he turned Moslem. At least they pay homage to a very great man. He must have been, since two religions claim him, and have canonised him.

Often, as evening falls, one can hear music from the great cathedral floating across the plains, and mingling with the voices of the White Fathers as they sing their Gregorian chants.

Père Delattre discovered the Basilica in 1920 and since then, by hook or crook, has managed to get together funds and helpers to re-establish a considerable portion of the ruin.

It was not until the excavations were over, and all the possible reconstruction finished that I heard him tell the story of its discovery.

There came a day, however, when the work was done, and a wall had been built around the site. The cost of the wall was borne by Marymount College, at Tarrytown, where my wife was for many years a student. It is an important wall, for it keeps out the goats and cattle that roam over the plain.

"Now," said Père Delattre, Archpriest of Carthage, "my work is ready, and we are to have Mass for the first time in fifteen centuries, since Augustine was here."

Père Delattre is two people. He is the priest and the archaeologist. With his flowing white robe and his almost whiter beard, and wearing the red fez of the continent, he is recognised and respected wherever he goes. The Arabs, who have little consideration for the "infidels," worship him. They call him "the marabout," an honour which is as deep as the heart of man, and as expansive as the Sahara.

He made the ceremony in the Basilica an hour of tremendous majesty. The White Fathers from the monastery, and the White Sisters from the convent, formed a long procession, carrying garlands of flowers to the resurrected basilica. For an altar, a few capitals had been gathered together, and the sacred vessels were placed on them.

The old Gregorian chants were heard again on the Christian site, and homage was paid by the vast company to the saints of centuries ago, martyred for the faith.

As soon as mass was over, Père Delattre, the archaeologist now, and as excited as a boy, climbed to the top of a column, and told us all how he found the ruin.

He is a picturesque figure, and a wonderful man, with undying enthusiasm. Though he is nearly eighty years of age, so excited was he to begin the tale that he nearly knocked the vessels over in his haste, and took an impetuous jump, incredible to those who are not used to him. An American youth with a mathematical mind did what I should never have done. He paced out that jump, and in amazement said to Père Delattre, who did not quite understand, "You ought to have been an Olympic champion, and not an archaeologist."

Père Delattre told us that, one day in haste to reach a sick Arab at Sidi-Bou-Said, he took a short cut through the fields covered with poppies. He could not waste time to go by the roads. In the midst of the poppies, his eyes ever alert for possible discoveries, he perceived a tiny bit of marble, which on examination he found to be inscribed with part of the Christian monogram.

"I had no time," he said, "to do more than put a stick into the ground, to mark the place, and then I ran on to my duties to the sick."

He is like that. That is why the Arabs adore him, and call him "The Saint." When he had ministered to those who needed him, however, he hastened back to his find, and on hands and knees, examined the field.

There were no further signs.

"It was not much to go on," he continued, "but the next day I went there with two Arabs and a pick and shovel, and we worked about the stick. Nothing was found before I went home."

The next day, *before mass was over,* an Arab interrupted Père Delattre, to tell him that, on the exact spot, two yards down, a mosaic floor had been discovered with the Christian symbol of the dove. The Arabs knew that such symbols were heart's delight to Père Delattre, and that they would be forgiven for any indiscretion in interrupting him.

"I have little more to say," added Père Delattre to the crowd that had listened to the enthusiastic saint with an intensity that the story demanded, "except that I set to work, and, due to donations from the Archbishop of Algiers, managed to carry away huge masses of earth, and to lay bare the skeleton that now you see. The discovery is especially thrilling because we know from history that the Basilica of St. Cyprian was by the sea shore, outside the city walls, and now we have it here, as it was in the days of the saints."

It meant the crowning of a long life to Père Delattre, and the old man cried with delight at the dramatic events of the day.

"To-day we are holding mass here again!" he sobbed, and only they who know the devotion of the man can really understand what it meant.

The men who are carrying on the work of St. Cyprian in Africa, Monseigneur Lemaitre, Primate of Africa, and Père Delattre, are of the rightful succession. They are of the race of heroes. It is no sinecure working on that continent. There are adventures and privations little advertised. When the news of his election was conveyed to the Archbishop, for example, he was in the Congo river, in a condition ready for a swim, but not a swim of pleasure for he was banging away trying to repair the propeller of his missionary ship. The messengers came to him there, to announce that he was elected Cardinal.

I have seen these two men in the desert, struggling with a disabled motor car; the Primate, covered in oil lay beneath the car and Père Delattre, Arch Priest of Carthage was struggling with a tire.

There was another great man associated with them, one who now rests in the Cathedral, who is linked with our work by a strange coincidence. Professor Kelsey went to Carthage some time ago. I believe it was on his honeymoon. In any event, a piece of pottery now in the University of Michigan provided the clue which caused the work of Père Delattre. Cardinal Lavigerie sent Père Delattre to Carthage. These two men had recognised the significance of the Christian monogram on the piece of pottery that Professor Kelsey took to his college.

Now Lavigerie is dead. He was the Abraham Lincoln, the Wilberforce, of Africa. It was he who caused the liberation of the slaves, and on his tomb in Carthage are two representative figures. One, the negro, with broken chains, mourns his champion, the other, a Bedouin, holds sheaves of produce, symbolical of the peace and prosperity that came with Lavigerie.

At Biskra, the monument to Cardinal Lavigerie, with marvellous fidelity, and true interpretation, shows him standing facing the Sahara, his robes flying in the wind, while in his hand, held high, as a Crusader held his sword, is the Cross.

In a measure these two have their reward, their lasting monument is the basilica of St. Cyprian. Not their only reward, and perhaps not significant in comparison with their human services rendered as ministers to the need of men, but humanity has a short memory and stones live long. Whenever future generations shall see, or hear, or speak, of the discoveries at Carthage, the ancient stones will speak also of the men who laboured there.

The basilica is the most impressive of all the ruins of Carthage, and stands in the midst of natural beauty. It is vast in extent, comprising seven aisles, with abside or presbyterium, ciborium, and atrium. Hundreds of Christian tombs surround the ruin, and over 9,000 epitaphs and inscriptions were found.

The inscriptions are now the especial pursuit of Père Delattre, who has a phenomenal memory and an uncanny skill in placing in order. He has discovered, and matched, over 13,000 fragments. It is, of course, the result of a life work, but nevertheless marvellous. I have seen him pick up a new fragment, recently unearthed, and run, in an ecstasy of glee, to an inscription that he had put aside, unfinished years ago, and fit the new section in.

It was in this way that he finally completed the Inscription of Saint Perpetua, the patron saint of Carthage, after seven years of labour.

Carthage has three great basilicas, which Père Delattre has excavated, and in addition to these the amphitheatre, several chapels, and extensive cemeteries of the Christian period can be seen. There are two other basilicas to be unearthed.

We shall hear more of the tombs, but one small point can be recorded here. It is a little for the imagination, and one cannot be entirely sure of the theory that some of us hold. It is this: in many of the tombs of the early Christians we have discovered huge nails. In the tombs of those who were buried normally there are four nails. There are other tombs, however, where we find only three, and they lie in such a position as would be expected if the tomb were that of one buried after being cruci-fied. The nails, and there are only three, lie where the pierced hands might have stretched, and where the crossed feet, pin-ioned by the agents of persecution, would have been. It is a little discovery which reminds us that Carthage stood second only to Rome as a center of persecution. We may, indeed, have discov-ered the tombs of the martyrs.

Relics of the early Christians are numerous, most wonderful of all being the famous statues of the Virgin Mary, dating from the fourth or fifth centuries.

Also, in the museum, is a great collection of Christian lamps, and a replica of an organ, dating from the first century A.D.

To speak separately of all the items discovered would be to make this story into a museum catalogue and one must be con-tent, therefore, to speak of representative items in each field.

Chapter 6

CARTHAGE: THE SANCTUARY OF TANIT

Without a doubt, the discovery of the Temple of Tanit is the greatest archaeological event of Carthage, or of the whole of North Africa, so far. It is the first link with the history of Carthage, and is the only discovery of a considerable ruin in position.

Tanit and her consort ruled the destinies of Phoenician Carthage, and her worship was characterised by lust and sacrifice nearly incredible. To her, little children were sacrificed, and in times of great national crisis adults were added to the victims.

The temple is situated on the side of a hill, not far from the supposed site of the gates of the city. Now, of course, it is covered with the dust of many centuries, but in the day of the goddess it was surrounded by trees, the sacred grove characteristic of the cult.

How we discovered the temple is a story not far removed from the exploits of Sherlock Holmes, or it might be better suited to the adventures of Pinkerton or Burns. It is a story that becomes usual, after a few years of exploration, for it is the tale of the beginning of most discoveries.

Information came to us that an Arab was selling "steles" of Punic origin, and we traced him to his home in an old cistern. By the assistance of a little anti-Volstead persuasion, we were able to induce him to uncover another stele which he had in the hovel. It was secured for the national museum at Tunis, and is one of the finest examples extant. But when we asked him where he discovered it, he sent us off on a fool's errand into the mountains, so that he might have a little longer time in which to work undisturbed, or perhaps in the hope that we should never discover his mine.

The two "detective" archaeologists primarily concerned were M. Icard and M. Geilly. The latter had found the Arab selling his specimens, and recognised the Punic descriptions.

We dug in the place indicated by the Arab, and kept at it for about two weeks, before we were certain that he had misled us. Therefore, one night, he was followed, and in the light of the moon was seen to be digging away like a rabbit in a hole. He was caught red-handed, and nearby lay ten votive stones.

The site he was working on warranted full excavation, so the land was acquired, and we set to work. The sanctuary of Tanit is the result. This, with the Punic tombs discovered by Père Delattre, and supplemented by the more extensive operations that have been possible with our wider organisation, is the most important addition to the knowledge we have of early Carthaginian life. It is the outstanding archaeological success on the isthmus. By its means we are arriving at some understanding of the language, customs, literature and civilisation of the city in the early periods of its establishment.

It seems to me, from the success which followed our later work, that if we were to take the Temple as our center, and dig around in ever increasing circles, we should finally unearth the whole of what remains of the early Phoenician settlement.

The sanctuary itself is remarkable, being on four distinct levels, or floors of votive altars. Each level belongs to a different period of Carthaginian history, and the sanctuary probably dates from the foundation of the city, having continued in existence until Carthage was wiped out by Scipio a hundred and forty-six years before Christ. We have discovered what remained after the fortnight of fire and the levelling plows of the Romans, hungry for revenge.

Thousands of urns containing the relics and bones of sacrificed children have been found. From anatomical comparison we know that the victims ranged from newborn babies to children of twelve years of age. They were put through the fires of Moloch and buried in the sanctuary.

Probably at regular intervals, intensified in times of national crisis, defeat, famine or reverses, these human sacrifices were offered to the goddess to appease and propitiate her and her consort.

Terrible as the idea is to us, it is not difficult to visualise the fierce intensity of the priests who performed the sacrifices. We know, historically, that the cult was one of abandonment, and that dances and orgies preceded the ceremonies. The people were driven to fanatical frenzy, the climax of which was the sacrifice. From Diodorus we know that when Agathocles menaced the city, in addition to the two hundred children sacrificed, three hundred men volunteered to suffer the same fate.

The monstrous brass figure of the Goddess towered above the altar, and before her roared the incandescent cauldron. Her arms were outstretched to receive the sacrifices, but the arms were hinged, so that the body they held rolled forward, and disappeared, to be consumed by fire.

Before her, raising a tumult that should drown the cries of the victims, in the dance, that still persists, were her priests and devotees.

The fanatical sect called the Aissaouas still dance a similar dance, remainder of the habits and customs of the days whose secrets we are now deciphering.

Beginning slowly, they work to a frenzied crescendo. We are able to witness the dance, and actually to film it, though modern susceptibilities are so fine that I have been denied permission to show the film.

It must be admitted at once that the sight was both repulsive and terrifying, but it gave us a better understanding of the frame of mind which permitted and even gloried in human sacrifice.

Prince M'Hamed, son of the Bey of Tunis became interested in our work. He knew little of archaeology, but quickly evidenced a great interest, and speedily acquired considerable knowledge of the subject. In the excavations of Tanit he had an especial interest, immediately recognising similarities between the cult and the habits of the Aissaouas.

He told us that on a certain day the tribe was coming to the palace, to attempt to persuade the Bey to abdicate as a protest against the French administration, and so to pave the way for the declaration of a holy war.

We were received at the palace in advance of the approaching fanatics, and, for our safety were surrounded by members of the Beylieal family, and soldiers. That may sound a little melodramatic to some people, but the precaution was not a jot more than was necessary. In addition to our being "infidels" we had photographic apparatus, which has cost many people their lives, but, fortunately for us, the cinematographic machine was new to them and did not at all resemble the hated cameras to which they were accustomed.

We were in the corner of the courtyard leading up to the steps of the palace. We were also as near to a door leading to the gardens as we could get. Here we mounted the machine, half in and half out of the door, surrounded by our guards and the Beylical family.

We heard in the distance, far across the plains of Carthage, the dull booming of great drums, the chanting of the priests and the "le-le" of the women on the housetops, urging the men to war.

Such must have been the sounds that assailed the ears of the Byzantines when the great hordes of the Crescent swept like a scourge to the walls of Carthage.

A cloud of dust presaged the advancing horde, and from the dust burst the sacred banners of the Mohammedans, waving backwards and forwards, in time with the rolling of the dance. My mind went to General Gordon, in his last stand at Khartoum, against these same fanatics. The followers of the Prophet, the followers of the Mahdi, or of Abd-el-Krim have one thing in common. Fanaticism is the secret of their strength.

Before we were ready, out of the dusty cloud figures had formed into lines outside the palace. They moved automatically. Men with drums on their backs stood for the drummers to beat the time of the dance. Priests walked up and down the line, urging the dancers on. The dancers gyrated with arms limp, their heads swayed backwards and forwards. Faster, ever faster they revolved, until hysteria caught them, and then, it seemed, hypnotised epilepsy. They foamed at the mouth, and as they reached the climax, priests caught them, and threw them almost at our feet.

I remember that the man at the end went first. He seemed to have much negro blood in him, and as he flung forward on the ground he began the most terrible contortions and rending of his body.

Soon he was joined by others who had reached ecstasy. The drums beat harder and harder and faster and faster, and the chanting rose to a sustained roar. The fanatics barked like dogs, and handsful of broken glass were presented to the delirious performers by the priests. As a famishing man would relish a handful of crumbs, the glass was chewed by the dancers. After the glass, nails, and after the nails the priests gave knives to the writhing madmen. The nails and knives were thrust through the flesh, and the dancers cried for more.

The priests maintained a certain poise throughout it all, increasing the frenzy and leading to more diabolical exhibition step by step. Even while the glass was being chewed, and the nails and knives were thrust into the living bodies of the zealots, the priests procured masses of live scorpions and plied the dancers with them. They might have been shrimps, so eagerly were they devoured.

Then the dancing became so devilishly possessed that the scene was simply a storm of dust and motion.

I was by this time almost as delirious as the dancers. Prince de Waldeck, who was filming the scene turned a white face to me and said "I can't go on."

For myself, I could imagine nothing but the return of Baal. Tanit lived in those moments.

Yet there was no blood. The dancers were before me with their cheeks and legs and bodies pierced by nails and knives. I saw one man snap like a mad dog at the ankles of a passing priest. Men on the ground writhed and rolled through murderous cactus.

Yet they seemed to come to no harm. The knives were still there, and the glass still being chewed when I left. I could stand no more.

In any event, we were forced to make a hurried exit. The Aissaouas had seen us, and in the rage of their frenzy charged at the company surrounding us, trying to lay hands on the infidels. We escaped through the gardens, but I was a wreck for three days after the sight.

Fanaticism is hereditary with these people. We, digging in the earth, are finding the first traces of its intensity. We have only unearthed part of the temple as yet, and have not found the actual image of the goddess, which must have been of gigantic size. Perhaps it will never be discovered, for what we have unearthed makes us certain that the temple suffered, in common with the rest of the city, from the fires lit by the Romans.

In the ruins we have found a layer of ashes, which seems to be the remains of the superstructures of the city. In the temple, beneath this layer of ashes, lay a misshapen mass of bronze that had been fused by fire.

Tanit ruled Carthage and her destinies, but she was held in abomination by the people of surrounding countries. Her abominations are recorded by many historians. They are cursed by the prophets of the scriptures. Diodorus Siculus tells of three hundred sacrifices being offered at one ceremony.

One of the most unusual terms of peace ever recorded is surely that made by Gelon of Syracuse on behalf of the Greeks. At Himera he defeated three hundred thousand Carthaginians, and demanded one single condition; that the people of Carthage should abolish the sacrifice of little children, and the eating of little dogs!

The Romans, when their turn came, finding that commands were not sufficient to stop the practice, hanged the priests on the trees of their own sacred grove, to serve as an object lesson, and to drive home the decree that human sacrifices should no longer be offered.

The Carthaginians themselves were not above duping the goddess. She commanded, through her priests, that no substitute should be offered, preferring first-born, and if possible, only, children of proud families. But the proud families managed, sometimes, to smuggle in the children of their slaves. Traditional history says that one of those who owes his life to this subterfuge was none other than Hannibal himself, who was represented at the sacrifice by proxy.

The Romans built over part of the ground of the Temple ruins, so that thanks to them we have in one place a Phoenician museum actually in situ. We have been able to preserve a vertical section of the earth, exposed, but guarded against the mole-like Arabs and other people of acquisitive tendencies. Here, at any future date scientists may come, and check their theories by comparison with things as they are found.

We excavated, working downwards of course, first what appears to be the Roman Temple of Saturn, built over the Punic ruin below. It was called so because we found a votive inscription in the débris of the ruined walls bearing the name of Baal Saturn.

The Romans had built there, but had disturbed the religious area very little, for they too were a superstitious people.

Under these walls were the first layer of Punic remains. This stratum is nearly six feet deep, and we found excavation very difficult, because water from what appears to be a hidden spring, constantly seeped in. We were able to rescue, however, vases of the most delicate workmanship, of graceful tulip form. In the vases were found exquisite amulets of the Egyptian deities, min-

gled with the bones and ashes of little children who had been
sacrificed.

Below this we found a very important silex of the Neolithic
age, an important find, showing that the peninsula of Carthage
may have been a home of prehistoric man.

In the Punic strata, besides the items already mentioned, were
found rough stones, placed in the form of small megalithic menhirs (giving the impression of a miniature Stonehenge), in
which, of course, North Africa is very rich. There is a hint here,
that the excavation of Carthage may even throw light on the
mystery of the dolmens.

People who have made voyages so that thereafter they may
write books, more for the sake of writing than for the accuracy
of information conveyed, have rushed home to say "There is
nothing to find at Carthage." This is, of course, where they who
know differ from those who neither know nor are teachable.

At Tanit we found these four separate levels, each of a different age, each with a new story. We found prehistoric relics.
Above them, we found vases and stones which, while treasures
in themselves and containing other treasures, told of probable
Egyptian influence of the people of the peninsula. These vases
contained real treasures of jewels, gold leaves, ivory masks,
gold ornaments, amulets with the heads of jackals and "the eye
of Osiris," the god Bes, and the Phoenician god Moloch, and the
sacred triangle of Tanit.

Above them, in turn, were altars still speaking of Egypt, in
obelisk form, and amulets composed of the Egyptian pantheon
rested in the urns surrounding the altars.

Still higher were purely Punic specimens, among which are
some steles in a stone of very fine grain, whose designs and
workmanship are varied and craftsmanlike. One was a finely
sculptured figure of a priest with his hands uplifted to his face.
On another a priest held a child prior to sacrifice.

Abbé Chabot, who is one of the foremost authorities on the
Libyan and Phoenician languages, immediately took a

"squeeze" or impression, of the inscription, and announced a new form of Punic calligraphy.

It is interesting to see the Abbé take a "squeeze" into his hands, and to hear him read off the message it contains, just as though he were reading the morning paper.

In this particular case he read an uncomfortable message for excavators:

Whoever overthrows this stone shall be shattered by Baal.

Within a few moments we had another curse levelled at us. The Abbé was reading off a malediction of Tanit, addressed to "the violators of the sacred silence of the area of the Temple of Tanit."

Here too, we found literally hundreds of lamps, which spoke of the nocturnal scenes at the feasts of the goddess. Babies' bottles, even babies' toys, Punic coins, the silent testimony of grim ashes, and a great variety of pottery were around the altars.

The altars are worth special mention. They stand in close formation in the temple, and under them are the sacred urns. They were covered with painted stucco, and several have been recovered absolutely unblemished, with the colours still showing after twenty-seven centuries. They range from one to five feet in height, and are made of sandstone from the quarries at Cape Bon, across the gulf of Tunis. Many take the shape of the "betel" stone, more have the shape of a mummy standing between columns. On others are the "triangle of Tanit." Others bearing the lozenge, the disc, the crescent, and replicas of temples, with steps, are quite common.

Yet there is nothing to find in Carthage.

Would that the man who said that had been at work in Carthage. Particularly I should have liked to have had him there when we discovered the "curse stone."

I am no more superstitious than any average man, perhaps less than most excavators, but I can never look back on the discovery of that stone without some shudder chilling me.

First, and perhaps foolishly, our Punic scholar read off the curse, and some enterprising individual translated it to our awe-struck, but inspired, Arab foreman, and he told the men. They promptly struck.

Your true Arab dearly loves a strike. It saves him working, at least for a little while.

These labourers, who stood by and listened, promptly hung their picks and shovels over their shoulders and, with affronted dignity, marched away.

"Discover curse stone," they said, "One franc a day more." Rapid reasoning, but effective argument.

Off they trooped until they got their franc. One is always having arguments which end with monotonous regularity "One franc a day more!"

One wakes on St. Patrick's day. Before the day is over, our Arabs steal away, having said "one franc a day more." As a matter of fact they struck because they were watched too closely, and had no chance to steal relics. So they demanded to be paid for loss of perquisites.

Or, the Arabs hear that someone else is paying a higher rate. It may be a hundred miles away that the trouble originates, but up they come, "one franc a day more."

They are really children, but cunning, astute, self-willed children, and in the matter of petty bargaining they are fit descendants of the people whose ruined city they help us to uncover.

Occasionally they turn nasty, and murder is not unknown. Not by any means.

But, to go back to the curse stone. Before the day was ended, the curator of the Tanit museum, while walking along the rim of the top of the excavation slipped. He had no foothold, and went over the edge. He dropped to the bottom of the excavations and knocked himself unconscious, with a terrible gash in his head, on the very stone that cursed us.

The first day he was up again, he was taking light duty cataloguing specimens in the museum, and a bust of the goddess Tanit fell on him from a top shelf, and put a gash in the other side of his head. Thereafter there was at least one of our number who half-respected the potency of the ancient malediction.

When he recovered consciousness for the second time, he feebly murmured "I've had enough of Tanit, damn it!"

Subsequent to the discovery of the Temple of Tanit, we made another ghastly find, illustrative of the eventualities that have to be met in excavation. It has been said previously that we are often coming into some sort of conflict with the freebooters, those amateur excavators whose sole purpose is the recovery of specimens for sale. There are many who follow this pursuit, and we have been confronted by them on more than one occasion, sometimes with guns, sometimes with cudgels. If a good opportunity offered, I have not the slightest doubt that the people of the locality, who think that we are robbing them of the chance to plunder, would deal swiftly with us, and not to our benefit.

One day there was found the mutilated body of a Tunisian woman in the excavations. Her hands were dismembered, the vandal had wanted her rings and bracelets. It is supposed, though the crime was never solved, that a local treasure hunter was responsible, having need of money to carry forward his private enterprise in search of the riches of the tombs.

The plunderers are acute, and quick to seize the immediate spoils. In most of the tombs that stand in museums, relics of the past, it will be observed that a corner of the massive monolith that serves as the lid of the tomb has been broken off. This in itself is no mean accomplishment, and is the ever recurring sign, easily recognised, of the looter, whether of this generation or of generations that recede into the dim distance, back to the time when the dead were first laid into the earth.

The marauders knew what archaeology has since discovered, that the treasures contained in the tombs were generally placed near the head, and they snapped off a chunk of stone, so that they might insert a hand and arm, and grope around inside, to obtain the jewels and coins that were buried with the dead.

The Arabs are always awake to any new venture that is to be undertaken, and in the silence of the night will try to steal a march on the official excavators. We look with intense suspicion on any newly turned earth that we see, wherever we may see it. Newly turned earth means Arab, and the Arabs seldom work where it is not profitable. We found them, once, tunneling away on the other side of excavations we were making on the Hill of Juno. For long we have used them as our signposts. They are prone to return the compliment!

They simply gouge out a hole big enough for a man to squeeze through, then, like ferrets, they work rapidly and silently. Before we know it, right under our noses, we are frequently robbed of contributions to science, so that they may lay hold on contributions to their purse.

Treasure of course, really valuable treasure, is to be found. I have seen several great urns of gold coins that were recovered, the contents of which must have been worth many millions of francs.

Treasure hunting means jealousy, and jealousy quickly leads to murder. The fate of the Marquis Puisaye d'Anselm's expedition is a graphic case in point. For years the story has been current that subterranean passages exist between Carthage and Tunis, under the lake. The beginning of the passage was discovered, leading from the exact site of the famous Temple of Eshmoun, whose treasure, associated with the treasure of Dido, was supposed to have been hidden in the rock hill that towers over the city, and approached by the subterranean passage.

The Marquis d'Anselm organised an expedition which, I believe, was financed by an incorporated company, for the recovery of this treasure. The attempt ended in disaster, though it is reported that the treasure was located. Several stories of the tragedy are told, but it seems most probable that the explorers were deliberately murdered by the Arabs, to prevent the treasure being taken away. It is generally believed that the Arabs bored through the walls of the tunnel, and let in the waters of the lake. The Arabs, doubtless, were afraid that the loot would escape them, and tried to make sure of a chance to dig it out, later, for themselves.

The Arabs in many ways contrive to hinder the work of our excavation, though it is not necessarily our own workers who are the culprits.

Once, I remember being taken across the fields of Carthage by a most mysterious person, who acted in a very nervous way, looking round every few yards to see if we were being followed. I was led to a small square shaft in the ground. It was the site of Arab digging, and of a most profitable find. The hole had been made by independent excavators, and the result, with some of the treasure, communicated to a local dealer in antiques. He in turn communicated it to others. One of "the others" was a naval officer, whose ship was anchored in the bay, and he came ashore with a companion in the night, and set to work. From the honeycomb of tombs to which the shaft led, priceless crystals were removed. It is said that, among other things, the naval officer carried away a crystal replica of the acropolis of Carthage.

Other trophies, which were still in the possession of the dealer, were ultimately secured at a tremendous price by a guest of mine, and are finally destined for a great American museum.

I have investigated the tombs, as far as is possible without further excavation, and found many of them rifled. They are undoubtedly Phoenician, and as certainly there are other terraces of tombs to be uncovered. For the authenticity of the site I can vouch, and in the shop of the dealer, carefully guarded, I have seen some of the priceless crystals, now in the Metropolitan Museum, New York.

And still some people say that there is nothing worth finding to be uncovered at Carthage.

Consult my Arab boys on that point! When we were digging away one day I noticed an Arab putting things into his mouth. The mouth of an Arab is of enormous capacity. We watched this youth for a while, and then turned him upside down, and persuaded him to cough. The result of that excavation has never been surpassed, even by a votive urn. There were coins and jewels and rings and amulets; treasures galore.

We let him go then, and the next day a marble column was missing.

Chapter 7

CARTHAGE: THE HILL OF JUNO

The Hill of Juno is another of the important excavations made in the early years of the work at Carthage.

This is the hill opposite the acropolis of Carthage, from which Scipio is reputed to have witnessed the destruction of the city, and to have wept over the spectacle of desolation. After three years siege, and the final onslaught that reduced Carthage and laid it open to the holocaust, the Romans poured through the streets on their incendiary mission. Fighting through the thoroughfares, and it was a city designed for terrific street fighting, with houses seven storeys high, the invaders came over the dead bodies of the heroic defenders who had faced famine, pestilence, and the weapons of their conquerors. Flames followed them, lighting the skies as never beacon shone to guide the fleets to harbour.

Up to the Temple of Eshmoun they came, where fifty thousand Carthaginians had taken their last stand. Here the last remnants of the densely populated city sought the protection of their remaining gods. Tanit had already yielded to the Romans, her temple lay in ruins.

Towards the last, Hasdrubal, commander of the Carthaginians, turned traitor, and threw himself at the feet of Scipio, pleading for his life. His wife was of sterner stuff, and appearing on the roof of the temple, her children with her, addressed the victor:

To you, noble Roman, I ascribe no blame. You have fought, under the rules of war, and nobly conquered in the name of Rome; but for that base fellow who has betrayed the cause of his people, there is nothing but malediction to fall on his head. Soon may he grace your chariot, in chains, through the streets of Rome, and end in misery!

Immediately thereafter, taking her two children in her arms, and clasping them to her bosom, she showed them to the victorious Roman and the debased Carthaginian, and leapt into the flames. So died the last heroic member of the mighty empire. The final chapter of the great drama of the Mediterranean was finished.

At this site, acting on the suggestion of Renault, we started the excavation of the little Christian church that had been erected, and here I got my first real thrill of discovery, finding the first objects that were the result of my own work as an excavator. The specimens were lamps, of early Christian manufacture. It was my first responsible piece of work, and though the thrill has become somewhat of a habit since then, I shall, I hope, always retain the memory of the feeling that came over me as I held the first relic in my hands.

From there we went to another site on the hillside above, a spot which Renault had also mentioned. We worked for a while in small groups a little apart, and I was up to my eyes in a pit, very dirty, but considerably urged, for things were being unearthed every moment, when an Arab, more excited (if that were possible) than I was, dashed at me, crying "Found Fish! Found Fish!"

He failed to move me. I was busy, so I said to him "All right! Keep your fish, or throw it away." I thought he *had* found a fish.

A moment or two later, having stood away till my anger had subsided, he came back at me.

"Found fish! Found fish!"

He was so insistent that I had to follow him for his very importunity's sake, and I too was infected when I saw what manner of fish he meant. There, at the bottom of a pit three yards deep, I saw the fish – a gleaming bit of mosaic, of superb workmanship.

Within two minutes we had everybody at work on the site. Père Delattre, hearing the news, came flying over the hillside like an angry prophet, his robes flying in the wind, and his tremendous beard waving like a flag, to see what we had discovered.

We had come upon our first example of ancient art. And what an example! It was the first one I had ever seen being uncovered. Inch by inch, at what seemed to be a terribly slow rate, the earth was removed from the surface. We were leashed by science that day, so that the collar cut into our necks. How we strained! How we wished that there were only one thing to think of, the mosaic. But the earth we were removing was precious. It had to be taken away and sifted and sorted for other objects, and they had to be recorded and the necessary but tedious, measurements taken. We were at it till late into the night, by torchlight, and design after design was revealed. There were garlands of flowers, baskets of fruit, and every kind of wild game. Like a majestic carpet, the floor of an old banqueting hall was unrolled before us. As each new section was uncovered we threw a pail of water over it, and the coloured marble shone like a collection of glittering precious stones in the glare of our torches.

These mosaics are the coloured pictures of the history books of Carthage. They tell us much of the civilisation and habits of the people. If ever stones spoke, these are the stones. This particular mansion belonged to the Romans who had followed the Carthaginians, and had, in turn, endowed the city with a prosperity and affluence second only to Rome and the Carthage it displaced.

We know the modes and fashions of the period from the mosaics. They are as interpretative as any photograph could be. Here are pictures of their sports, their occupations, their athletic and other games, their home life, their horse races, gladiatorial shows, and their campaigns.

In one room we uncovered a mosaic, intact, depicting a hunting scene. It remains as beautiful as the rarest tapestry, with a fidelity to form, and a wealth of detail that is amazing. The picture shows a boar trying to escape from dogs and hunters. It taught us something new about ancient hunting. The hounds are partly clothed in armour, and are driving the boar to the nets held by beaters. The hunters bring up the rear of the chase.

One room led to another, and we found many mosaics. Also we found frescoed walls, which, though not so well preserved as the floors, yet showed that the Romans painted their walls to simulate marble, with graining and veining finely imitated, much as is done to-day.

In some places, as would be expected, we found the scribbling of naughty boys, who had left the usual contribution of boys to walls, when there is a crayon handy. Elsewhere we found where somebody had been checking over his accounts, and had totaled them up on the first convenient place, in this instance the wall. There are multitudinous scrawlings, which range from the humorous to the obscene.

Sometimes we find inscriptions on parchment as we excavate, and by now we know that the inscription fades as quickly as an unfixed photographic print. So we copy those inscriptions with the utmost rapidity. Once, I am sorry to say, we failed to do so, and the next morning there was no inscription to copy.

The Abbé Chabot mentioned that incident when he was lecturing to the Académie, and he was later somewhat taken to task by a fellow scientist for not having made a copy at once. Now we never omit the precaution.

Singularly enough, we once found the reverse of that when we were preparing an excavated wall. It had been *papered* with old parchments, and when we removed the parchment we found that on the plaster wall there was the "carbon copy" of the messages the parchments carried.

We pushed ahead with the work on the Hill of Juno, and in one of the rooms found a passage to the rock wall of the hillside. There were steps leading to the wall, which sent old Hassan, our foreman, into paroxysms of joy.

"Tomb! Tomb!" he yelled. "Punic tomb!"

I was again highly sceptical, I remember.

"Ung chose! Ung chose!" he insisted, growing more excited every second, screaming things that meant there would be many things to discover there. He was in full cry, and as hot on the scent as the dogs we had seen on the mosaic floor close by.

He did not fail us, but put my scepticism to shame. These Arabs have a very *practical* knowledge of archaeology. It is not essentially scientific, but it has a very clear eye to the main chance. Punic tombs mean gold rings, and jewels, small loot that can be secreted and smuggled to the dealers. Many a time we have bought back our own finds from the dealers, well knowing that they are ours, but having to pay good money for them again.

Hassan was so jealous of his discovery that he would permit none but himself to excavate the passage. All other work was suspended. The Arabs crowded round, almost in tears, but really relishing the opportunity to pursue their favourite occupation, which is to sit by and watch other people working. I remember, when I tried to get them back to work their answer was to the effect that the thing simply wasn't done when a Punic tomb was discovered.

For three hours Hassan wormed his way, like a human mole, into the clay, with only his feet sticking out of the soil. How he breathed baffles me, but at last we heard a muffled, but triumphant yell from the bowels of the earth, and the toes we could see wriggled until they got purchase to lever their owner back to life and light again. He backed out of the burrow, like a ferret in reverse gear, covered with mud, and holding in his hand a tiny bit of rotted wood.

I was unimpressed, but Hassan trembled like an aspen in his excitement.

"Coffin! Coffin!" he screamed.

I crept in, myself, and looked around. All that my torch lit up was a thin outline of wood in the clay, but it was enough for the moment.

We dug away with our knives, in turn, each one working until he was either almost suffocated, or quite exhausted. We kept constant relays going, and at last we discovered a beautifully graceful piece of pottery lying near a crumbled skull.

That was *our* first Punic tomb, though Père Delattre had, of course discovered many before us.

What we had discovered, however, was important. It disclosed a new necropolis on the Hill of Juno, dating from the very foundation of Carthage.

Above our workings was the site where Scipio stood, and from which spot he had cursed Carthage. The text occupies some fifty lines in the original text of Appian of Alexandria, and, since it has done duty for many cities, including Corinth, it may be worth while to give a precis of it.

Scipio, you will remember, sent a laconic message to Rome. "I have Carthage. What shall I do with it?"

The answer was sent, equally laconic, "Curse it!" and Scipio, who seems never to have done things by halves, responded with this malediction over the place.

God of Death and War, bring infernal terrors into this cursed city of Carthage, and against its armies and its people.

We curse with the utmost might of our being this people and this army. We curse whoever occupied these palaces, whoever worked in these fields, whoever lived upon this soil! We implore that they may be deprived for evermore of light from above.

Let eternal silence and desolation remain here. Cursed be they who return! Doubly cursed be those who try to resurrect these ruins.

That curse. It has its significance for all who work there. I remember Renault's last words: "The curse of Scipio has. . ."

When we opened the very next tomb, the Arabs thought it was working! I had been into the tomb, and had investigated it, temporarily. Then I came out again and took a breath or two before carrying the investigations further. Above the entrance was a massive slab of masonry that looked as though it was absolutely immovable. I suppose, however, that we had loosened the supporting earth, and had not taken as many precautions as we are now in the habit of taking.

On the next journey, excited at a find I had unearthed, I rushed back to the people waiting outside. Almost simultaneously, the tremendous slab dropped with a crashing explosion, like a small bomb, and cut me off from the tomb. It almost cut me off from any further excavations too! It missed me by the fraction of a second, and the fraction of an inch. If I had been standing there, the rock would have gone through me like butter.

It was on the Hill of Juno that we discovered the Roman palace, whose rooms on the ground floor numbered seven. The palace was probably several storeys high, since we know that the Phoenician houses were frequently on seven floors.

The palace generally brought to mind the villa at Bulla Regia which was excavated by Dr. Carton, and gave us light on the entirely adequate domestic arrangements of the Romans. At Bulla Regia, Dr. Carton unearthed a complete system of central heating, which was carried from the hot baths to the private villas of those citizens who were rich enough to afford the luxury. From the Boiler room, or "caldarium" of the baths, water, boiling hot, was delivered to the private houses, and passed through similar lead pipes round the rooms, and to the private bath of the citizen.

I suppose that modern civilisation really could teach these ancient hedonists very little indeed.

Underneath the Roman villa, in a subterranean passage, we found quantities of pots and pans, all of terra-cotta, with the bases burned, as they came from the fire. There were strainers too, and spoons and knives.

It must have been a Roman kitchen. Possibly we found the cook, too, for a woman's skeleton lay among the débris of the pots, and, when by chance the curator of the museum, Mr. Groseille, tipped up a slab of stone, we found her savings near the fuel. There were arrayed eighty coins, neatly arranged, so that she could see exactly how rich she was. What dreams imagination weaves. Perhaps her dream was of freedom, for the price of which she saved, or even she might have been saving to go to her husband with a respectable dot.

The bricks of the building were stamped with the seal of the brickyard, and by this means Père Delattre was able to tell us its date: the first century A. D. The bricks correspond with those of a house on the Appian way, a fact also verified by Père Delattre. They probably had a Roman architect for the building, brought over by people who, fired by Virgil's famous description of the wonders of the city, and Caesar's exhortation to refound it, had settled there.

Near the palace on the hill, we unearthed what must have been the site of a great battle in later days, for we came across a burial ground of the Vandals, where the corpses were as thickly clustered as on the fields of France in 1914-1918. With them were their swords and other weapons, and a multitude of lamps, of distinctive Vandal design. I have said before that the history of Carthage could be written from the lamps we unearth.

Near the palace fortune favoured us, and we excavated a considerable number of Roman cisterns, which undoubtedly have a significant historical value. We knew that we were excavating not very far from the scene of the great debate between St. Augustine and the Donatists, whose arguments took place in the year 411 A. D. in the baths of Gargilius. The terrific crises of the Christian Church was fought out between some five hundred representatives, two hundred and sixty Christian bishops, and two hundred and forty Donatists. For three days, in the Baths of Gargilius, the controversy raged, and Augustine's oratory and

erudition ultimately prevailed. Had it not been for him, it is safe
to say that the Christian Church as we know it to-day, would not
have persisted. But he did prevail, and we were working on the
land near to the site of this encounter. Some day, perhaps we
shall be so fortunate as to uncover more intimate relics, but so
far we have to be content with the discovery of the cisterns
which, apparently, may have served for the baths prior to their
abandonment. The cisterns that we have excavated are of enormous extent, and may have been the water supply for these
baths. In addition to the cisterns, we found the aqueduct which
leads from them to the great aqueduct, which was the source of
supply of the water of the city.

There is still a useful quantity of cool, fresh water in the cistern, and perhaps it is not out of place to mention that the
younger members, and occasionally the older members of the
excavation party, used the cisterns as the "old swimming hole."
They are extremely welcome after a day's work in the ruins.

In the course of our excavations, on the hill, we have been
able to reconstruct, for the benefit of tourists and the advancement of knowledge, a very complete museum of Carthaginian
life throughout the centuries. We have recovered, and preserved,
tombs of all the succeeding inhabitants. Here, in the stillness of
death, is the history of Carthage, from the time of prehistoric
man.

Fully restored, and carefully preserved are the tombs of man
before he was civilised. Beside him lie, just as they were laid
into the earth, the remains of Phoenicians, Romans, early Christians, Vandals, Byzantines and Saracens, so that within a few
moments the visitor, who has little leisure and less opportunity,
may appreciate the progress of the isthmus. The tombs lie there
as we discovered them, and a significant tale they tell.

This area is actually the site of our headquarters on the field.
We have had electric light installed here, carrying it from Tunis,
sixteen kilometres away, and, so far as is possible, we have
made the site worth visiting, even from the standpoint of the
searcher after beauty.

Up the hillside we have made paths, with steps to cover the more difficult approaches, and now, through paths that are lined with flowers, the tourist can see history more graphic than can be written. Often we have had nearly a thousand people in the day to see what we have done, and are doing.

Other important fields of excavation in and around Carthage include the tremendous edifices erected by the Romans.

"By the Romans?" perhaps you say, remembering Scipio's curse. The Romans respected the curse, but narrowly. Their settlement touched the cursed site, but perhaps never invaded it. We find their structures just outside the city that must have been the purely Phoenician settlement. Their buildings cover the necropoli, which were always outside the city proper in Punic times. So Scipio is evaded, and the curse avoided.

Chief among the discoveries dating from the Roman period, is the Amphitheatre, which was discovered by Père Delattre, and which was restored under our joint direction. This edifice is of considerable size, and must have enjoyed a great repute in Rome. It was one floor higher than the Colosseum at Rome. The walls are now reconstructed, and Cardinal Lavigerie has erected a Marble Cross and a chapel in honour of the countless martyrs who, for the sake of their faith, suffered and died here.

A grim chapter of Christian history is contained in these reconstructed walls. Here the Vandal Genseric had the Christian bishops who were sent out from the city to intercede with him, trampled to death. Here, too, the martyrs were fed to the beasts, while the populace sat, amused and hilarious, in the serried tiers, watching their torment; a true Carthaginian holiday.

The area of the amphitheatre is vast. Between sixty and eighty thousand people could be accommodated. The spectacle is easily imagined, for we have discovered the cages, with their trap doors, which held the ravenous beasts, deprived of food that they might be the more ferocious, before they were loosed upon the martyrs.

Here Saints Felicitas and Perpetua were gored to death by a wild cow, and here a buffoon was engaged in the pleasant pursuit, for the delectation of the unsatiated Romans, of prancing among the unconscious Christians with a red hot iron, to see if the searing metal would stir them to new activity, or if they were really dead. What roars of laughter, what obscene jests were flung, from safety, to the tortured victims is told by Tertullian and Augustine.

The Romans were enthusiastic theatre-goers, They loved a spectacle dearly. Carthage possessed, in addition to the amphi-theatre, a circus, a stadium, and a hippodrome.

We have already prospected the Circus, which measures seven hundred and forty yards by three hundred and fifty yards, and had accommodation for three hundred thousand people.

Three hundred thousand people! They must have catered for the whole of the free population of the city at one sitting! One of our next tasks is to excavate this site, which lies between the amphitheatre and the Temple of Tanit. All outside the walls of the Punic City. All escaping the curse.

There must have been magnificent spectacles there. The way to the hearts of the populace was the provision of a spectacle. Graft was easy then. A politician, wishing to be sure of a follow-ing, provided the cost of a performance in the amphitheatre, and, as one would say in America, so he made himself solid. I am not sure whether they had the equivalent of the vernacular, but it is safe to say that they had, for much that we have recovered leads us to believe that humanity changes slowly or as William Wat-son put it, "by how slow degrees!"

The American Partisan of sports, the "fan," had his exact counterpart in Carthage, but his name was not worthy of abbre-viation. He was indeed a fanatic. And he had little to learn from his later compeer.

Not even the Hippodrome of New York offered greater spec-tacles. We have discovered the sluices and the canal to the sea, which provided the water for the transformation of the arena into a naval stage. Here the Romans produced their naval battles in miniature, while the spectators cheered. We know exactly how these spectacles, and the arena and amphitheatre appeared, for there has been unearthed a mosaic, which is now in the museum at Tunis, which gives to the minutest detail all the things we need to know, for the ultimate reconstruction of the building.

What a chapter of popular history this represents, coupled with the other items of our collection. We can reconstruct, from our specimens and from the verbal records of the historians, the life of Carthage almost as exactly as though we had a motion picture taken at the time, and on the spot.

How they worshipped sport! Père Delattre excavated the house that was given to their popular idol, Scorpianus. It was the palace of the ancient Dempsey, except that he was their champion charioteer. We have also excavated the tomb of a ballet dancer from the Theatre. Item by item we are learning every detail of the fashionable life of the city.

In the excavations we have discovered the reserved seats that belonged to the magistrates and the plutocrats. Their names are carved into the seats lest some interloper should come and usurp them.

Probably the chariot races ranked next to the slaughter of the Christians as a popular sport. From the number of indications we have found, I should judge that these contests were frequent, and that the teams visited the various cities in turn. The champions of Utica were the nearest rivals to those of Carthage, and how dearly they loved each other!

The teams were distinguished, much in the modern fashion, by the colours they wore and we have record of teams whose colours were Green, Red, Blue and White. The prize money was no inconsiderable item, and not infrequently amounted to $70,000 for a day's contest. The statesmen of the period, incidentally, felt much as modern statesmen do, when they compare their remuneration with professional sportsmen. One protested, and his protest has a familiar ring, that Scorpianus received three bags of gold for a day's work, while he, poor man, received less for the total of his year's service to the State.

The partisans organised their campaigns carefully. The main idea was to "get the goat" of the other fellow, just as the "bleachers" try it in modern ways. Only, if anything, they did it more thoroughly. In the humorous section of the Lavigerie museum is a multitude of "maledictions," which the various factions scattered broadcast among the contestants. They are in lead, thin sheets of inscribed metal, fortunately for us, and are in excellent preservation. There would be parchment duplicates, doubtless, but they have gone and are not to be found. We can be content with the specimens we have.

When Utica came to Carthage, Carthage was determined that no effort should be spared to put Utica off its game. So we have maledictions hurled this way and that against the visitors. These "goat getters" knew their way about. Their maledictions were definite, very much to the point.

"May the chariot of the Blues have a wheel come off at the third corner!" says one leaf of lead. It is worth noticing, from a psychological point of view at least. The suggestion is there, to carry fear into the heart of a superstitious individual. The place where the fans wanted the accident to happen is stated. Possibly it was the point where a good view of the catastrophe could be obtained.

"May the champion of the Blues be taken with cramp in the middle of the race!"

"May his horses be seized, so that they cannot start, cannot bound, cannot run!"

And, finally, "May he suffocate the night before the race!"

Truly modern in outlook. And truly modern in popular reaction. Tertullian recounts the battle of the fans. Excitement ran high, there were favourites to cheer, there were rivals to discourage.

On one occasion the visitors were driven to the top tiers of the amphitheatre, and there a pitched battle took place, all arising from a love of sport. How essentially human these Romans were.

For the theatre, too, every provision was made. There were travelling troupes in those days, who made their "one night stand." And doubtless there were "stars" and barnstormers, idols and idlers.

Everything was done in approved style. The Romans anticipated our magazine programme, which was again, either of thin sheets of lead, or of parchment. The lead programmes have survived, and give an account of the performance of the day, and of following attractions. Interspersed were jokes and obscenities. The theatre programmes of Carthage are amongst the world's most obscene literature.

Around the walls of the monastery, Père Delattre has a unique collection of the minor pursuits of the Romans, the little games they played, perhaps while waiting for the spectacles to begin in the arenas or on their quiet evenings when there was nothing much of interest in the public places.

It may be too much to say that there is the ancient equivalent of the cross word puzzle, but one of the slabs reminds us of the modern craze. There are the squares, to which we are accustomed, and in some the letters have been placed, while other spaces are blank. It is a game, of course, and not a puzzle, for cross words were not done by sculpture!

Innumerable little round discs have been found, some red and some white, which we are convinced are checkers. The steps of the temples at Dougga and at Timgad are worn away, very much as though they had been used as a checkerboard. It is impossible not to think of the regulations of a certain austere and ancient English university, whose students are still ordered not to "play marbles on the steps of the buildings."

We found multi-coloured marbles, too. They could hardly have been anything but the toys of the children. They are of white, gold, black, with even an inferior quality in granite, identical with the marbles of to-day.

Here is the minor tragedy of excavation. Much of the work was done by Père Delattre, on "excavating lease." It was then impossible for him to acquire lasting rights to the land, and when excavation has been made, the site has had to be filled up again. The villa of Scorpianus, presented to him by an admiring city, was uncovered, its magnificence was revealed, with mosaics and frescoed walls. Such material as could be taken was removed for the national museum, and then the earth was replaced. Père Delattre had only a four months' lease. But it is safe, as are so many other sites which have been filled in again. They wait for other work, when funds permit.

It is a little disappointing, but that is only one of our troubles. A much more irritating thing is the real estate boom!

The speculative builders and gamblers in land are apparently determined to raise a new city over the site of these old civilisations, and, judging from the start that has been made, we shall before long be confronted with the need of buying a "desirable modern villa" before we can get at the earth beneath, for the relics of the past. If the real estate agent is allowed a free hand, or if we cannot raise enough money to forestall him, in a few years Carthage will become a seaside resort.

It is not entirely a question of preserving only the land from their exploitation. The name of Carthage itself may go, for one dealer, richer and perhaps more enterprising than the rest, has already staked out his suburb, and re-christened it after himself.

He is doing his best to get the name established in the minds of the people, and in the deeds of sale.

But he was generous. He offered the use of his land for excavation on condition that the name of Carthage was changed to shall we say "Smithville." He is a regular Mr. Babbitt, so perhaps we might say, and euphonically, it is nearer the Tunisian corruption, Carthage may ultimately become "Babbittville."

Science has realised almost too late, that this danger exists. Our expedition came in time to preserve some of the land, particularly that under which is believed to lie the Punic Forum and other important sites, but other areas of equal interest are already gone, and it will need much money and more legislation, to expose their treasures to the sight of man again. The land which is still undisturbed by the builders of "attractive villas," and can be purchased at a reasonable price, is year by year becoming more restricted.

Less than twenty years ago, we could have saved the whole area intact, and the peninsula might have been made into a national reserve, the greatest natural museum the world could know, an international monument of tremendous interest.

Then one could go from the fishing village of La Goulette, at the southern extremity to the charming Arab village of Sidi Bou Said, which is the ancient Megara, Phoenician suburb where Hamilcar lived, and Salammbo too, without encountering any buildings except a few native huts, the Cathedral and missions of the White Fathers and the White Sisters, and a palace or two belonging to the Beylical family.

It was a great opportunity, but it has escaped the attention of everyone, save the real estate people. Building operations followed the projection of an electric railway through the Carthage area, and the real estate agents saw that rapid transport meant rapid profits. There was not even an element of risk. A lot at Carthage might be above a mine of treasure. The lure must work. It has worked, to our sorrow.

That electric railway. It must be unique. Its track is ballasted with antiquity. Bits of columns from Christian Basilicas and pagan temples, fragments of cornices and pilasters, even Roman inscriptions are to be picked up between the rails.

The speculator sees his opportunity. Coupled with the natural beauty of the site, which is entrancing, is the promise of intrinsic worth under the earth. He even capitalises history, and draws on classic names haphazard, for suggestive titles. Those names! Hamilcar, Salammbo, are now stations on an electric railway. Hannibal has not yet appeared, but his turn will come.

Less than a dozen years ago this land could be bought for twenty-five centimes a square metre. The poorest is now worth ten francs.

And we, unavoidably, play into the hands of our enemies. Every treasure we unearth sends up the price of land. Tourists by the thousands come to Carthage now, where few came before, and where there are tourists, the Arab is shrewd enough to realise there is money. There are a thousand ways of getting money from travellers, and the Arabs know them all.

We hope, however, that the most important of the territory may yet be saved, and we are straining every nerve to defeat the commercial genius of the peninsula, and to preserve the historic values.

Chapter 8

THE HOME OF THE EXPEDITION

There is another side of excavation. We are not always digging, but we are usually either comparing notes or planning new fields. Life is as comfortable for our off duty hours as we can reasonably make it. It is not so festive or elaborate as life in Paris or New York, but it has its charm.

Our home is an old Arab palace at Sidi Bou Said and overlooks the plains of Carthage, with the sea on either side. The palace is several hundred years old, and belonged to a Mohammedan prince. We have called it Palais Hamilcar, and have made an effort to restore some of the atmosphere of an ancient Carthaginian home, which is not so difficult, considering the specimens we have around.

It is supposed to be on the site of Salammbo's palace, overlooking the Megara, the suburb of Carthage, and therefore, fortunately for the superstitious, outside the sphere of Scipio's curse. The palace has actually been built over Roman ruins, the cisterns of which we still use for our water supply. In the gardens cypress trees make a stately avenue to the gateway, while bougainvillea, daffodils, primroses, violets, flowering cactus, cornflowers, poppies and lemon trees blossoming in the spring, contrive to make a riot of colour commensurate with the landscape.

Our garage also is an old Roman cistern, and there is something which occasionally strikes a grotesque note in the sight of a palpitating, if ephemeral, Ford, chugging up the driveway and disappearing into masonry that has stood for centuries.

In the courtyard, which is an exquisite example of Arabian faience, there are ancient marble columns, and a fountain plays cheerily. But even here we are not free from the thirst for excavation. Père Delattre found a Vandal tomb, in a fine state of preservation, and in the tomb an emerald necklace, which is now in the museum at Tunis, in company with the gem-studded breastplate of the warrior. These two items are probably among the finest of the collection in the museum.

Mosaic floors and ruined tombs crop up everywhere, and, inside the palace we classify and argue about them and the results of our work.

The interior of the palace is very much like a school, and life goes on under routine that is also reminiscent of school days. Rooms are set apart for drawing, classification and measurement. Our photographers have a dark room and studio, and we all have a share in the council room.

Visitors remark on the notice boards. They are there, containing instructions, minutely detailed, of the duties of the day.

When the members of the expedition come down from their dormitory in the morning, they scan the boards to see what is apportioned to them for the day. Some are detailed for duty in Utica, others for the various nearby fields, and occasionally a lucky individual or two may be sent to Tunis for further equipment. The youths of the party evidence a justifiable rivalry for these journeys to Tunis. I am afraid that the Patisserie Royale has a lure second only to Tanit.

Routine must be maintained, and the day begins early. Breakfast is at 6:30 for those who go far afield, and at 7:30 for the rest. The culprit who is not down in time for breakfast finds breakfast gone. Luncheon we take with us to the scene of our work.

After the day is over, we return to the Palace, and dinner is served when we have sluiced off the immortal dust of Carthage. After dinner we sit around and discuss the day's results, what we have done, and what objects we have found. Dimensions are checked, and photographs of the previous day are talked over. Everything is classified.

During the council, Professor Peterson takes down the reports in the journal of the expedition, and thereafter it is "free for all," frequently resolving itself into a debate, with the architects and surveyors, the various specialists and Abbé Chabot as the principal characters.

In this way students from the various universities become familiar with every phase of the operations, and acquire highly specialised knowledge under the most ideal circumstances.

Sometimes too, we have visitors. Very often they come in considerable numbers, and add somewhat to the cares of housekeeping. I am afraid I am to blame for their coming, and that it arises out of a habit of mine. When I am lecturing I invite people to come and see us at Carthage. It doesn't seem possible that everyone will come, at least within the next few weeks, until I get back to the field, and then it seems as though they all came at once, and brought their friends with them.

We do the best we can however, and usually it is a happy thing for us, and for them. And it is all good for the cause.

Once in a while there is a strange consequence to such enthusiasm for Carthage as I may have been able to arouse among my audiences.

One zealous amateur nearly precipitated a general strike. She hove to in front of our party one day, dressed for the part in a velvet hat, blouse and corduroy trousers, adorned with a gorgeous scarf for waist belt, and announced her intention to begin excavating!

Work came to an abrupt halt. The Arabs struck at once, it seemed so opportune a moment. They neither could nor would understand this apparition in their midst. Père Delattre went into a hysteria of amazed protest, and the strike almost extended to the actual members of the expedition. By superhuman tact and machiavellian diplomacy, the catastrophe was ultimately averted.

Close to our home is the veritable Aladdin's Palace of Baron d'Erlanger, and it is a wonderful relaxation to spend an hour or

two, in the quiet of the day, in surroundings that speak so eloquently of the spirit of Hannibal and the great Carthaginians.

It is an immense palace, with endless rooms and corridors,
built of seventeen different kinds of marble, and furnished in
glorious Moorish fashion, with carpets of Mecca and cushions
of the Tunisian souks. Its soft lights and gentle shadows invite
rest and speak of peace.

In all the courtyards, between columns of marble, hang gilt
cages containing singing birds. The air is fragrant with the perfume of incense and the odour of orange trees and lemon blossoms. A fountain plays in the great room, and the water, that has
its source in a basin beautified by lilies and tulips, flows through
the middle of the luxurious chamber. Here by the laughing
stream, reclining on cushions, one hears the mysterious music of
the country. The musicians and singers are hidden, but, in the
half light, from a seemingly great distance, comes the muffled
drumming, eloquent of the retreating Moors leaving Granada,
wailing the loss of a great empire. Nearer and nearer it comes,
and new instruments take up the theme. The cymbals clash and
the flutes wail, and the voices of the singers intone the minor
chords of the chant of retreat.

Magnificence upon magnificence, both of eye and ear, lead
the mind across the centuries, until it is necessary only to be
tranquil in order to appreciate the tragedy that has flowed over
the isthmus since Carthage first struck awe into the minds of the
people of the ancient world.

Through long avenues of dark trees, cypress and myrtle, is to
be seen a limpid pool, in which gold fish lazily turn, and on
whose surface is reflected the whole of the village of Sidi Bou
Said. The gleaming white houses, with their brilliant blue windows, fresh and untarnished, are reflected here and the towering
minaret of the mosque whence, at night, the voice of the muez-
zin calls the people to prayer. It might almost be the voice of the
Phoenician priests, exhorting the moon, while Carthage was still
their city.

Sunday is our rest day. It is essentially the day when we let excavation cease, and remember that we are human beings and not moles, when we wander down to the Monastery gardens, having been to Mass. To hear the White Fathers singing the old chants, is to listen to the most inspiring and beautiful music I know, and the spectacle of the rites of the early Christians, preserved here as nowhere else in the world, is sufficient to carry us back in body as well as in spirit to the great days whose ruined memorials we are recovering.

The monastery gardens are the loveliest spot in Carthage; the only place where peace is never invaded. They lie crowning the top of the hill, enclosed by a wall.

Really the gardens are a park of ruins. The hoary old stones are softened by the brilliance of a profusion of flowers, creeping vines, and the venerable Père Delattre. He is the whole spirit of the place for us. When he is gone, I hardly like to think what will happen to us all.

Innumerable trees are here, and great pyramids of ruins, secured from loss, piled up, waiting for the time when there are sufficient workers, and sufficient knowledge, to fit them again into their proper places in the great work of reconstruction.

Moving quietly among the trees are the white-robed Fathers. It often seems to me that nowhere in the world do the birds sing quite so sweetly as in these gardens, gardens which themselves are a monument raised on the blood-soaked earth of Carthage after untold generations of merciless warfare, persecution, disaster and pestilence. Out of Christian martyrdom has prevailed Christian peace.

From the gardens, wandering through the columns of the acropolis, it is only a little way to the museum, on the steps of which a White Father will doubtless greet you with a Christian welcome, and offer himself as a friendly guide. The first things he will show you are the tomb stones of Saints Perpetua and Felicitas.

Through a doorway is the great Punic room, where the dead of Carthage speak of the past. The sun strikes directly on to the lid of the sarcophagus of the Carthaginian priestess Arizat-Baal, an exquisite sculpture discovered by Père Delattre, forty feet under the clay of the hill on which Dido is said to have landed.

The original colouring is unimpaired, and the priestess seems to be alive. Before amazement at her beauty has passed away, the White Father will probably say "That is as she was, twenty-five hundred years ago. There she lies to-day." His hand will fall to his side, and, following the gesture, your eyes will be arrested by the open sarcophagus, which contains the grim skeleton of the dead priestess.

Nearby is the tomb of a young girl, with the hair still clinging to the skull. In a little box is incense that was found in the tomb with her. When it is burned, the old scent still rises.

In a case are a pair of spectacles, with the lenses in position. I never see them without imagining an old Carthaginian merchant adjusting his spectacles before signing a cheque with one of the quill pens such as those near to hand, which were found in the tomb of a scribe, perhaps a poet who paid tribute to the beauty of the priestess.

Around are a variety of cases containing personal objects: different kinds of rouge, vanity boxes, bronze mirrors, nail files, scissors, scent bottles, combs, hair pins, incense burners, and all those trifles that contributed to the happiness of women of fashion when Carthage ruled.

In a way, one is glad to come out of the museum again, to see the sun, and to catch a glimpse of the sea.

From the terrace one can gaze down to what were the old gates of Carthage, and the little ponds, so small and forlorn looking to-day, speak of the time when the sea came round to the Admiral's palace, of which, now, only a few columns marked with the triangle of Tanit, still remain. It is astonishing that nothing has yet been discovered of the great walls of the city, which were at once fortifications and granaries, or, beyond a few pillars, of the Admiralty and the harbour, which was enclosed by three-storey high buildings, where the people could witness the manoeuvres of the fleet as they sailed by, saluting their Admiral, before putting out to sea on a mission of war.

Despite the edict of the self-assured, there is much yet to be discovered at Carthage.

Chapter 9

THE DEAD CITIES

Burned by the blazing sun, and scarred by the hands of man and passing years, the martyred cities of Africa lie half buried in the sands from one end of the continent to the other. Their golden ruins are silhouetted against a sky that once looked down upon a land of beauty and luxuriance and is now left a wilderness.

It has been a hobby for the last five years to wander along the half-deserted trails of the ancients, over mountains and wilderness into the deep shadows of vast ruins, the skeleton of the work of the Empire builders, cities whose scattered stones are the bleaching bones of history lying gaunt in the sunlight.

North Africa is an archaeological park stretching from the Atlas mountains to the Syrian coast, the trail runs through an almost endless series of triumphal arches, by aqueducts, bridges, forums, fortresses, basilicas, palaces and temples. Sometimes the ruins rise like mirages from the shimmering sands, sometimes they are half-hidden in mountain mists, and at times it is possible to see them reflected in the clear waters off the shore.

From Carthage, which was the metropolis of them all, the old roads of the legions lead north, south and west, in some cases for so many hundreds of miles that they are finally lost in the sea of sands that is the Sahara.

To me, Carthage is the city of Basilicas and the place of the cult of Tanit, full of memories. Utica is the city of the Phoenician treasure tombs. Dougga is the city of matchless temples. Bulla Regia means that adventure lies in the mysterious underground palaces. Timgad was the garrison town. Gigthis and Djerba are the dead cities of legend and sand.

Each has its own distinct and personal character. No two are alike, and yet there are hundreds of these now silent habitations of forgotten peoples only waiting for the pick and shovel of the excavators to make them reveal the glorious past.

Only the surface has been scratched, in a small attempt to penetrate some of the mysteries and the history of Africa, and, though the pioneer enthusiasm of the old school of French scientists has done wonders, their efforts and those of the Services des Antiquités have never been adequately seconded. There is no field on earth so promising as Africa. Nowhere are the ruins so abundant, speaking eloquently of the population that once filled the country.

Population must have been dense indeed during the time of the Romans. In very restricted areas I have counted several hundred important ruins. Gsell enumerates 264 in the neighborhood of Tebessa alone, and Boissiere speaks of 300 ruins in the region of Mateur, where to-day there is one solitary little town of about three thousand inhabitants. Several archaeologists and historians have calculated the population of some towns in proportion to their size. Thysdrus, with its colossal amphitheatre had a population of 100,000, Sufetula 30,000, Thelept, whose vast ruins are yet absolutely untouched, had 60,000 and Meninx 40,000.

It is difficult to calculate the population of Africa in Phoenician times. My friend Stephane Gsell treats this subject fully in the second volume of his monumental *History of North Africa,* as well as the list of cities that bear Roman names of Punic origin. The works of Ptolemy, the nautical instructions called Stadiasme of the Great Sea, the outline of Peutinger, and the famous itinerary of Antonine serve as my authorities in the study of the old cities and the various routes.

Whether we can ever approach exact figures or not, an immense population lived in this region in both Phoenician and Roman days, covering the country between the Mediterranean and Cyrenia. Surprise awakens when the size of these empires is considered in the light of the struggles that were everlastingly continued, both against human enemies and the ravages of nature. The opinion is generally held that the climate must have suffered great changes during the last two thousand years, but, the more I see of Africa, the more I am convinced that men adapted themselves to the country, and made it flourish by their own ingenuity and patient labour.

From one end to the other, there are traces of aqueducts, cisterns, and irrigation works. The question that arises is never to be avoided in sight of these works. If there used to be a heavier rainfall, then why all these vast constructions? When Marius made his famous march to Jafsa (Capsa) he passed through uncultivated, arid deserts (Sallust Jug. 89). I have crossed this region, and have seen it thick with buildings and towns that were built after his march. If the wilderness blossomed like the rose, it was through the work of men.

France to-day is following in the wake of her great forerunners of fifteen or twenty centuries ago, and I am firmly convinced that her fight against the desert will be as successful as was that of the Romans.

Some hundreds of times, after lectures, I have been questioned about the climate, and if the changing climate is not responsible for the ruins being in a desert country. I believe that if the waterways and other works were restored, Algeria and Tunisia could become the granary of Europe as it was for three hundred years under Roman rule. This opinion is, of course, a matter which would need to be supported in a long and reasoned argument, but in the course of my wanderings I have collected sufficient notes, and made enough comparisons, to form the basis of a later report on the question. Stephane Gsell, Carter, Th. Fisher and A. Knox have all expressed their opinions on the matter, but the field is still open. While at Tebessa lately, Maurice Reygasse and Stephane Gsell started a discussion that we continued in a lively fashion until the early hours of the morning.

However, the basis of that discussion may well be the starting point for one who would wander through the dead cities. Civilisation is a question of water-supply, and we can start along the great aqueduct to find the cities that profited by it.

The Great Aqueduct leads from Carthage along the Imperial Way south. It stretches across the plains like an old dragon that is still master of its land, to the source at Zaghuan; eighty kilometres of raised waterway, which was capable of delivering six million gallons of water to Carthage daily.

For twenty centuries the natives of the plains have looked at the monument to pre-Christian engineers, have seen it in its splendour, when the brilliance of a setting sun outlined it in crimson against the sombre purple of the Atlas mountains.

The explorer of to-day follows in the train of earlier expeditions, which had no reference to archaeology, but whose object was plunder. From the ravaged plains, and the desolate cities, stones, monuments, and even buildings have been wrested to ornament the cities of the Mediterranean, whose power waxed as the days passed. Many an Italian and Spanish city boasts as its own gems that had their origin along the Imperial Way.

At Zaghuan the furthest point of the aqueduct, on the side of the mountain, the temple through which the stream flows still stands. It is called now the "Chateau d'eau" but for the Romans it was a holy place. The temple was in the form of a semicircle of worked columns, between which stood statues dedicated to the water divinities. Year by year the people assembled here for the rites and ceremonies of blessing the water, whose volume kept the cities supplied. Perhaps the Romans had an eye for the picturesque, as well as for the utilitarian value of the place, for, from the flower covered ruin the broken aqueduct can be seen twisting its way across the plains to Tunis, and beyond that to Carthage.

Not far from Zaghuan, but a little off the track and needing a special journey lies Thurburbo Majus, just awakened from the sleep of centuries. Its excavation and restoration are part of the work of the Services des Antiquités, which has been going forward in Africa during the last twenty years.

This city has been called the Pompeii of Tunisia, a name well earned and appropriate. It lies, in the springtime, in a bed of many coloured flowers, which carpet the earth and grow in wild profusion round the ruins. The magnitude of the remains of the old city and the glory of the countryside make an exalting spectacle. Thurburo stands beside a river, surrounded by a circle of fantastic mountains, the jeweled tomb of the dead, sunk in a deep setting.

Seeing the city for the first time, one is impressed by the variety of marble that has been used in its construction. Much is coloured, and the colouring has mellowed and softened with age, so that the Forum, the Capitol, the summer and winter baths, triumphal arches, market place, temples and cemeteries combine with nature to suggest that the city is only in repose, and not desolate or dead.

It might only be waiting for the dawn to spread fully across the sky, before the city awoke and the streets filled. It is even almost gay. The tones of the marbled walls, staircases and even roads, hint at the brilliance that once existed, as the buildings change in hue, and almost texture, with the varying light and shade of an African day.

I have seen the ruins at night, violet toned against the moonlit countryside, with shafts of polished silver here and there, and the mountains beyond like towering giants brooding over the city that speaks of the genius of Rome, now silent and melancholy, but immense and grand.

South of the aqueduct lie the lead workings of the ancients at Djebel Resses, the lead mountain that was mined by Carthaginians, Romans and Vandals. In our excavations we have found a great number of slingstones which were made at Djebel Resses, and are inscribed with the curses of the slingers on their enemies. The stones vary in size from that of a pigeon's egg to a walnut, and their messages read "May this rest in the skull of my enemy" with an additional burst of profanity, or "I hope this gets him!," "let this bring my enemy to the dust." The additional and purely personal remarks are quite unquotable.

With Djebel Resses on one side of our way and Bou Kornein on the other, the road winds to the "canyon of the Hatchet" where Hamilcar penned in the revolted forces of his own mercenaries, and met them with Carthaginians.

It is the easiest thing in the world for us, knowing about the great battle, and identifying the place, to say how obviously it lent itself to the purpose. Any general would, if he could, have preferred such a spot for the battle, especially if his forces held the upper reaches and guarded the passes. Hamilcar compelled the issue at this point. There was no way of escape for the rebels, and they were reduced to hunger, and finally to cannibalism, before they surrendered. Surrender was no escape, however, for with Punic thoroughness, they who escaped their companions were crucified by their captors. It served the Phoenician's purpose, of establishing discipline and authority, but it has left its memory here, and, despite the surrounding beauty, one is quite willing to leave the spot which even the natives call accursed to this day.

It served too, for the great climax of Flaubert's masterpiece *Salammbo*. Tissot places the actual site at Ain es Sef. We have planned an exploring party for our next season's work, to search for traces of the battle, the most ferocious in history. Polybius calls it the "inexpiable war" and certainly its horrors have never been equaled in the history of warfare. (Poly. I, 88, 6-7.)

On the way South by Bou Kornein lies Hamanlif, where extensive ruins have recently been found. Bou Kornein was the sacred mountain of the Carthaginians and the Romans. On its twin summits stood the "high place" of the Canaanites, when the cult of Baal flourished. In Roman days the holy place became the temple of Saturnus Balcaranensis, and traces are still to be seen of a sanctuary, which was excavated by Professor Tontain, and whose specimens are now in the Bardo museum.

The fires of Baal are cold, and from the sacred place looking down the green slopes and across the Gulf of Tunis one can see

the cathedral of St. Louis of Carthage, symbol of peace and
charity, where once ruled Tanit, Moloch, Baal, synonym of all
that was merciless and vicious in pagan horror.

It is a strange thought, but many an Arab dwelling must be
built on the ruined altars of the Phoenician sun-worshippers in
this land of dead empires.

Bou Kornein means twin-horned, and the name may possibly
have some reference to the horns on the head of images of Baal-
Moloch.

Travelling south, near the gully of Hamamet, at Bir Bou
Rebka (Saigu) are the ruins of another temple which was dedicated to the gods of the dead past, Baal and Tanit, whose fires
have smouldered long, but now no more.

A little further journeying on the Roman Road brings us to
Aphrodisium, whose name speaks for itself, and at once sug-
gests the cult it commemorates. Here and at Sicca Veneris (now
Le Kef) the worship of Venus reigned. Many relics of the orgies
have been discovered, as well as the indications mentioned in
Stephane Gsell's History of Africa. They who would know more
about the practices and their historical setting are referred to that
authority (Cults, Vol. IV, 402 ff.) and Valer. Max. (II, 6.15).

We pass from the site of the "abominations of the Sidonians"
down the coast to the old tower of Ksar, now Menara, on the
way to Sousse, the ancient Hadrumet. The roads are magnificent, and it has been great relaxation for us, year by year, to
make expeditions from Carthage through this region.

In the spring, the great Bedouin migrations take place. The
caravans come north for the greener pasturage and for the harvest, and their travelling hordes bring to mind others who have
followed the same route. The picturesque groups come trekking
towards the mountains with their herds of camels and dogs and
mules, and their women and children. The nomads use the
Roman highway that leads from Tripoli and the Sahara to
Carthage, the same road that served the ravagers questing for
pillage, in the days that stretch to the forgotten years. The blue
robed, tattooed Bedouins recall the tribes of the past; the Merce-

naries of twenty centuries ago, the Nasamons, Getulians, Ethiopians, Garamanteans and Libyans. All these have trodden the road before us. This is the street, it seems, where history was born.

In the sunset along the trail we have camped by the old circular tower, and watched the twinkling lights of nomad fires on the shadowy horizon, and dreamed in the dusk of Hannibal's elephants sweeping past us in the night, their trunks swinging and their mahmouts shouting, passing on in scores from the Sahara to Carthage, then on to the eternal snows of the Alps, or to die in Trasimene and Cannae.

Here Hannibal himself journeyed, on his flight from the city, and here, by the tower waited for his ship, the way to safety. Perhaps the story we told by our camp fire is worth retelling, of the day when the emissaries of Rome came to Carthage to demand his surrender.

In the year 195 B.C. Hannibal fled, after careful preparation. That none should be suspicious of his intention, he showed himself publicly in the Forum, but when night fell he made his way to the gate of the city with two companions. Horses awaited him there, and the great Carthaginian galloped for a night and a day, to a lonely tower by the shore of sea. Whether the tower at Ksar Menara is the one he used is uncertain. Historians say the spot was between Thapsus and Acholla, but the last named city has never been identified. Be that as it may, there is a great tower here, like the tomb of Cecilia Mettala on the Appian way, and it never fails to awake the thought of Hannibal's last ride.

At the age of fifty-two this iron man rode nearly a hundred miles in fourteen hours, and at once sailed for the Kerkenma Isles. Michelet said that he would like to have seen Caesar galloping, baldheaded in the rain, through Gaul; but I would rather imagine the Carthaginian General galloping straight and furiously along the great way through the plains, from power to exile.

Years passed, and on this road came the turbaned Saracens on their camels, spears shining and banners waving, outlined like shadows on the crest of the hills against the clear light of the African sky.

On the crest over that horizon, pale-faced and baldheaded, Caesar galloped to the field of Thapsus, towards Utica, where Cato, unwilling to await his arrival, died from the dagger thrust, before Caesar saw the walls.

Caesar suffered from cold and rain on the fields of Gaul, but here he rode through the searing breath of the Saharan land.

One remembers too that the victorious "white prince" Belisarius drove this way, and that the imperial Byzantine icons stood clear for the world to see, heralds of the end of blood and fire, and of the defeated Vandal empire in Africa.

The clattering mail of the past legions is heard no more on the Roman road, going south, to Sousse, and there are sentinels no more on the walls, watching for the advancing armies.

Sousse, the first city after Tunis, and capital of the rich Sahel land, is a magnificent walled citadel to-day. The massive fortifications were built by the Aghlabites, and bear the sign of many assaults and sieges. From the parapets of this African Carcassin can be seen the site of the ancient Phoenician harbour, and memory is active again, reaching to the day when Hannibal sailed from the region of Hadrumet-Thapsus, to an exile which was never broken. From the battlements one looks over to the Kerkenna isles, where Hannibal feasted before sailing again for Tyre (Titus Livy XXXIII 48.3). The banquet ended in a drunken debauch, and in the midst of the coma that ensued, the wily strategist slipped anchor and sailed for the cradle of the Phoenicians.

In Bithynia he died, at a place called Lybyssa, fulfilling the oracle which said that the old warrior was here to find his last resting place. Appian says "Lybyssan soil should one day give shelter to Hannibal," but it was not his native land, only a far and lonely spot on the sea of Marmora. His last words are supposed to have been said only a few moments before the Roman soldiers arrived to take him captive.

"If one old man can still make the Roman Empire and the whole world tremble, it is better he should die. . ." Then he took the poison that he carried in the ring which he always wore, and died, to disappoint the Romans of a triumph (183 B.C.).

Sousse, the ancient Hadrumet, is the city of the African catacombs. It was here that the Christian troglodytes lived in unending subterranean passages, and here ten thousand rock tombs have been discovered. These melancholy hiding places of the persecuted Christians are as awe-ful and depressing as those of Rome. They were excavated by the Archbishop of Algiers, Mgr. Lenaud, and by the military authorities. Here is a well sculptured stone of the Good Shepherd carrying the Lamb, as well as engraved symbols of the early Christians on the walls. There are many tombs and inscriptions, and always bones. Nothing could be sadder than the dark corridors lined and sealed with death.

From the corridors one comes to a field thick with flowers, and surrounded by eucalyptus and cypress trees, beyond which the minarets of Sousse gleam above the camp of the dead.

From Sousse, moving further south, we come to the desert, and suddenly see, outlined against the clear sky, the vast ruins of the amphitheatre at El Diem, the ancient Thysdrus, one of the most extraordinary sights of all the magic land of sand and gold and ruin.

The gigantic pile seems even to dwarf the desert itself. It is astounding as the pyramids, so vast and so silent, rising like a mountain over the squalid Arab town. This was the Cloaca Maxima of African passions; the stage of terrible scenes, the cesspool of Roman brutality. Its accommodation was for nearly eighty thousand spectators, who thronged the place to see the slaughter of Christians; most thrilling sight of all to the frenzied populace. But, by contrast, we camped here in the quiet of the night, when the moon had softened the gaunt outline, and turned its windows and terraces into the eyeless sockets of the head of death.

Only the rough outlines of its history are known. The intimate tale is yet to be discovered, though we had with us Gaston Boissier's "Afrique Romaine," and turned to the great chapter in which he describes the amphitheatre of El Djem (pp. 251 ff. See also Andollent, *Carthage Romaine*, pp. 688 ff.)

I had "Manfred" with me, and surely the description of the Colosseum fits even better the ruined amphitheatre here:

I stood within the Coliseum's wall
'Midst the chief relics of almighty Rome:
The trees which grew along the broken arches
Waved dark in the blue midnight, and the stars
Shone through the rents of ruin; from afar
The watch-dog bay'd beyond the Tiber, and
More near from out the Caesar's palace came
The owl's long cry, and, interruptedly,
Of distant sentinels the fitful song
Begun and died upon the gentle wind.
Some cypresses beyond the time-worn breach
Appeared to skirt the horizon, yet they stood
Within a bowshot. Where the Caesars dwelt,
And dwell the tuneless birds of night, amidst
A grove which springs through levelled battlements
And twines its roots with the imperial hearths,
Ivy usurps the laurel's place of growth;
But the Gladiator's bloody Circus stands,
A noble wreck in ruinous perfection!
While Caesar's chambers, and the Augustan halls,
Grovel on earth in indistinct decay.
And thou didst shine, thou rolling moon, upon
All this, and cast a wide and tender light,
Which softened down the hoar austerity
Of rugged desolation, and fill'd up,
As 'twere anew, the gaps of centuries;
Leaving that beautiful which still was so,
And making that which was not, till the place
Became religion, and the heart ran o'er
With silent worship of the great of old! –

The dead, but sceptred sovereigns, who still rule
Our spirits from their urns.

It is not at all difficult, in face of this giant of the empire
builders, softened by centuries to a real orange colour, contrasting with the dull glow of the sands and the shimmering salt
patches, to imagine the efforts that went to its construction, or
the crowds gathering for holiday.

Time was insignificant to the builders. The stone for the Colosseum was hewn along the coast, and in gigantic slabs carried
over the intervening twenty miles of desert. How numberless the
slaves who toiled at the rollers, and how interminable their
work! But after them, when the building was complete, one
standing on the upper tier of the amphitheatre would see the citizens of distant places coming in droves, across the sand, on foot
or in chariots, on their camels or on horseback, eager for the
spectacle. The watcher would have seen the long trails, dust-
clouded, leading back to the horizon; have heard the cries of
excitement, rejoiced in the magnificence of this people who
governed the world, but came to make holiday. To-day it is the
very absence of the people that hurts. All is so silent, so
deserted.

Rome built the amphitheatre, but people who followed, used
it. Here the Kahena made her last stand. The Kahena was Boadi-
cea and Joan of Arc in one, one of the heroines of the world,
fanatical undoubtedly, but shrewd, courageous, far-seeing and
determined. Her story stands the peer of all in history.

In 705 A.D. Kahena, Queen of the Berbers, fought the invading Arabs under Hassan, the last destroyer of Carthage. She was
called Dahiah, the queen, and Kahena, the priestess or sorceress.
She was one of the Berber tribes of the Djavinrah, and swept
down from the Aures mountains ablaze with fanatical enthusiasm, to defeat Hassan. Her followers in the lust and insanity of
war slew forty thousand of their enemy in one battle alone.

In times of stress she rode through her country, a marked figure on a white charger, her spear shining and her armour bright,

urging her people to valour, born of desperation. On either side rode her sons, a group whose presence was in itself sufficient to arouse the smouldering flames of patriotic fire.

Her land was harassed by the ravaging Arabs, who foraged and looted when they would. The Kahena, believing that it was the richness of her territory that invited the marauders, did, more thoroughly than they, the work of destruction.

"They want our gold, our cities, our trees, and our riches!" she said. "Let us destroy everything, that none will desire our land, and we shall be left in peace."

It was done. The Kahena put her own land to the torch, and left it desolate. She destroyed crops, forests and cities, till the land was barren. Then she turned upon her enemies and drove them back to Gabes, and beyond.

Legend says that the present desolation of the land around El Diem is the work of the Kahena, and few can remain long in the neighbourhood without hearing of her. She was at war most of her days, and the Berbers unfold their legends of "the sorceress" on the least provocation.

The Kahena was ruthless, devastating, terrible in her devotion, yet withal a woman, discerning and temperamental, calculating, shrewd and emotional. Epic of woman, and the very torch of independence.

When eighty knights of the Emir Hassan fell into her hands, she played the woman. Perhaps on any other day she would have sent only their heads back to the Emir, but, on this day, there was one of their number who somehow reached her heart. He was Khaled, son of Iezed, of the tribe of Cais, and pleasing to the eye. The seventy and nine were sent, unharmed, back to their prince, the one was kept behind, the adopted son of the Kahena. Before the departing knights, Khaled was nourished by the breasts of the Kahena, the sign of adoption among the Berbers.

Whether the statesman or the woman was uppermost in this moment it is difficult to say. The tie of adoption might have been a diplomatic effort, or it might have been the desire to retain such a son by her side. Yet in the warfare of her people it proved of no consequence, for the Emir Hassan returned with a mightier company, and the Kahena was besieged in the great amphitheatre of El Diem, whose ruins stand in the midst of desolation, raised by the Romans ere they were swept from power, to remain as a memorial to this woman.

For three years, it is said, she withstood the siege. The armies of the besieger were encamped round about her, and her own forces stayed within the walls that made an impregnable fortress, so well had the Romans built. It fared ill with Hassan. All he could do was to sit and cool his heels in the parching desert. Entrance to the citadel he could not contrive, and his troops suffered hunger and thirst, though they held on. The story runs that the Kahena, vaunting her security, and dramatic as any Oriental, threw fresh fish, once a week, to the starving besiegers at the base of the walls.

Fresh fish, in the very heart of the desert, twenty miles from the sea! It must have meant the very epitome of discouragement to the waiting soldiers unable to move, and themselves nearly starving in the midst of a hostile and desolate country. It is said that the Kahena was using the great subterranean passage to the sea coast at Salacta, for the replenishment of the larders of the besieged troops. The passage was built by the Romans for the purpose of flooding the amphitheatre, that aquatic carnivals might be presented to the populace, and the Kahena had discovered them. The tunnel is wide enough for three horsemen to ride abreast.

The siege terminated in betrayal. The Kahena was delivered to her enemies, even as was Joan the Maid, and was beheaded in battle. Her head was shown to the warriors and then thrown into a well. The Berbers will show you the well, still called "The well of the Sorceress."

The Kahena went, but still many a scar on the columns of the amphitheatre speaks of battle subsequent to her time. Succeeding people used it as she had, as a fortress, and found it a safe haven; while the attackers found it a rock on which they threw themselves, to break in futile effort. Its day as a fortress passed when one Bey of Tunis placed cannon before it, and bombarded it methodically until he blasted a way through the walls, that it might no longer serve as a refuge for rebels. He made a way in, it is true, but it is much more of a testimony to the Roman builders than to the efficacy of the artillery of the Bey!

The whole of this region abounds in signs of Roman labour, and at Foum Tatahouin and Gigthis are Phoenician ruins also. Further down the coast of Tripoli lie the ruins of Sabrata, Olea and Leptis Magna, from which is derived the name Tripoli...Tripolitain, the "three cities."

I have little doubt that the Greeks also traded with and colonised this locality, and probably came to blows with the growing power of Carthage; possibly simultaneously with the great wars in Sicily.

One of the most important trade routes from Carthage to Tripoli and Cyrenia passed by Gabes Medenine and Ben Gardane, the frontier post.

Passing Gabes, one sees the ruins of Ksar Koutine (the ancient Augarmi). There are ruins on many of the hills; guardhouses and outposts of the Roman Empire on the fringe of the desert. Gigthis, Zarzis, and Villa Magna were themselves great cities, and Zarzis (Zian) lies in the neck on the road from Medenine to the Island of Djerba.

This was the great oil centre of the Romans, and is a romance in itself. It is a desert now, but then it was the scene of a great enterprise that must appeal to the oil magnates of the world. The Standard Oil Company, with its miles of pipe line was anticipated here. Tissot speaks of the "oil pipes" that led from Zian to the sea, and Dr. Carton recently found traces of the canalisation.

It is a unique chapter of mercantile history, and full of significance for the present generation. We are used to the magnitude of our own organisation. We have rapid transport. We carry our oil and our water overland through great pipes, for the benefit of our people. There is little that is new in this. Remembering the great aqueduct, which is not superseded to this day, we now have a view of the ingenuity of the traders of the ancient periods.

Numerous ruined oil presses have been found, which, in conjunction with the pipe lines, speak eloquently of the size of the commerce. The oil was pressed at the olive orchard, and then carried through pipes to the waiting galleys, prototype of modern tankers. At the quayside, the oil was run into giant amphores, sealed with the mark of the producer, and hastened to Rome, which, as Cato, in his spleen pointed out, was only three days sailing away.

There are three temples yet visible at the spot, doubtless enriched by the offerings of the oil traders.

We have no proof that there was a Teapot Dome scandal in those days, but one is certain that, since sport played its part in politics, trade would be even more powerful.

Chapter 10

GIGTHIS

They say that North Africa has nothing more to offer! Who they are matters little, and what they say matters less. Nor would they say it if they could have travelled for days along an uninviting route partly by the sea shore and partly through the desert, desolate, uninviting, and sinister.

There are times when the desert is inhuman, when it appears like a gigantic menace, withdrawn a while that it may the better engulf the unwary.

We had travelled south in the cars, exploring the country, collecting our facts, reviving our geography, drinking in the setting of the great movements of history, but the journey had not been entirely enjoyable. We had lit up the face of the desert with our searchlights, we had dared it, and so far had conquered its discomfort as well as our own apprehension. For days we had been riding over the barren plains, unrelieved by vegetation other than the wiry tufts of coarse grass, the drinn of the Arabs. Sand was everywhere, in our eyes and in our food. It would have been in our water and our wine, except that these were securely sealed. Another night, like the preceding nights in every solitary and uncomfortable detail, had fallen and we turned on our headlamps. The younger members of the party were playing the searchlight in every direction. Doubtless there was pleasure in thus awakening the shadows, each more weird than the last, and in lighting up the scurrying form of some vagrant, half-wild dog as it hunted alone. It is surprising what one will do to relieve the ennui of a long journey across barren places.

We knew we were near Gigthis, but did not expect it quite so suddenly as it appeared. We rounded a rocky shoulder, and were instantly aware of a fresh sea breeze. Our lights caught the glint of little salt lakes, turning them into silver shields on the flat of the earth, and then, swinging into the full beam we saw the Forum. The situation was almost ludicrous in its contrast. There were we, a few men coming out of the wilderness, standing in front of the deserted work of the empire builders. We had brought our own illuminations with us, and lit up Gigthis more brilliantly than her own revelers ever had been able to do. We camped on the steps of a temple, probably erected to some long forgotten sea divinity, and there we held a modern riot.

It was the coming of age of one of the members of our party, and we had carefully preserved a few bottles of champagne for the event, that it might be done with due style and ceremony.

That was a night to be remembered. Our city was either bright light or intense shadow; there were few soft tones for the moment. Our lamps threw a beam that cut clean, and left no frayed edges. They were strictly utilitarian and not at all romantic, but along the line of the shore lay a camp of the Bedouins, their skin tents stretching long, and low, like shadows between us and the sea. Their camp fires burned fitfully and contested the brilliance of the stars reflected in the gulf of Bougara.

Our modernised feast may have compared but poorly with the genius of the Romans in these matters, but we had one satisfaction at least. We were discovering their city, and not they ours. When it was over, and we had switched off the brilliance of the lamps, we gathered odd bits of brushwood, prowling around like thieves in the night, and lit a bonfire for the sake of its effect on the ivory toned marble.

One of the rewards of exploration is that the explorer may try effects like that, but before lighting a fire on the steps of a temple, it is first necessary to find your temple, and then your wood. Having found these necessities, the dead awake. The softer light persuades the stones to live again. It catches them unawares, the long shadows are gentler and the ruins more friendly. Imagination becomes a possibility when all things are congruous. We forgot our motor cars.

My bed was on the steps of the Temple, and temple steps are about as useful for a bed as a marble capital is for a pillow. They do not induce sleep. Sheer fatigue overcame the hardness of the stones at last, and I slept to the sound of the moaning of distant waves lapping the shore, to dream of processions of elephants padding their way through the streets of the city, laden with gold and ivory, to be shipped to Carthage.

When daybreak awoke me, I saw, like an island hung between sea and sky, the land of the Lotus Eaters. It hung like an amethyst and emerald pendant, supported by two graceful ivory columns tinged with the first blush of sunrise. It looked as such a land of enchantment should, enticing us. We accepted the lure later, and made a wonderful find.

Gigthis is built between two hills, and once a river ran through the valley to the sea. The bed is now only a dry and rocky gully, but on the banks used to stand the palaces of the rich citizens, from whose windows the same view that we enjoyed could be seen. Time has made a great difference, however, for the walls of the harbour gleamed in decay through the unclouded waters that have now submerged the port.

Away from the city stretched the forbidding waste of the desert. Nothing lived, save the Bedouin camp and our little party. These, and a bird that perched motionless on a stone by the water's edge, looking out to sea. It had found a place for the sole of its foot, but no companionship, and probably little food. Gigthis was dead. It is dead. Even its echoes are voiceless, but in death it has a soul, and character. Its marbles conceal in ivory and gold the secret of the ages, the warfare of man against time, of beauty against decay, inviting the dreamers of to-day to think of the time of glorious companies, whose relics now are crumbling stone.

If decaying columns can speak of tragedy, or battered cornices stage the drama of civilisation overthrown by war, then Gigthis is eloquent. Once the gateway of the Sahara, warehouse

for Carthage, where rested the treasures too stupendous for
Rome to conceive, her treasures are now forlorn, or driven deep
under the silt and accumulation of centuries, waiting for light.

Let there be no misunderstanding of these dead cities. The
galleons of Spain carried in their hulls not more than the fraction
of the wonders lying under the loam of North Africa. There is
work for many generations. There is value, scientific, artistic,
intrinsic, to be dug from the dust. I should certainly never be surprised to learn that enterprise more commercial than academic
had been launched for the exploration of these easily mined
places.

Particularly I would like to begin to dig, at once, at the bend
of the river, before it reaches the sea, not far from the Marine
Gate. Let me say why, but to explain I must tell a little of the
history of Gigthis as we know it.

Gigthis is mentioned in the famous Periplus as being a city
half a day's journey from Djerba, which establishes its Graeco-
Phoenician origin. Greek influence is found in all its buildings,
and that is not surprising, when we remember that Greece colonised all this littoral. It was undoubtedly the clearing house for
trade between Carthage and the Sahara, ultimately being left to
the Phoenicians without interference from the Greeks, a com-
pact being made that there should be no infiltration of the
respective territories beyond the altar of Philenae.

Herodotus speaks of the Garamantes being thirty days
beyond this area, which he called the Land of the Lotus Eaters.
In the fifth century B.C. trade to an enormous extent existed
between Leptis, Sabrata and Gigthis, and the mysterious capital
of the Garamantes, called Ghadarmes, whose influence spread
throughout the Sahara.

The ancient Nasamons also traded along the Syrtian coast,
and it is reported that a Carthaginian, one Magon, made the trip
across the Sahara three times (*Athenee* II., p. 44). Herodotus,
fortunately, in his romantic manner, gives us a light on certain
aspects of trade, speaking of the raid made by the Garamantes
on the Ethiopians, who were pursued in chariots drawn by four

horses, raw material of the slave trade which prospered Carthage considerably.

These slaves were probably brought across the caravan routes to Gigthis, there to be transshipped (Gsell IV., 140). We hope, in the trip to the Hoggar which is being planned at the moment of this writing, to find traces of these old routes, along which the produce of the desert, in human material, gold, and ivory, came to civilised men. Some encouragement is given in this direction, for Barth found illuminating sculptures in the rock caverns of Tibesti.

Hercules was the chief god of Gigthis, and from the little excavation that has been done here, a head was recovered, giving some light on the religion. The head was found by G. A. Constans, and is in the Bardo museum (cf. G. A. Constans' Gigthis, pp. 44-46).

After the Greeks and Phoenicians came the all-conquering Romans, who made Gigthis even more powerful and important, and used the city as a centre for their own trade.

The Marine gate of this city of ivory and gold leads up from the ancient quays, and stands to-day as one of the really imposing relies of the city in its prime. Gigthis was essentially a sea port, and the harbour promises a rare field for excavation and investigation. Fancy can still play on the old scenes, and imagination reconstructs the city, looming up on the coast, gleaming in the sun to beckon the ships of the Mediterranean as they make for port. The full tale and the clearer vision wait until science has taken in hand the weapons of the navy. History will be hewn from the earth by pick and shovel.

Still standing, and cleared of débris, are the ruins of the triumphal arch giving on to the Forum. These ruins were brought to light by officers and soldiers of the French troops stationed at Medenine. Even warriors are now detailed for archaeological research! The arch is not large, but is of considerable beauty, and its proportions are so exquisitely balanced that it seems rather to be a graven jewel than a mass of hewn stones.

From the steps of the Forum, which are undamaged, it is possible to visualise the grandeur of the past. Votive stones and pedestals in the forum bear inscriptions which are easily legible, bearing testimony to the march of time. One is inscribed "In the reign of Aurelius."

Greek inspiration is easily recognisable in the Forum, and in many unidentified temples. It will not be long, perhaps, before we unearth evidences and stones that will enable us to write a new chapter in the history of the seaport.

Beyond the temples are the palaces of the wealthy, the traders and profiteers, the usurers and slave dealers.

Mosaic floors in colour that defies time are still intact, and throw an unwavering challenge to sun and tempest.

The villas are well planned. Actually they are riverside mansions, and full use was made of the river for every convenience the architects could imagine. Vast cisterns were built, in themselves indicative of the condition of the city. It does not rain often at Gigthis, nowadays, and apparently the original residents suffered from drought also, hence these huge reservoirs, wherein a supply might be laid against the reverse of a rainy day.

Under the soil of the hill overlooking the sea are the Phoenician ruins. A few stones may be seen, mutely imploring the work of the excavators, and these few are enough to start any thorough-going red-blooded archaeologist on a work that merits the devotion of a lifetime, for they bear undoubted signs of Egyptian influence.

Gigthis, seaport, storehouse, cosmopolis, drew from all the known lands for her trade and her culture. The few capitals discovered still carry their brilliant colouring of red and gold. Gigthis must have invented the phrase "The Gay City."

In one of the palaces here was discovered the strange scientific freak to which reference has already been made. A rain storm, rare event, soaked one of the walls, peeling off the "wall paper." Left on the wall was the writing from the parchment, the world's first carbon-copy.

The characters, but this is for the scientifically-minded, were Neo-Phoenician. The rediscovered documents are in the hands of Professor Dussand of the French Academie des Inscriptions et Belles Lettres, and are now being deciphered by him.

Rain, and not archaeological excavation, may yet be the means of wresting the story of Gigthis from her present demolition. Rain has helped on many occasions. It is the prime cause of several discoveries in North Africa. I have, myself, seen many mosaics come up fresh and smiling, like carpets from the cleaners, after a rain storm, and of course, at Carthage, rain means a crop of coins, glass globules and many other small relics of the past coming to the surface and simply asking to be picked up.

From the Phoenician ruins on the hillside at Gigthis the paths lead down again to the sea, and on the way down stands another little Forum. They are like that! Day after day I see something I want to uncover, read some sign that indicates museums of rare things just under the earth.

But that path to the river recalls me to the statement I made earlier in this chapter. It leads back to the one spot in Africa where I would like to start digging at the earliest possible moment; the bed of the river.

It is sheer tantalisation. Remember that the houses of the wealthy citizens of Gigthis stood on the riverside. Think of all the devastation, both deliberate and unintentional, the ravages of looters and of time. The river bed must be filled with treasures of the old commercial city, the waters of the river must have received many works of art dislodged by the Vandal and Moslem scourges and by the weight of years.

I picked up many coins in the river bed, and sheets of wonderful arretine pottery, though I was only gleaning for a few moments. Under the silt may lie a Venus of Cyrene. One can say little that is impossible in the city of the Gods and the men who vied with them for splendour.

One's steps lead to the grey blocks chafed by a million tides, ground into shapeless masses, the old port. The sea is tranquil now, there are no ripples breaking the surface, and the sun touches the flat expanse. A quivering mist rises. For eight yards one can walk out on the ancient piles over the waters that once carried the galleys of Tyre and Rome, but now are shallowed and undisturbed.

How great the contrast is. Colour, baffling to modern utilitarianism, must have made the scene a panorama of extravagance. Galleys with furled sails and glistening oars, with gold figure-heads, and banks of swarthy rowers, came in here, smoothly and easily, sidling to the wharves, there to be laden with the wealth of Africa. The races of the Mediterranean must have jostled together on the quays, their feet wearing the stone smooth. Getulians, Libyans, Garamanteans, Numidians, Carthaginians, and Tyrians, Greeks and Romans, black slave and white free, senators, soldiers, ebony African chieftains and hook-nosed, bartering, Phoenicians, all were here, haggling and commanding, dealing in gold dust and ivory, slaves and elephants, precious stones, oil, and produce of all the provinces.

Through the streets came the procession of elephants, massive hulks on cushioned feet, in single file and tricked out in splendour, swaying in slow stateliness through the Marine Gate, urged by the hoarse clamour of negro mahmouts.

Behind the galleys and the kneeling elephants, patiently waiting for their unloading, rose the golden city on its crescent hill, its river running between marble walls to the Syrtian sea. Its temples and palaces outlined, with forums, baths, statues and arches, against the olive green of the hillside and the vivid sky.

Such a spectacle greeted the returning seafarers, and for greater magnificence duplicated itself in the quiet waters of the land-locked haven.

To-day, nothing stirs. All is gone, faded like the dream of a century in the night of a thousand years. Only the spirit remains, and yet the dead stones vibrate, trying to recapture the glory as they lie there, ground by the hand of man and the heel of time, burned by an enduring sun. The stones of Gigthis are her symbol of the beauty and genius of man opposed by the restlessness of centuries and the engulfing African desert.

Chapter 11

DJERBA:
AND SUBMARINE EXPLORATION

From Gigthis it is necessary to double back a little round the peninsula, to reach the narrowing part of the Straits between the mainland and the Island of Djerba. The straits are approximately three miles wide, and in the days of the Romans a bridge connected the island and the mainland. It seemed to us, as we made our way to the point of embarkation, that we could walk right across without difficulty, but that was only an impression gained by the peculiar perspective of the island.

The coastline is almost flush with the sea, and in the distance Djerba looks like a floating breastplate, heavily jeweled, floating on the pale blue of the waters, with a thin ridge of white sand around its edge.

The mainland is almost denuded of vegetation; the island is an oasis torn from its place and sent floating out to sea.

Our motor cars had to be transshipped, and the question of their transport was by no means easy to solve. It was finally accomplished by tying two Arab feluccas together and building a platform wide enough to take one car at a time. We wedged the wheels with stones, and pushed off, but the felucca has a contrariness more irritating than that of an ass, and we were no sooner adrift than each boat wanted to take its own course, and leave the motor to fend for itself. As soon as we had overcome this tendency we found ourselves aground! It was useless waiting for the tide to float us, because there is no tide. Therefore we harnessed two score Arabs to drag the transport into deeper water.

The channel presented little difficulty thereafter, and in due course our expedition was all safely landed on the opposite shore. But we wished that the bridge still remained. Only the traces of the causeway could be seen, however, whose foundations gleam beneath the clear sea like submarine temples.

The island is about three hundred square miles in extent, and at the present time has a population of nearly fifty thousand people, who are the Puritans of North Africa, never mingling with the people of the mainland and inordinately proud of their pure blood and untarnished ancestry. In religion they are unorthodox Moslems, called Kharedjites, and are industrious and skilful farmers. The island is very fruitful, and well covered with olive trees.

Just the same, I am afraid that Ulysses was not factually correct in his romancing. The people are ignorant of the Lotus! They are serious inscrutable individuals, most of whom, from their skill on the water, must have been born sailing a boat. And, to sail a boat there seems to be the ideal of the children. One is not surprised, for there is a brisk, clean wind off the island, and the sky and sea make for complete satisfaction. Probably I am unduly susceptible to colour, but I feel that a sky actually orange toned, and a sea whose waves shade into deep purple, to become almost black in the shadows of the troughs, would tempt most people to sail.

Djerba has not yet been spoiled by the tourists, though it is a tourist's paradise, for here are habits and customs, and people too, who have not changed for more centuries than can be comprehended. The villages are all of a pure silvery whiteness, which gleam brightly in the sun, and many of the inhabitants are attired in vivid blue. The effect is almost cubist, especially when the women join in the processions, wearing their fantastic cone-shaped "tanagra" hats. When there are strangers about, the women keep themselves hidden, lest they should be seen. The men, however, are not so bashful.

Our photographer nearly stampeded the whole population, so eager was he to get a photograph of the women. They were terrified at the thought, and scampered away from him, across the fields, and he, now doubly determined to obtain the photographs, ran after them, with his large camera at the "ready." That made them more frantic than ever, and it took us a little while to persuade the men, who resented this attention, that nothing serious was intended. Perhaps they thought we had a plan of abduction afoot.

The incident brought a new topic to the villages, at least, and probably that sudden inrush of the new world has aroused the sleepy silent towns more than anything else could.

It is hardly permissible to call the groups of houses towns, for the population is far from urban. The towns are only market places, where the people come occasionally to buy and sell. Their life is mostly agricultural, though there are potteries, and some work is done on looms, which provide the white burnooses and striped blankets which are acquired by foreign traders.

Success has had to be dragged from a reluctant earth, for life on the island is not so simple as fable would have it. The huge old olive trees which are scattered over all the island are often gnarled and hideously contorted, but they do bear olives, and that, according to the people, is all that is required of an olive tree.

For excitement, the people come into the market places, and watch, or participate in, the sales of donkeys, sponges, dates, figs, and dried orange blossoms.

In the court-yards of the Foudouks or caravanserai, where the arched colonnades give a welcome shade, doves coo and lazily swoop in quest of food, while the unladen asses lie in phlegmatic content.

Quaint camel-driven mills and oil presses in the storehouses do duty to-day as did their replicas in the days when Gigthis was the centre of the oil trade of the Empire.

Time has been gentle with Djerba, and it has not shared the fate of its neighbours on the mainland. To-day it is a flowered palm garden, with a beauty hard to parallel, and it is studded with innumerable and magnificent relies of all the ages that have gone over the head of man since he first learned to scratch a picture in the rock, or to light a fire for his own comfort.

Signs of vengeance and destruction are not entirely wanting, of course. Only recently the French, for reasons of their own, have given proper burial to the ghastly memorial Dragut raised to the overthrow of the Spanish, made from the remnants of his massacred prisoners. Five thousand Christian skulls were piled high; graphic and barbaric monument to the thoroughness of victory and the hopelessness of defeat.

The ruins of Djerba have not, so far, been studied archaeologically. The island is a virgin field for the scientist, though it figures prominently in legend and history. It is "the low lying isle" of the Periplus of Seylax, "the isle of the lotus eaters" of the Greek authors, "Pharis" of Theophrastus, "Meninx" of Polybius, and "Phla" of Herodotus. The Periplus records the beauty of its gardens and the splendour of its cultivation as far back as the 4th century B.C. Our party can echo that praise after twenty-five hundred years.

It is, however, from an archaeological point of view that Djerba is most interesting. On the island are the signs of many civilisations, some open to the sight of man, and many more needing only a little work for their excavation.

Hercules, identified with the Phoenician God Melcart, was worshipped at Djerba, as indeed in all the Phoenician colonies, and an altar existed in the isle of Meninx (Gsell, Vol. IV., p. 306).

In 253 B.C. Rome sent two of her consuls, C. Servilius Caepio and Sempronius Blaesus to plunder the Carthaginian coast. The fleet at their disposal is said to have consisted of two hundred and sixty vessels (Eutrope, II., 23 and Orose, IV., 9-10), and were on the point of leaving for home, heavy with booty, when they were driven aground at low tide in the Gulf of Bougara. By throwing everything overboard they were able to

lighten their quinquiremes, and escaped just before the
Carthaginian fleet came on them.

Two hundred and sixty ship loads of the riches of Phoenicia
lie off the coast of Djerba.

Archaeologists are neither fugitives nor necessarily adventurers, they may have little in common with Ulysses, but it is as difficult for me to leave Djerba as it was for the hero of Homer's
tale. No one offered me the tempting flower, but Djerba offers a
field almost unknown, and the sea round about offered more.

It is a fabulous isle in a fabulous sea.

Tradition says that Djerba was an Aegean colony. It is obvious that both Greeks and Phoenicians have contributed to its
development, and in addition there are the usual Roman buildings. Everywhere there are piles of marble dust, broken columns, and mosaic floors. We have explored the site of many
cities, whose ancient names we do not know. The Phoenician
city, which is still unlocated, we know was called Tipassa. It lay
in the southwest part of the island, and Stephane Gsell suggested
to me that it may well be the ruins of that city that we partly
explored, under the sea. The clues of the lost city seem to coincide with the site where we discovered certain specimens. (See
Gsell, Vol. II., pp. 124-5.) Tissot believes that Haribus, another
city on Djerba is also of Phoenician origin, while Gesenius (pp.
220-1, 227) mentions a neo-Phoenician inscription found on the
southwest coast of the island, near Adjim.

There can be no doubt of the immensity of the discoveries to
be made, for the slight excavations that have been made by
occasional explorers and the military authorities have established the fact that there are strange tombs outside the city of
Meninx, and a few objects, such as mosaics and a beautiful baptismal font have been recovered, and are now at the museum in
Tunis. A careful survey needs to be made, for the island is practically covered with Phoenician, Roman and Spanish remains.
The ruins are on either side of the roadways that lead through the
island, and before Djerba gives up its information nearly all its
area will have to be worked.

In the very centre of the island is the famous Jewish Synagogue of Hara Srira, to which a great pilgrimage is made annually. In the library there is an old scroll of the scriptures, dating from the second century, and which is held in reverence throughout Africa. The priests who seem to belong to the time of their manuscripts are jealous of the old library, and though with difficulty they can be persuaded to show the ancient scroll, none is allowed to touch it. It is handled with silver tongs, if it is handled at all.

The priests, however, will tell of the history of the synagogue, and its accompanying monastery. Ages ago, the Jews, being driven out of Palestine, came to the island in the course of their wanderings, and asked permission of the inhabitants to settle there. This was given, on condition that they did not live at the capital, Meninx.

The wanderers had carried with them a stone from the temple, and, with that as talisman, searched the island for the place where water was most plentiful and sweetest. There they built their temple, and around the sanctuary grew their town. They prospered so well that an Arab Caid protested against their wealth, which was due to their shrewdness in selecting the site and controlling the sources of fresh water. The Caid argued that, since the Jews were traders and not agriculturists, they had no need of the best water supply on the island, and gave them notice to quit. The Jews pleaded that they might be allowed to keep the temple of their fathers, and the Caid so far relented.

To this day the temple stands, but round it are the ruins of the first city, which had to be dismantled, because the sacred stone had found the only pure water on the island.

Here the pilgrims come from all over the continent, and here the Jews are unmixed, unchanged, proud and exclusive. Not bowing to the conventions and customs of other countries, where prosperity has often led to dissimulation, the Hebrews of Djerba are a distinguished and noble company, with little but scorn for their co-religionists who have ceased to be their co-nationalists.

Not far from the synagogue is the village of Guallala, the pottery centre of Djerba. It is surrounded by palm trees, and, to the traveller, is a living specimen of antiquity. Pottery is still made in the same way as was the pottery which we unearth in our excavations, and one can sit and watch the potter at work, learning from the very conservatism of the island much that is valuable in reconstructing the life of two thousand years ago. I noticed that most of the potters' houses are built of material recovered from the adjacent ruins of a Roman settlement.

The kilns burn day and night, and nothing has changed through the years. The old potters might have furnished the Persian with his poetic inspiration, Omar would have found examples here. The modeling forms might have served the Phoenicians or the Romans.

Djerba would be a happy hunting ground for the ethnologist, as well as the archaeologist. Its present, as well as its glorious past, has much that is suggestive for the observer, for the student of history, and for the excavator.

The depths of the Mediterranean hide many secrets, and much archaeological treasure. Its shores are covered with ruined cities, and its bed is paved with the loot and vessels of many civilisations. During the Punic wars hundreds of vessels were sent to the bottom of the sea, and while Carthage was yet the glory of the Phoenicians and when she became the metropolis of Roman civilisation in Africa, great fleets and treasure ships were sunk.

It was the lure of submarine archaeology that drew our expedition to Djerba. Other fields of similar nature will be explored before many years are passed, such as Mahdia and Carthage; signs lead the imaginative to think that perhaps the legend of the lost Atlantis is not entirely unfounded, though imagination is sometimes overtaxed. There are so many offspring of Atlantis that if every suggestion were founded on even a shred of possibility, not a city, not a continent, but a whole universe would be insufficient to contain the fabular past. There are cities off the Norfolk coast, rumour says, and some off Brittany, others off

Holland. Rumour has a diplomatic passport, and travels free. So, when I first heard of a sunken city near Djerba, I thought for a while that it was no more than another version of the old, old story.

The Djerba story, however, seemed so circumstantial and arose out of so prosaic an adventure that there was more than a touch of probability in its presentation.

A sponge diver had reported the discovery to M. Renoux, governor of the Isle of Djerba, who gave me a copy of the diver's statement, which said that, one day, while diving for sponges off the island, and in the gulf of Bougara, he came to the walls and windows of a sunken city. He estimated the depth at sixteen yards, and said that he had seen the fishes swimming in and out of the windows.

The ruins, he said, were situated between Djerba and the mainland at Gigthis, and as soon as a party could be organised he would show us the place. For verification during my American lecture tours, I asked the Governor to corroborate the diver's story. I was going to Missouri.

The Governor willingly sent me an affidavit in due and proper form, and with that document as evidence I began the organisation of an expedition under the sea, and was fortunate enough to find people willing to subscribe several thousands of dollars for a preliminary survey of the locality.

When I returned to Djerba, however, the diver had unfortunately died, and the former Governor, M. Renoux, had been promoted. A new governor was in charge, and I had to begin the survey with a very slender indication of the exact site of the city. The new Governor, M. Pagnon, courteously assisted us, and put me into touch with Dr. Rhossetos, a Greek sponge merchant, who in turn immediately communicated with the Greek Sponge Divers' Association of Sfax, with the result that, after a customary fortnight's parley, we obtained the ships from Sfax and several expert divers.

We were ready to begin as soon as the authorities would let us, but time was lost in obtaining official permission. It is quite proper that there should be official cognisance taken of such expeditions, and proper that work should only be permitted under certain conditions, but in this case our contact was with two widely different departments. The Services des Antiquités knew us, and understood our mission, but the department of Travaux Publiques looked at the enterprise from another angle.

The trouble was, of course, that we were going to explore in a region of sponge fisheries, and as it was the breeding season the authorities thought we might damage the fields. Finally everything was explained to the satisfaction of every official of every department, and I received the necessary permits and documents, while the officials protected themselves by detailing a coastguard officer to watch us and our operations.

In a few days we interviewed all the local authorities and I had the satisfaction of seeing the first diver go overboard.

It is said quickly, but, unless you have worked with sponge divers, whose imagination is baffling, it is difficult to convey all the excitement of the preliminaries. Every man had seen "walls and windows under the sea," and the dean of divers had seen them several times. He was a wrinkled old buccaneer, who looked as though someone had dealt with him as the Romans dealt with Carthage, plowed up his face. Everlastingly he was gazing down into the water, wildly gesticulating, and incessantly shouting "Houni! Houni!" (here, here), but if every place he "hounied" had been part of the city it would have put New York to shame for dimension.

He was ably seconded by the Caid of Adjim, a jolly old rogue, who considered us insane to the last man, especially when, one day, a member of the expedition asked him if it was possible to get a collection of scorpions together, to be sent to New York. He ordered the "round up" of the scorpions, and turned to his under-caid saying "Can you beat it? Half these people are hunting for a city under the sea, absolutely useless as a city, and the other half want to send scorpions to their relatives! Madness and murder!"

Doubtless you are waiting for that diver to come up again, and feel that he has been long enough under water, but these divers can stay under a long time, and before we let him rise again I want to say a word of thanks to MM. Renoux and Pagnon, the former and the present Governors of the Isle of Djerba. They gave us unstinted help, and put all the officials of the island at our disposal. That was great friendship. The Greek ships and the divers were at Djerba, but it took us several days to round up the members of our crew from the cafes of Houmt Souk, the capital, which appealed more to their imagination than the submerged city. Not the Lotus flower, but Chianti Rosso was the lure of the crew of our ships. Ulysses fared better.

But the diver has been down long enough, and several others with him. I am afraid the disappointment was great. They rose having discovered nothing except that the currents were strong, even down on the sea floor, and that it was not going to be a very easy treasure hunt.

Still, we made a picturesque scene. We sailed out of Adjim five vessels strong, quite a fleet. There were three Arab feluccas and two Greek ships, and the Greeks had their flags flying, and their crews were vastly excited. Weather was fair, but the sea choppy after a heavy wind.

For three days we had no success. Our divers went gaily away in their bright-sailed Berber boats, and we followed after, accompanied by a sixth, the cat-boat of the Government's observer, who proved to be a great discovery. He was a jovial Breton from Lochmariaquer, near Carnac (the land of the Dolmens), and it was not long before we found that we had friends in common. Thereafter he never missed a moment of the hunt during the whole of the ten days we were occupied. He was a most interesting character, a hero of the submarine war in the Mediterranean.

Success became distant, and we fell back on to our own preliminary explorations, made while we were waiting for the officials to give us permission to go ahead.

We had used those days in scouting around and questioning the natives, who, as usual sent us off on many a wild goose chase, and put us once in a while into real danger, just for the fun of the thing.

Every nation has its own peculiar sense of humour, but for sheer peculiarity commend me to the Arab. We set out from the shore where we believed we were at the site of an old Spanish fortress, and pulled away. Our diver went down, not naked as the romanticists would have it, but clad for his work in the modern accoutrements. We put him into his clumsy suit, and screwed on his heavy helmet, adjusted the massive shoulder weights and leaden shoes, and started the pump before we closed the window of his headgear. Then, with the life-line round his waist clear of all obstructions, we lowered him.

The Arabs had made no mention of the sudden change of current, nor had they given us any indication of its force, and we were calmly working away, trying to lose no time. I suppose, in all, we were there several hours, and engrossed in the work, when a sudden squall struck us. There might have been warning enough for the weather-wise, but we had not seen the clouds banking up, and the tempest hit us, full and heavy. Our anchors dragged, and our motor failed to start. Some of us tried to get the diver aboard again, while the rest pulled like madmen at the oars. We boarded the diver after I firmly believed that it was too late, but happily the man had suffered no harm.

It took us all our time to keep the little ship from being pounded on the rocks, and nothing could get near us, for we were in the very middle of a nest of sharp-pointed crags, and the way out was narrow.

The ropes of our anchors nearly broke, and the ship gradually drove nearer to the shore, dragging the anchors from their hold. The engineer was frantic, the motor positively refused to budge, and we could see the rocks waiting. We actually hit, and began to pound. The weight of the sea and the force of the wind swung us against the points and washed us off again, to bump once more. And then the stubborn motor relented, and we breathed.

But there was hardly enough strength left in the lot of us to steer a course to safety.

It was a good joke, from the point of view of the Arabs, but, as I said before, humour is a peculiarly national matter in application and appreciation.

When the early attempts of the bigger expedition brought no results we began to ask questions again, and gathered that we should stand as good a chance near the scene of our adventure as anywhere.

It was at four-thirty in the afternoon of the 24th of May, 1925, that Michael Cocinos went overboard there, and my eyes watched first the thin stream of bubbles that broke on the surface, and then the horizon, to see if anything threatened to break in that direction. Cocinos was assisted by two other divers, and I felt a weight of responsibility that was hard to bear, at the thought of three men risking their lives for us, and had a moment's regret that I had ever undertaken the expedition to discover a ruined city at the bottom of such a depth of water.

Naturally, I remembered the Governor's story of how one poor man had lost his life down there, his air tube and life-line entangled somehow in what might have been the doorways and windows of the lost city. Another man had struggled for five hours, and even the casual Arab divers, who go down naked, said that they had lost a friend in the mysterious ruins.

At the end of ten minutes, the sailor standing in the bows with the life line felt a tug, the signal that the diver was coming up again. We crowded into the bows, and our cameras and moving picture machines were concentrated on the silvery bubbles that told where the diver was. In the clear green we could make out the great helmet, and we began to hope. We could hardly wait to get him out of his gear, to hear the tale of his discoveries. Everybody helped to get him aboard, and we were extremely solicitous for his comfort. No company ever hung on the words of Demosthenes so eagerly as we did on the faltering account as it was translated by Dr. Rhossetos.

All we learned was that the currents were still strong, and that the diver had been carried off his feet by the eddies, sometimes falling into deeps, sometimes scrambling up the shallowing earth.

Another man went down, burdened with our hopes and fears. He went over gently, down, down, unceasing in his descent. The record showed five, ten, fifteen, twenty metres. It was too much, we held our breath, hoping that the rope would stop sliding into the sea, but it went to twenty-five and then to thirty metres.

"He has fallen into a hole," said Dr. Rhossetos, and we believed him, but the bubbles began to spread on the surface, and we knew that the diver was being carried by the current. Orders were quickly given to haul him aboard again, and he was white and exhausted when we saw him.

"Too fast a current," was the verdict of the experts, and I am afraid our hearts fell as did our faces. We were very downcast, and the practical Greeks did not help us to great enthusiasm when they said we should have to wait for the changing tides, so that the men could go down in safety. The currents cease for one hour between ebb and flow. That meant we could work for about three hours a day.

Of course, everything was done at the wrong moment. Our kind advisors said that we had chosen the wrong time of the year, we had chosen the wrong time of the day, and apparently we had chosen the wrong place.

The currents between Djerba and the mainland are strongest in May. It was May when we found that out.

It meant that fifty men would be idle for the greater part of the day, and few expeditions can afford to have fifty men idle. That must be the prerogative of commerce. We held a council of war, and decided to make as thorough an exploration of the neighborhood as possible whilst waiting for the tides.

In that, at least, we were well advised. Gigthis, Zarzis, Meninx, Tipasa, the villa Magda, were all within easy reach, and, with one of the ships, we visited the ruins of the old Spanish fortresses, one of which is still standing, Bordj-Castille. The other lies in the water, a complete ruin.

In addition we were able to make some survey of the submarine ruins of Guallala, a town of the island. These particular ruins had been seen by the Berber sponge divers and proved to be something of a reward for our disappointing efforts elsewhere. The ruins are regular in size, and lie about three hundred yards from the shore, at a depth varying from two to ten yards. I followed a rectangular wall for many yards into the sea, and was amazed to find that the point furthest from land had a great circular wall, which could clearly be seen. Our divers immediately followed up this discovery, and reported that the wall was composed of white stone blocks.

The walls were amazingly constructed, and beautifully regular, and the reports were so enthusiastic that I decided to go down and investigate for myself. Everybody told me that it was sheer folly, but neither threats of deafness or promises of paralysis deterred me, and I was soon being screwed into the stuffy suit. The sensation corresponded exactly with my idea of being buried alive. The more they screwed me in the less confident I felt. The neck pieces were assuredly heavier than usual, and the shoes were precisely three times more cumbersome than the occasion demanded. Of course, Mr. Kellerman would not reject the opportunity for a picture, and asked me to smile nicely for the camera, which I did, but he later told me that it was about the best imitation of a man en route for the scaffold that he had ever seen. I did my best for him, though. The more I looked over the side into the sea the darker it seemed, and the more I wished I had listened to the warnings of my advisors. At that moment, however, they were adjusting the lifeline, and the full weight of lead was on my shoulders. To this day I have full sympathy for rats in traps.

I knew that I had to press a button in my helmet, with the side of my head, in order to let out the air and descend, and that was a useful thing to remember. Two men lifted my weighted legs over the side, as though they were preparing to bury a dead man, and the crowd at the side of the ship seemed as much like mourners as possible. I suffocated, and fancied that the air pipe was out of order, and was quite certain that the life-line would break on the slightest provocation.

The heat was dreadful, and I made frantic signs that I wanted to take off my helmet and get a drink (which I had forgotten). The crew, who had been so excited by the idea of my going down, were jumping all over the place in glee, including everybody but the moving picture operator – it is strange how these movie men can keep to the main idea – and he wanted to get the best possible view. He did.

My signs had at least some result. One man at last went back to his job, just in time. He went to the pump and gave me air. No wonder it was hot, and I was suffocating. Evidently the poor man, in the excitement of the moment, had lost his head, and my life didn't count for two hoots in comparison with the opportunity for a gorgeous film. They had forgotten that one must breathe.

The next act was equally to their liking. I was dropped over with a splash, as though I were a corpse. I really believed I should be, for I was more miserable under water than I had been on deck. Everything was green and strange, and there was a loud clatter in my ears. I moved my head, and found the valve to let out the air, and down I went the faster, watching the bubbles climbing up to the surface. I hit the sea floor, and though I would, I may not express my consternation when I found I could not walk. Was it necessary to hobble me with so much lead?

I looked through my window, and everything was grotesque, in green and blue. Since I could not walk, I tried to crawl, losing hold of the life-line, and grew a little panicky in consequence. I could not regain the line and therefore could not signal to be hauled up, though I was quite ready to go. I wondered then what they would do, how my wife and child were, and what would happen when the news came. Those crack-brained zealots upstairs might forget to keep on with the air supply. Then everything went dark. I managed to look through the top window, and found I was under the ship. How funny it looked. Then I thought I had found the life-line, and pulled hard on it, three times. There was no answer. I was sure the watcher in the bows had gone to sleep. The perspiration rolled off me. I felt a trickle down my neck, and was convinced that the water was leaking through the rotten old suit, and that I was to be drowned like a rat. Why?…well, just why didn't they pull me up? Then I found out. I was tugging away for dear life at the cords that held the weights round my neck.

After the Romans and the Vandals, and all the other inhabitants of the island had been resurrected and lived and died again, I found the life-line. If the watcher in the bows were asleep, I guarantee that my signals waked him, for more trickles were running down my neck.

Something went crack, it was my helmet fouling the ship on the way up. That ought to have been the finish, and I was reconciled to death, except that there was plenty of air coming along, and I could still breathe. My suit bulged like a balloon, and I must have resembled a long dead hippopotamus when I reached the surface, skimming the side of the hull as I rose. I was hauled up the ladder, but, since I could not move my feet once they came out of the water, I was ignominiously dragged aboard.

My helmet was whisked off, and I took a long, deep breath, gave thanks for my restoration, and looked around.

"How long have I been down?" I gasped.

"About five minutes," said the Captain. "What did you come up for?"

Thereafter I took a much keener interest in the scaphanders, as the professional divers are called, who live their lives in diving suits and work on the floor of the sea.

They repaid the attention, for their life is interesting even if it is hazardous. It is worth while watching them as they go out, from either shore or supply boat, to their tasks. They are rowed by Arabs, who manipulate their boats much as the slaves of Carthage and Rome must have done. The native oarsmen use gigantic sweeps, which must be between fifteen and twenty feet long, and they row with all their might, and with every muscle of their bodies. Standing, barefooted in the well of the boat, they grip the thwart with their toes – toes that have not been demuscled by civilisation – facile, easy toes that grip like fingers. Then they bend over the shaft of the sweep bent close to their chests, slowly rise, gripping the oar tightly, and, grunting in unison, they fling themselves backwards with all their strength and energy.

The scaphander is, of course, the hub of the sponge trade, and, being the hub, seldom makes much personal progress. The result of his efforts goes to the rich merchants who handle the immense trade in sponges. The divers get fairly good pay, but are so much at the mercy of their overseers that it is not uncommon for them to make private bargains for lenient treatment.

It is easy to recognise the diver ashore. He drags his feet with difficulty; sign of diver's paralysis. Paralysis claims many victims. The percentage of death in pursuit of their occupation rises to nearly ten per cent per annum. Sooner or later, the effect of working for long stretches under terrific pressure is apparent. Local anemia and general disorder show their hateful signs, but, singularly enough, even the most paralytic of the divers recovers the use of his limbs when he gets to the sea bed.

The French and the Greeks have co-operated in the main sponge fields for the welfare of the divers. A hospital ship is in attendance, and there is a divers' hospital ashore, but for all the precautions many cases escape the attention of the authorities. The fixed limit at which men may work, by law, is established at thirty-eight metres, but the overseers have a way of their own in manipulating the recording instruments, so that they show a different pressure. It is known that frequently the men work at fifty metres, and occasionally at sixty, and, if the overseer thinks they haven't worked long enough, he ignores their signals to come up. The divers try to get even, and inflate their suits, when they blob up like corks, only to be driven down again, if the foreman thinks fit. These little antagonisms cost the divers much more than they cost the men on the ship, for, by forcing himself quickly to the surface the diver hastens paralysis, if he does not break a few blood vessels on the way.

Tales are told, on the coast, of divers who have disappeared, and of others who have been "buried at sea" sewn up in coarse sacking, and whose death has never been reported. The tale still persists of an old diver who was left down below, because he was too old to carry on his work.

When the sponge fleet is at work, if one can forget the miseries of the workers, or if by good fortune the captain is one of the humane men who looks after his crew, it is an interesting sight.

There are humane men in the sponge trade, and some captains run for fifteen years or more, without losing a man. They never have difficulty securing a crew.

The sponges are sorted, roughly, before they are gathered, for the divers are able to recognise the good and the unmarketable. Working along the bottom for about forty minutes, they collect their haul, and tuck the sponges away into a net. When they come to the surface, the divers give their first attention to their catch, for often they work on a profit-sharing basis. Then the diver gets out of his gear, but one is hardly out of his suit before another is over the side. Time is precious.

The sponges are trodden out by barefooted sailors, and strung on lines, to be trailed behind the ship for several hours, after which they are soundly beaten with heavy sticks, to clear them of shells and other refuse, soaked again, and bleached in a tub of weak oxalic acid.

With the big fleets there are supply boats and tenders, and the divers' boats frequently stay away from port for several weeks. The supply boats, or cutters, come to port with nearly every inch of their rigging hung with dripping sponges. To the sensitive nose there are disadvantages.

The native Arab divers, called "common" divers, escape the ills of the scaphanders, since they work for only a minute or two before returning to the surface.

Clutching a small boulder in their hand, they dive straight down, often to a depth of thirty-five to forty metres, and, working rapidly, bring up their haul. One who has never seen them at work before is likely to imagine that some dogfish has got them, for they can stay under water several minutes. I think the record is five, but I have seen them stay down for three minutes, and a terribly long time it seems.

We had several exhibitions of their extraordinary skill in diving for sponges and for fish. They go hunting for large snake-like eels that live in crannies, where the octopus also makes his home. They catch the fish by tickling them.

As specimens of humanity, these naked divers are magnificent. Their heads are worth the artist's inspired moments, for they are pure Berber, descendants of the native sea-farers of the Mediterranean, and they swim and handle a ship as though they were born in the sea. I made good friends with them, and as a parting gift when we left I gave them our tiny portable gramophone, in memory of our quest for a city under the sea. In return they made me a present of enough sponges to serve me and my family, and my friends and their families, for the remainder of our natural lives.

Endless are the stories of their endurance, and many a terrible tale we listened to over our evening meal on the way back to Djerba. The divers have to diet strenuously, but no such restriction lay on us. We parted from them, eventually, on the eve of their departure for the high seas and the greater fields, where they work at a toil unceasing, under the fierce glare of the midsummer African sun, to gather sponges for us who seldom give a thought to the trade, if even we know how to think about it.

Frequently now, when the soft texture of one of their sponges helps me to enjoyment and cleanliness, I think of their hard lives, of the diseases that wait round the corner for the scaphanders, of the dangers that lie hidden; a choked air pipe, a vicious dog fish, a tangled life-line, and the great silence, the intimidating enormity of the isolation of the sea bed. I wish that Hood had known. Then, perhaps, a world that takes most of its boons casually might have learned of the terrible monotony and hardship.

Not "Stitch, Stitch, Stitch," but, "Dive Dive, Dive," for sponges that are won at the risk of a man's life.

Chapter 12

THE CITY UNDER THE SEA AND THE SUNKEN GALLEY

After my short apprenticeship to the life of a scaphander, we devoted our time to the investigation of the curious sea walls, and made several excursions into the island.

There must have been a Roman settlement just below Guallala, the potter city, about three miles from El Kantara, which is the ancient Meninx. Rich marble ruins strew the ground, and one of our party dug up a beautiful Roman lamp dating from about the first century. Some of the stucco we found, resembled closely that at the Punic temple of Tanit in Carthage, and it is quite probable that we shall discover what remains of a Carthaginian storehouse here. That remains to be proved, of course, but when time and our arrangements permit, we shall make a complete investigation.

The walls commanded our most earnest attention, for we had allotted little time to the expedition, and much of that had been lost owing to the exigencies of the conditions under which we worked. The submarine works of this city whose name we do not know, are very similar to the drawings made by Daux of the Phoenician structures on the North African coast; good examples of which can be seen at Utica and at Carthage. We even hoped that the circular building under the sea at this spot might be the admiralty tower of the Tyrian or Carthaginian settlers.

The place is certainly worth a complete examination, and when we reported these well-preserved walls to the Governor of the Island, he promised his full co-operation for a complete examination next year. It will benefit the Island, incidentally, for visitors to be able to see submarine traces of the greatest sailors in the history of the Mediterranean. That possibility always is uppermost in the minds of the inhabitants, for wherever exploration is going forward, if it is within any reasonable distance, tourists flock in considerable numbers to watch progress, and tourists are a valuable commodity to the natives.

We returned to Adjim, about fifteen miles from El Kantara. This we had made our headquarters, and we spent some time in charting the currents, and working out the tides, that we might discover the best time to work.

While we were sailing through the straits, on these preliminary surveys I had noticed, nearly opposite the place where we believed lay our greatest possibility of success, traces of ruins in the clay cliffs. We landed, and our surmise was affirmed, there was undoubtedly another settlement here, for the ruins we had seen were fragments of Roman masonry and cisterns. Then it seemed quite feasible to suppose that it was traces of this dead city that had been found by the divers, continuing to the sea. We hunted for signs of roads on the summit of the cliffs, and picked up old coins and pottery in the mass of powdered ruins. This city, like Meninx and Guallala, looked as though it had been ground to dust and ashes. By whom this was done, and how, and why, probably we shall never know.

It is obvious, however, that the crumbling rocks of the place are filtering slowly into the straits, due to erosion by the violent and rapid currents.

With this additional clue, we continued in the straits, and soon found more encouraging signs. But news of the work began to get around, and the usual congregation of sightseers, tourists and others, made the island their rendezvous, often to the embarrassment of our work. They came out from the mainland in Arab dhows and nearly crowded us into the sea.

A storm suddenly broke one afternoon, and the tourists found themselves drenched to the skin. Our moving picture operator on another occasion used language strong enough to keep off a troublesome party, and finally we were compelled to make it plain that tourists would not be permitted on the spot when work was actually in progress.

On the sixth day, our second diver reported that he had at last seen what he thought was an object imbedded in a stone wall.

It was little enough of a discovery, but it filled us with intense excitement, which rose higher when the diver went down, to return again with an object that we could recognise as the work of man, even while the diver was yet below the surface. We restrained ourselves sufficiently to be careful in hauling the find aboard, and then we minutely scrutinised it. The one question that was in everybody's mind was "Have we found the lost city?"

The object brought to the surface was actually the remains of three amphores imbedded in six inches of sea growth, barnacles and molluscs. Time, and the weight and flow of the sea had ground them into a solid mass weighing about sixty pounds. The diver explained that it was only with extreme difficulty that he had been able to detach this significant relic, but he believed that with a pick-axe he could dislodge some of the stones and bricks of things he said looked like walls.

Our first task was to film and photograph the first clue, after which we buoyed the spot, and then Cocinos went over the side armed with a pick-axe, and carrying a rope.

He went down slowly, as if to torment us, and we read off those metres much more eagerly than we had ever read measurements before. When he had gone five metres, there was a slackening, and it was not till he reached fifteen, that we were halfway satisfied that he was doing his best; but when he was at sixteen, we shouted. The recorder stopped there, the exact depth that had been given by the diver, since dead, who had reported his find to the Governor.

Then we forgot to watch the diver, and waited for the man in the bows who was holding the life-line. We saw the line become taut. It was the first signal, and eagerly we hauled on the loose rope. An object was coming up, slowly. It had little shape or form, but when it broke the surface, we saw with unutterable delight that it was another marred piece of pottery. The cheers we raised were unintelligible, but they were at least expressive. The sea was yielding some of its secrets. All the long days of hard labour and keen disappointment were forgotten. Only the whole-hearted explorer can realise what our satisfaction was. We had striven hard, and for reward had recovered two or three bits of useless earth. But that earth had been worked by men who made history, and they turned surmise into certainty. No man, I suppose, ever wishes to undergo a past effort again, or to suffer even the echoes of his disappointment, but I would willingly take all the hardships of five years of intensive exploration again, to recapture the thrill of satisfaction that went through me then.

Even the most sceptical was satisfied that we had hit upon something tangible, something that marked an epoch in archaeology. We had, however, to guard against too high hopes, and to damper our optimism, lest we should announce as an established fact what after all was only a very strong indication. Mr. Streit, the correspondent of the New York *Times,* who was with us, sent a very guarded telegram to his paper, announcing the result of our work.

The tides and weather then turned against us, and we had to go ashore, a bitter necessity indeed, but we used the time to good advantage by finding another ruined city several miles northwest of the Adjim landing. Here were evidences of rich buildings, and the outline of a temple on the water's edge. Nothing has been discovered concerning these towns or villages, there is no historical allusion which we can definitely ascribe to them, names are wanting, and the archaeological department of our expeditions knows very little of the region. Djerba offers a huge study; in less than a month we located half a dozen ruined settlements.

May the twentieth saw us again on the sea, and gave us our second great thrill. Our diver had been down only eight minutes when he sent up a series of tugs on the line.

"This looks as though he had really discovered something," said the captain.

At that Mr. Kellerman jumped forward. "Clear a space for the camera," he shouted. "If anything does come up, Pathe News gets it first!"

But the New York *Times* correspondent was alongside, and I believe the rest of us gazed into the sea at the spot where the bubbles were rising, just as though somebody had hypnotised us.

A blur showed through the green, and then the blur took shape, and I saw, far down in the clear water, a beautiful Phoenician amphore, sea-encrusted. As though it were the slenderest glass, it was lifted from the water, to be followed by the diver, who came up with his pick-axe in his hand, and showed by very definite gesticulations that he wanted his helmet off at once, so that he could share in the excitement.

The atmosphere and the sun seemed to realise that everything must contribute to the importance of the occasion, and the scene will live in my memory for many years: late afternoon with the sky cloudless, and the sun bright; an excited group of men in the bows of a tiny ship that lay on a sea so calm as to rebuke our noise, and the low-lying shore of the Isle of the Lotus Eaters outlined like a great jewel on a silver strand.

We put the amphore on a mat in the centre of the ship. It stood about four feet high, with its two handles still intact, and its pointed base undamaged. Its perfection testified to the extreme care of the diver who had recovered it, and for which I was more grateful than I knew how to say.

Sea shells, fungi and sponges clung to the sides, but its general form and its dimensions were identical with the amphores discovered at Carthage by Père Delattre in the earliest Phoenician tombs. An important feature, which aids in identification of the period, is the opening. In this respect the Phoenician amphores differ from those of the Romans.

The Arabs and Berbers were all amazed at the vase, and were unanimous in declaring that no such pottery had ever been made at Djerba.

On the way back to Houmt Souk, we informed the Governor of our find, and he instantly asked if he, with the Caid, might be present at the following day's operations.

The next day, however, was very windy, and the Governor postponed his visit, but nothing short of a hurricane would have held us back. The divers themselves were urging us on, and piling up excitement on excitement. They were real hunters after treasure.

Just the same, when we reached buoy, we decided that it would be better not to send a man down, as the seas were breaking over our little vessel, but nothing on earth could stop our No. 2 man from going over. The result was that we only barely escaped disaster.

He had been down a while when we received the signal to haul him, but when we tried to raise him, the rope would not give, and we knew that our man was caught, deep down. With our hearts in our mouths, we started the motor, and bore against the current, which, lashed by the wind, was stronger than usual. The Greek members of the crew were pale and anxious, they needed no interpretation of the misadventure. We pulled at the life-line again, and doubled the men at the pumps, but to no avail. For ten minutes that we counted by the seconds, we stared at the bubbles that still rose to the surface – our thoughts on the tragedy beneath. We knew that our diver was seventy feet down, and wondered if he had got caught in the windows or doorways of the submerged ruins. Such a case had been reported only a few years ago.

We were just on the point of sending help down, as a forlorn hope, when the line jerked, and the sailor holding it, screamed for very relief. The diver was loose at last. A few moments later, we saw the motionless form of our explorer rise to the surface, and float face down. Our hearts stopped beating again, for fear he had been wounded. We hauled him in, and saw his deathlike face through the window, and I saw a trickle of blood at his nostrils.

He lay absolutely motionless for several minutes before he gave any signs of life, but we did all we could, and after administering a strong stimulant, saw the colour begin to come back into his face.

He had had a terrible struggle for life. The current had carried him under the overhanging rocks, in utter darkness. Imprisoned there, he sensed that the current had changed, and was growing stronger every moment, lessening his slender chance of escape. We learned, afterwards that he had tried to make steps in the sand, to get leverage so that he might push himself out, but as often as he braced himself, the sand gave way, and he was washed back again into the recess.

It was the changing of the position of our ship that helped him, finally, and as he swung clear, he lost consciousness.

Naturally there was no more diving that day, and we returned to Adjim.

Work began again on the twenty-second of May, in glorious weather. M. Louis Pagnon, the Governor of the Isle of Djerba, the Caid, the Greek Consul of Sfax, and many other people paid us an official visit in the afternoon.

Before they arrived, in our morning's work, we had recovered two more amphores, and several bricks of varying size, which the divers said came from walls that were approximately six feet high at that point. The most wonderful of the specimens we brought to the surface that morning was a six-handled vase, which the diver reported to have been lying about a foot below the level of the sea floor.

We called a halt, to give the men a rest, for the work was strenuous, and they had had a continuous battle against tides and currents for some days, and were driving themselves that morning, without any urging from us.

As a relaxation, we busied ourselves tidying up the ship, for it was something of a gala occasion, and almost anybody would have enjoyed the delightful luncheon, acquired by our divers, that was spread out on the canvas-covered deck.

The sea behaved excellently for our visitors, for when work commenced again, the divers made one extraordinary find after another. Pieces of corroded bronze, shoals of bricks, remains of a large number of amphores and one undamaged specimen were raised, to the astonishment of the Governor and the Caid.

The Governor grew increasingly excited.

Even so slight a thing as the broken lip of an old pottery vase brought exclamations of rapture from him. He is one of those rare men who has a flair for excavation and gets the maximum of adventurous enjoyment out of the work.

The Caid was a little more matter of fact, but every bit as impressed, and gave us his considered judgment on our finds, insisting that every relic was of a manufacture unknown, and never seen before on the Island. He said he had seen ancient vases somewhat similar to ours.

The Governor, becoming the Official again, saw to the documentation of our finds and questioned the divers, taking their statements. The Greek Consul then formally took the divers' sworn affidavits.

It was our last day's work, and our little expedition was being disbanded for the while. The professional divers were due to depart for the main sponge fields, and our own time was ended.

Before we left, however, we photographed and filmed the entire party, and all our specimens, in which figured six amphores, four vases, eight bronze pieces, and a score of bricks. All these, with the mass of fragments of pottery, were measured and catalogued.

Then we sailed back to Djerba, our expedition under the sea finished for a while. The little phonograph played Hawaiian music, while the Greek crew and the divers sat around, smiles lighting up their weather-scarred faces. As we sat there after dinner, Michael Cocinos told us the tale of the sunken Treasure Galley at Mahdia, and how he, himself, dug out and saved the beautiful ancient Greek statues now in the Bardo museum at Tunis.

We filled our pipes, and sipped Samien wine, and Dr. Rhossetos interpreted the tale as Cocinos told it, more like a bed-time fairy story than actuality.

Cocinos has a mind for the spectacular, but the story would have been thrilling if it had come from the mouth of a much more phlegmatic person. It worked me to a pitch of excitement that only my friends can imagine, for I have long believed that the bed of the Mediterranean is as rich in archaeological treasures as is the soil of North Africa, and my hope has been that some day I might really attack that field in earnest. To hear the gnarled old diver talking along, and to see Dr. Rhossetos grow excited in his haste to keep up in translation, was glorious. It certainly gave me the last word in a few discussions that had taken place between the skeptics and me.

However, listen to Cocinos.

"It was in the spring of 1907 that a party of Scaphandra, or sponge-divers, sailed over a spot a few kilometres northeast of the old Phoenician ruins of Mahdia. They saw a row of long cylinders in the mud at the bottom of the sea.

"When they got back to Sfax they told the authorities that they had seen a lot of cannon at a depth of thirty-nine metres, and were laughed at for their tale. A few days later, though, native sponge-divers, who took their naked plunge to the spot, came back terrified. They swore they had seen sleeping giants down there, and they were so certain that the Government Official at Sfax made them make a statement on oath.

"That brought in the 'Services des Antiquités' from Tunis, who started to verify the tales. They worked under the direction of M. Merlin.

"M. Merlin had trouble in getting divers. I knew he would."

There are reasons for trouble with divers. They go on strike if they have the opportunity, as quickly as our own Arab workmen strike at Carthage. And they are every bit as superstitious. The sleeping giants of the sea were as good an excuse as a curse stone!

"M. Merlin very nearly had a serious mutiny. That is where I came in, for it brought him to use this very ship, and so I was sent down to investigate the galley."

Cocinos was very proud as he continued his story. "We had nearly as much trouble with the currents," he continued, "as we have had here. They were very strong and we worked at a great depth."

He rattled on at a great speed. I have given a little of his story, because it *is* his story, and much of the credit for the final salving of treasures, whose worth cannot be measured by money, is due to him.

The discovery of this sunken galley is actually one of the most outstanding archaeological finds of the century.

Mahdia, for such as wish to trace it on the map, is a small Tunisian town, located near the promontory between the ruins of the ancient Thapsius and Sullecthum.

When the first reports came through to M. Merlin, of the Services des Antiquités, he instantly commanded a full investigation, and the so-called "cannon" or "Sleeping giants" of the divers' tales were resolved into a number of beautiful marble columns. Investigation showed that the columns were lying on the deck of the sunken vessel.

The galley was situated about a quarter of a mile off the coast, at a depth of about one hundred and twenty feet. The depth of the sea, and the peculiarity and strength of the currents made exploration dangerous, and it took considerable time to find divers willing to undertake the work. In fact, at one time, the ships were anchored above the sunken wreck, and the divers refused, point-blank, to go down.

Further pressure was exerted by the Services des Antiquités, and great help was given by two Americans, Mr. Hazen Hyde and the Duke of Loubat. The French Academy of Inscriptions and Belles Lettres also co-operated, and work was recommenced, culminating in a successful descent, and the recovery of certain objects.

It was from M. Alfred Merlin himself that I learned of the supposed conditions which sent the galley to the sea floor. The vessel was probably a raider, laden with booty, from the siege of Athens by Scylla, in 79 B.C. It is well established that several ships were blown out of their course and lost, and the galley off Mahdia may well be one of these.

Roman senators and wealthy citizens in those days used to issue their orders, commissioning certain objects and possessions from the officers, well in advance. And the army did its best to keep the bargains. The treasures on the galleys were destined to ornament the country homes and palaces of the cream of Roman society, but the old chap who was waiting for these particular columns, had a long wait.

It was difficult for the divers to unload the weighty masonry from the galley, but thanks to the shipwreck, what was to have been an individual possession, now occupies a place of importance in a national museum. The trophies already recovered from the wreck are housed in the Bardo museum.

The first great difficulty was the removal of the columns, which occupied part of the deck of the galley. It was their weight, most likely, that caused the vessel to capsize.

Divers went down and attached cables to the pillars, and they were slowly raised from their muddy bed.

"After we had got several columns," said Cocinos, "we started to dig away tons of mud."

At the end of ten days, working in torrid heat and squally weather, while his divers had been digging away in relays, M. Merlin had the great satisfaction of seeing the first of the treasures rising to the surface. They were priceless vases and statuettes, and Cocinos had had a difficult job putting the wraps and ropes around them, working at that great depth.

The actual recovery of the first specimen created a change of heart in the workers. Men who had been hunting for an excuse to strike much more eagerly than they had hunted for the galley, suddenly became violently enthusiastic, and the excitement of the treasure hunt became personal and intense.

Through the days, M. Merlin stayed out on the ship, in the scorching sun. The divers hoped that they might discover gold, and when they were only rewarded by the discovery of vases that are more to be desired than gold, from an archaeological point of view, they went on strike again.

The depth was too great, and their nerves began to break. By promises and encouragement, however, M. Merlin kept them at work during the summer months, while the scientists of France anxiously waited for further news.

A month to an eager explorer is as short as the twilight, and certainly no disciple of Isaak Walton ever fished so patiently, or cast a line in greater hope than did M. Merlin. The result is said so briefly that my fear is it will not be appreciated. To give the due importance to each find, one would have to take a book of a thousand pages, and in it write, as for the exercises imposed by a stern schoolmaster: "In 1908 was recovered from the bottom of the sea, the glorious Aphrodite, which now stands in the Bardo Museum."

When that book was complete, in fine copperplate, another should be started for the immortalisation of the "Eros." And so on, to make a library.

It must fire the imagination of any amateur of the fine arts to realise that from the mud, where it has lain for centuries, a marvellous bronze "Eros" has been recovered. It is believed to be a duplicate of the Eros of Praxiteles. Several of the other specimens are signed by Boethus of Chalcedon, a sculptor of the second century B.C.

Among the collection are the grotesque dwarfs, magnificently modelled, dancing, and holding castanets. Also, two heads of extreme beauty were found, which are believed to have been the figureheads of the trireme.

I asked the diver what he felt like, having brought up these treasures more than two thousand years old, and he replied in one word "Fine!"

He was silent for a moment or two before he continued. "But," he said, "it was only when, a few years later, I saw the dirty things I had tied to a rope, shapeless and caked with shells and mud and sand, that I knew how wonderful they were. They were all cleaned up, and on fine pedestals, in a beautiful room. Then they looked magnificent." He smiled as he said that. I really believe that he thinks archaeologists have a little right to live, mad as they are.

The incrustations on the objects were, of course, extremely difficult to remove, but with care and patience they have been cleaned off, and several of them are found to be intact.

Ever since I heard of the discovery, I have been hoping to organise an expedition to make a complete recovery; not only of the contents of the galley, but of the vessel itself, which is every bit as valuable as the cargo it carried. It is only in the last few months that the matter has even been mentioned by the newspapers, but we have high hopes of ultimate success.

There has been more interest in the proposal to raise the galley lately, and if only Cocinos could tell the tale again, of how he went down and groveled along the bottom of the sea, finding bulky objects covered with sand and mud, there would be even greater interest.

I am waiting for him to have another opportunity, so that he may come up to the surface, and tell us how he scooped off the sand with his hands, to see the metal faces staring up at him from their beds.

M. Merlin has promised his full co-operation if ever we raise the necessary half million francs. Divers, ships, equipment and all are ready, and if we are successful, the job can be finished in the months of May and June of 1926.

The French Government is also actively interested in the project, and gave us a favourable answer when we asked for permission and their co-operation. The Government has been unable to do anything since the outbreak of war in this direction, but there is every probability of our receiving good help when we begin exploring.

The statues, vases, massive candelabra, and the many other relics brought out of the sea are only an earnest of the amount yet remaining submerged, for so far, only the deck cargo has been touched. The more valuable cargo lies in the hull of the galley, and it should be possible to recover nearly everything.

We are hoping that Michael Cocinos will go down again in the early summer. And when this wreck is dealt with, there will be more work for him to do. Of that there is no doubt, for we are only on the threshold of the treasure house of the Mediterranean. There are secrets there for whose solution many people eagerly await.

Chapter 13

PREHISTORIC MAN IN AFRICA

The Sahara is at once the largest and the least known of the deserts, and its actual exploration was only commenced in the seventeenth century. Since then, however, the company of heroic adventurers has steadily grown. Caille first reached Timbuctoo, Speke and Grant traced the course of the Nile, and many others have added something to the little store of knowledge we possess. Von Rolls and von Nachtigall, the intrepid Germans; Duveyrier, Flatters, and the heroic Père de Foucauld, all three of France, complete the list of the original pathfinders, whose names are history.

To them we may now add Hussenein-Bey, General Laperrine, and Mrs. Rosita Forbes, people of our generation.

A great deal still remains to be done, vast tracts of territory must yet be uncovered. What many of these originators did, must be verified; their findings supported or corrected as the case may be, and there are regions whose extent is enormous, and are as yet utterly unknown.

There are, I imagine, millions of people who picture the Sahara as one vast seashore, a monotone of sand. Actually there is abundant colour there. The desert can be rainbow-hued, and it is by no means so derelict of human interest as its name would imply. In the most desolate regions of the Sahara, the traces of pre-historic man are multitudinous. Specimens of his handiwork can be found by thousands. I know one tract of the desert, covering an area of nearly five miles, where the surface is nothing more nor less than an arrow-head factory. Here are flints partly chipped, in every stage of manufacture, and scattered among the arrowheads are the very tools, also made of flint, which were used in the manufacture of pre-historic man's weapons.

Undoubtedly there have been climatic changes which amounted to a revolution of nature, but they still remain to be studied and documented.

Fortunately for the work to which I have laid my hand in this direction, two of the foremost scholars of the present day are collaborating with me. Professor Gautier, the greatest authority on the Sahara, is doing the Geographical and Geological side, while Maurice Reygasse, certainly the foremost scholar on pre-historic times, is helping on anthropology and kindred subjects.

Up to the present moment I have only visited the extreme south of Tunisia and Algeria, but year by year we get further into this fascinating land.

As far as the Tripolitan frontier, we find traces of the past peoples; Neolithic man, the Berbers, Phoenicians and Romans have left their mark, half buried now in the creeping sands of the desert, and in the mountains that rise austerely from the plains.

I propose to tackle some new site each year, always working south.

The Matmatas are interesting. The people who live in the region of this great range are pure Berber, and their habits and customs are reminiscent of the life of man in the undated past. It is here that we go back to the people of to-day, leaving awhile the dead civilisations for one that is alive, but older. We actually do go back to these people, for they are a backward company, and have nothing whatever in common with civilisation as we know it. The region was called, by the ancients, the land of the Troglodytes and the Garamantes. Here men still live as did their ancestors of prehistoric periods. Between Gabes and the Tripolitan frontier in a wild and forbidding land, abounding in mountain fastnesses, the harassed Berbers have found refuge for centuries in rock caves, persisting in their habitations though the Phoenicians have been dead so long, and no more ravage the country. But perhaps some of the people of to-day do not know that it is safe to be abroad. Their legends live for history, and the fears of the past are crystallised into the habits of the present.

For three years I have wandered among the strange dwellings of the Troglodytes, and each new expedition reveals some new phase or peculiarity of the "lizard eating" people. The Arabs call the locality the "Djefara," and the total population, almost entirely of pure descent, numbers nearly one hundred thousand. The Accara tribe have held the peninsula of Zarzis, which lies opposite the Isle of Djerba, from time immemorial. The famous Touazine live near the Tripolitan frontier, the Khezeur have the marvellous mud city of Medenine. The Ghoumrassen are the mountain folk, and all combine in the powerful confederation of the Ouerghamma.

It is convenient, and scientifically correct, to divide the people into three categories: the mountain dwellers, who live in almost inaccessible eyries such as Douriat, Ghoumrassen and Ksar Beni Baicat: the subterranean people, to be found at Hadege and a score of similar villages in the Matmata region: and the people who use habitations of the "Ghorfa" type, to be found at Ksar Medenine and Matameur.

In 1922 I worked over the region between Hadege and Foum Tatafoum, inspecting many of the rock dwellings, hewn out of the mountain side. Ages of insecurity drove the Berbers to seek refuge in these places, and it is only since the French occupation that they have even felt the fringe of the garment of peace. They are afraid of peace. Quiet for them is only the threat of impending danger, the lull before the storm. It will take generations of peace to dispel the dread of attack which is the age-long heritage of the Berbers.

Their eyries are approached by a single narrow path, winding up steep slopes to a dizzy height, and there is not the least doubt that the only way an invader could enter would be in the wake of famine. We found evidence of prehistoric man in several caves in the Djefara country, and at Gafsa and Tebessa we have palaeolithic and neolithic sites as rich as any to be found in France.

During the peaceful periods, the natives began to build lower down on the mountains, and in the soft clayish rock near the valleys. Also at Hadege we have a whole town absolutely underground.

The traveller may walk along, or ride, and see practically no indication that some four thousand people are housed in the vicinity, under the ground. The earth dwellings are open to the sky, and built around a central shaft or courtyard, which sometimes reaches to a depth of five stories, which are terraced. The town is still increasing in size, and nothing changes from century to century. The inhabitants dig and build according to type, and that type began when their history began, before history was. There is usually one entrance, or hole in the ground, and the first floor is the stable. Bedrooms are on the same floor, and it is a familiar sight to see cattle filing through the bedroom!

The cupboards and beds are also cut out of the rock, and at Douirat I saw rooms whose furniture too had been hewn from the stone. At this Troglodyte city I believe there must be a good mile of houses underground, complete with roads. Each year we are taking photographs of the strange people in their stranger abodes, a difficult problem, as they are not even modernised enough to want to be photographed. Last year the expedition camped in the ancient rock caves several hundred feet above the Troglodyte city.

The military commander of Matamata lent us twenty of his convicts, to carry up the camp material. Most of these Berbers were doing servitude for a strange reason, an echo of which we had seen the day before, when a hand to hand fight took place in the subterranean streets. There had been a bad epidemic of smallpox in the region, and military doctors had been sent from Tunis to vaccinate the Troglodytes.

They were not at all well received, so the men had to be handled by force, or the doctors themselves would have been seriously injured. When an attempt was made to vaccinate the ladies, the Berber feelings were utterly outraged, and rather than let the Doctors drive out the menace that threatened the whole community, the Berbers tried to drive out the doctors. Though smallpox was killing them by scores, they refused to be treated, or to let their wives be treated, and fought tooth and nail.

It was far from a joke for the doctors working in the dim labyrinths, digging out the human moles. The Berbers carried their antagonism so far that the riot was only suppressed by the intervention of armed forces, with the result that some of the population had to go to prison.

The children, of course, make a joke out of their habitations, and think them no end of fun. They go to school, such as it is, chattering and laughing like any normal run of children, but we got a most illustrative film of their activities, by the cunning of our operator.

Naturally it is not easy to take films of the Troglodytes; the darkness of their city and the antagonism of the people, contribute to make a picture-man's life anything but pleasant, but, by secreting the camera first on the top story, and then on the ground floor, Mr. Kellerman got the city from top to bottom, which is to say he got it from end to end.

The school in the community is a rough and ready affair, and so is the instruction. The children learn to repeat a few lines of the Koran, and they are educated.

To reach school, they simply flop out of the windows of the upper storey, and drop, sometimes fifteen feet to the refuse on the ground beneath. They laugh and chatter as they pick themselves up, shake off the dirt and troop along together.

The road up to the Matmatas was bad, several years ago, and in places consisted of the river bed, pure and simple. The colouration is a dull brick-red and grey during the hours when the sun is strong, but at twilight, whether morning or evening, the place is lit with hues as vivid and primitive as can be desired. The mountains are fantastic in shape, resembling hundreds of giant pyramids, barren and gaunt, with only a few signs of vegetation here and there, a few palm trees and poor wheat growing in the valleys around the abode of some solitary cave-dweller.

The whole area is intensely unreal and sinister, a region which might well be the land "on the other side of the moon." The town of Medenine is the example of the third group of habitations. It is hard to imagine anything stranger than the collection of cylindrical chambers, built one on top of another straight up to the sky. "Ksar" (fortress) is the plain type of fortified town. There is a single door into the Ksar, and the minaret is the only point that rises over the skyline of the city. In construction, the city recalls nothing so strongly as a beehive, except that the bees are more regular in the construction of their cities than are the Berbers of Medenine.

Take several hundred "Ghorfas" and place them in a circle, so that the doors face on the area enclosed, build cells haphazard, one on top of the other, and in the crevices throw a few handfuls of mud, haphazard again, and you have Ksar Medenine.

The houses form the wall of the city, and are blank to the outside world, all doors looking out on to the space that corresponds to the "village green." In times of war, the town is instantly closed, and becomes a fortress, sufficiently strong to hold off the marauders, though it would offer no resistance whatever to modern armament.

To reach home, the tenant of a house on the fourth tier, and there may be as many as six tiers of mud houses one on top of another, has to crawl up a narrow staircase, not more than a few inches wide in places. More often than not, he has to be content with an odd stone projecting from the wall here and there, and his entry to his house is more like the ascent of a monkey. The houses have no windows, and when the door is closed the interior is dark and rather airless. The doorway is about as high as a man's chest, and is certainly not constructed for a fat man. The inhabitants crawl in on hands and knees, and instantly close the heavy door, and bolt it against all intruders.

When the house is to be left, empty, the door is locked in a primitive, but satisfactory manner. On the side of the hasp is a hole, which penetrates the wall, and is large enough to admit a man's hand and arm. Reaching through, the householder pulls the trap to after him, and locks it with a massive wooden key, which he then withdraws and takes with him. The lock is a heavy wooden bolt, the key a long stick with pegs at the end which fit into holes in the bar, and so enable the bolt to be pulled backwards and forwards. If you should see an Arab walking with a cudgel over his shoulder, with ugly spikes on it that look dangerous, it may be only a patient householder carrying his key, and not a marauder with a bludgeon.

To live in such a city is undoubtedly bad enough, but it has at least one advantage, one does not have to climb to an eagle's nest in order to roost for the night.

The uninitiated, however, will be nervous at times, for the houses look as though they were in danger of collapse, but, being uncertain which way to fall, decide to remain upright.

In former days bandits roamed periodically from Tripoli to ravage the whole area for slaves. The people lived in constant fear of the raids; nothing was ever spared. This apprehension is the reason for the strange construction of the villages. Medenine is called the Skyscraper city of Africa, and its people live in buildings six storeys high, or just by way of contrast, six storeys deep. Twelve storeys, in Africa, beats even Woolworth.

Throughout this territory, as would be expected, are traces of all the civilisations that have passed like slow-drifting glaciers over the continent. Phoenicians, Romans and Greeks traded and worked here. Ruined towers and guard houses, of outposts erected by the Romans, crop up frequently, and are worth investigation. But my own greatest interest lies in the possibility of discoveries relating to prehistoric man, on the edge, and in the centre of the desert.

It is for this cause that I have devoted all my leisure during the last five years, to studying the works of men who are really great in this world, Reygasse, Bordy, Gsell, Capitain, Père Huguenot, Gobert and De Morgan.

The principal prehistoric sites of Africa are those round Gafsa, including Tamerza, Radeyef and Seldja, the area in the neighbourhood of Tebessa, and the district which ranges from Southern Algeria to the great Central Sahara, especially the plateau called the Hoggar.

To the region around Gafsa in Southern Tunisia they have given the name Capsien, and in this region Reygasse is working, establishing the theory that this is the locality whence came the earliest types of stone implements. Here, he has collected a series of instruments numbering at least 6,000 which are all worked stones, and which I have seen, belonging to the Chellean and pre-Chellean periods. They are mostly "coup de poing" blocks of silex, nearly oval, and their date, on a conservative basis reached by archaeologists and geologists, is about 125,000 B.C. Some authorities give the date of this period as being 200,000 to 300,000 B.C., but I lean personally to the more moderate estimate – though why one should quibble over a mere hundred thousand years is, perhaps, inexplicable.

Signs of human life indicative of every one of the known periods of prehistoric life, dating from two hundred thousand years B.C. are to be found here, and I had the wonderful experience of discovering, under the guidance of M. Reygasse, some fine examples of rock sculptures, those first attempts of prehistoric man in the realm of artistic expression. These abound between Tunisia and Mauretania, and merit independent research, since the work of Reygasse has almost established the similarity of African and European periods.

Prehistoric man is supposed to have travelled to Africa from the North, perhaps migrating as far as Siberia. Certainly there is a close similarity between the implements of this area and those of the Esquimaux.

A word concerning Reygasse may not be out of place. He is certainly the outstanding authority on Africa, in relation to prehistoric eras. He has explored all the fields and has crossed the Sahara in order to locate neolithic man in the most remote places. There are few rock sculptures that he does not know, and he has included in his research the Dolmens, tumuli, and menhirs which abound in Africa. For fifteen years he has been studying the question of the origin of man, and year by year, with almost uniform regularity he startles some scientific congress with new discoveries he has made. In his home at Tebessa he has a collection of some 150,000 implements of the stone age; the greatest private collection in the world.

During these years he has been working quietly, almost in secret, and now he has entrusted me with the task of presenting his discoveries to the world, and to collaborate with him in the continuance of a gigantic work, of which, he says, he has only scratched the surface.

For two weeks he took me and our moving picture operator all over the scene of his great finds, an excursion into the habitat of prehistoric man, an almost unbelievable region where man has lived ever since he first came out of the twilight of animalism.

Reygasse is in a peculiarly happy position of being able to make his own investigations, as Administrator of the Commune of Tebessa, a huge region containing most of the known prehistoric sites. He has all the forces needed in his excavations and explorations. As Governor of a peaceful region, he has been able to execute all the duties of administration and use his leisure for archaeology. His discoveries in this direction have won the unreserved approval of the French Government, which is encouraging him to go still deeper into the subject.

In my recent tour with this great enthusiast, we had all the local Caids and authorities at our disposal, and they welcomed us at every village and outpost. Horses, mules, guides and military escort met us at the different halts, and gangs of men were put to work on the excavations several days before we arrived. In this way I was able to assist in the uncovering of some of the oldest specimens of the handiwork of men.

For the tour we left Tebessa at daybreak, and followed the old Roman road to Bir Sbeitla, where Reygasse made the spectacular find of several thousand marvellous "coups de poings" some years ago. Before reaching the Bordje, we were met by a striking cavalcade of mounted Arabs, who surrounded our cars and gave us a typical salute, firing their guns into the air and performing a veritable "fantasia" for our especial benefit. I was glad when it was explained that they were peaceful in their intentions, and were showing their pleasure, but all the same I wondered, if this were peace, what they might rise to in anger!

It was a thrilling exhibition, and the moving picture man secured a great picture of the turbaned knights of the Sahara, as they tore around us on the dead run, with their gold-braided, scarlet capes flying in the wind.

Then, because a picture man is a genius, and a genius, all separate and alone, the camera was moved to the back of one of the cars, and Reygasse and I were filmed driving along at full speed surrounded by our whooping escort.

Caid Lakal Ben Tayab entertained us at length, and a regal entertainment he provided. Champagne, wild game, kus-kus, peculiar dishes of the people, roasts and entrees purely Arabian, and the envy of every chef who ever hears of them, liqueurs and cigars were forthcoming; surely a feast not generally found on an exploring expedition. Our host had a row of decorations, including the Legion d'Honneur, and was the idealisation of the Sheik of legend and romance.

The Caids are sticklers for ceremony and etiquette. Even in the heart of the desert, it is expected that the traveller, when the guest of a Caid or chief man, will wear his decorations. The ribbons are not enough, and we have had to include in our equipment, miniatures of whatever decorations we possess.

Like many of the Caids and Sheiks of North Africa, our host was a cultured man, and thoroughly aristocratic; he was soon discussing our expeditions, both intelligently and enthusiastically.

The site we were to explore lay on the banks of a river, and the prehistoric implements are found imbedded in the alluvial deposit about two hundred yards from the fortress. In a few hours we recovered fine examples of the work of Acheulian and Chellean man, which Reygasse was kind enough to let me keep. There is something especially exciting in digging out of the mud a pre-historic axe-head, a weapon that has been lying there for something like a hundred thousand years. It equaled the moment, almost, of our own discovery of the Temple of Tanit, at Carthage, the uncovering of the "dancing girl's" tomb at Utica, and the raising of the first sea-incrusted amphore at Djerba.

From El ma El Abiod, we continued south to the important proto-solutrian site of Bir Sbeitla. All this region is full of ruins of ancient Roman towns and settlements. It used to be a great oil producing country (olive, not petroleum), and Stephane Gsell has discovered something like two hundred and fifty ruins in the neighbourhood, together with some remarkably well-preserved ancient oil presses. It is far from an exaggeration to say that you stumble across a ruin every five minutes.

At Bir Sbeitla, we had another cavalcade. Probably the Caid here had heard of the entertainment of our earlier host, and intended to outdo him. He assuredly gave us a wonderful show, though horses can only run at full speed, and man can only eat till he can eat no more! But our host provided us with a novelty. It was under his entertainment that we first had "meschouie." This is a great feast, like an ox-roast, save that a whole lamb is roasted and the company sits around on the floor, and then it is each for himself, with due deference to etiquette and precedence. But, it is an absolute scream to see otherwise sedate gentlemen tearing away at a roast lamb with their fingers, and gurgling "bismillah!" between mouthfuls.

"Bismillah!" was the only word that fitted. It gave me a real insight into the peculiar sense of the fitness of things that I had often remarked among certain Arabs.

The country around was wild, with grandiose mountains, veiled in purple shadows, and from this point we continued our journey on Arab horses. It took me a long while to get accustomed to the high Arab saddles, and longer to get over the effects! The saddles are far from soft, being made of wood, in conformation much like the saddles of the plains of Western America.

An exhilarating ride took us up to the gorges of Saf-Saf, and the prehistoric site of the "escargotiers," or snail-eaters, where Reygasse had a gang of men at work. Here we found a whole hillside, just one mass of prehistoric hearths, ashes mixed with flints and millions of snail shells! We were lucky enough to dig out quite a representative collection of Aurignacian relics, far better worked than those of the previous epoch. The long "lames," which may have been razors, and which were worked on both sides, were specially well made. These things belong to the "Capsien" or "Getulian" periods, to give them their African names.

Standing on this hill, with all the legacies of prehistoric man around me, I tried to imagine the scene so many thousands of years ago. Here are the remains of the famous Cro-Magnon type of human beings, and Reygasse and Capitain are convinced that they migrated from Africa to Europe. The Asiatic explorers claim them for that country but there is no doubt that Africa by the work of her scientists, has proven that by far the most numerous traces are to be found here.

I saw literally millions of snail shells in this region, and I can imagine how they must have hated their daily meals, after the million mark was passed!

All is silent here now and desolate. The jackal can be seen often enough, slouching around like a cur, or loping off when he is disturbed; and flying in the face of the sun are falcons and eagles. The massive animals of other years have disappeared with the changing climate. Long ago it was wet and cold here. Rhinoceros and elephants abounded, and it has been established that bears, bison, deer and the felinae were also common. It would be a great thing if a systematic dig, on a sufficiently extensive basis, could take place here every year, searching for what must be somewhere near by, skeleton remains of these fore-runners of the solutrean race.

From the fill of the snail-eaters, we continued up the valley between precipices, like the walls of a canyon to a series of rock caves, with images sculptured on the entrances. We camped in these caves, and filmed the rough carvings of antelopes, bison, deer and elephants on the smooth rock. There is something extremely fascinating in the study of these primitive efforts at design, and the subjects are really well-designed and arranged, though Africa has yet to equal the marvels of the caves of Altamira, in Spain.

Pressing through the valley of Saf-Saf, it grew terrific and almost suffocating, the heat was so intense. Our Caids dropped out one by one, because they could not stand the heat. The going was rough, and that added to our discomfiture, but it was surprising that we should be able to go on, while the Arabs were overcome. Perhaps if they had had the same incentive, they might have stuck it out.

We filmed the canyon, the stronghold of our forerunners, though we did not always climb to the caves. The view from the ledges in the rock which pre-historic man enjoyed must at least have instilled in him a sense of the spectacular.

We broke camp at Sbeitla to continue across the mountains south to the "great atelier," or "flint factory" of the Jhedir Safia. Here we reconstructed and filmed the arsenal of the pre-historic people. Imagine a series of small hills covered with the débris of a million broken flints, near to the scarred faces of the rock where the flints had been chipped out by the ancient "Aurignacians." Reygasse collected thousands of specimens here, and we found some beautifully worked flints of every kind.

Among the specimens we took away were complete ranges of arrow heads, axe-heads or hand hatchets, scrapers, razor flints, and many nuclei (flints from which the tools had been chipped). Moreover, and perhaps the most beautifully worked, we found the tools with which the various instruments were made. They were, of course, also of flint, but must have been worked with infinite care and considerable judgment, their serried edges proving admirably adapted to the finer work of finishing off the rough chippings.

Not a sign of life now animates the land. It is deserted and savage. Only at times nomads of the south pass over it, never dreaming of the ebb and flow, and ebb again, of civilisation that began with man's dawning intelligence. There must have been a merry row going on when the Cro-Magnons were having a field day at the flint workings on the hills of Safia. I wonder if they were actually so deformed as their rock drawings show them. The negroes in parts of Africa to-day are peculiarly formed, physically, their hips and shoulders being rather exaggerated, and we suppose the Aurignacians were also.

On the way to Bir Ater, Reygasse talked for hours of how he had explored this region mile after mile, and so came on these classical epochs. It was a tale of patience and endurance modestly told, but the more thrilling because of the hesitation with which he spoke. I had to draw him out for a while, and then he came into the full stream of his narrative. I was actually sorry to see the welcoming riders who interrupted his tale.

Our hosts met us in the customary lordly style of the hospitable desert Arabs, and we slept in the bordj of the Bir Ater in splendid safety, as all these resting places are small fortresses, with loopholes and towers of defense.

These caravanserai are built by the French for defense, but contrasting with Morocco in this particular, they have rarely been used for actual warfare.

Reygasse is naturally proud of his "mousterian" discoveries here, especially of silex pedoncule, that up to the last few years was generally thought to have been Neolithic. In this locality, too, Reygasse has established the direct transition of the Acheulian to the typical Soluterian periods. Instruments we found on the surface below the Ced Djebanna, were typically mousterian, and made of a bright yellowish flint.

In the curve of the river we found flints mixed with the ashes and bones of pre-historic horses, and it is here that we hope to undertake a large excavation soon, with the object of discovering human relics. There are great possibilities, and the field shows unbelievable richness.

It is impossible for me ever to thank Reygasse sufficiently for the whole-hearted way in which he helped Kellerman, our moving picture operator, to take a detailed film of all these sites, and the discoveries of a lifetime. All the epochs and the best examples of the periods were taken, and I am sure we have a unique documentation of this great African field of the men of the old stone age.

The Dolmens and Megalithic remains. From the Atlas Mountains of Morocco to the yellow sands of the Nile, and from the southern shores of the Mediterranean to the jungles of central Africa, man has lived since the dawn of humanity. It is only since the territory was occupied by the French that this land of wonder and mystery has been opened to scientific research. The Moslems have no interest in the history of the past, or in the preservation of what remains of former civilisations.

In the last five years I have visited all the great ruins of North Africa: Carthage, Utica, Uthnia, Aphrodisium, Bulla Regia, Timgad. . .I am sure I could name a hundred in Tunisia alone. Yet little is known of them by the outer world, less is known of the mighty builders who came before the Phoenicians and the Romans.

There is nothing stranger in the vast natural museum of North African territory than this immense collection of the remains of the Megalithic peoples, whose works are to be found in the Atlas Mountains.

It was the late Dr. Carton who took me first to the fields of the Dolmens. He took me to the specimens at Bulla Regia, which I have already mentioned elsewhere in this chronicle, the place of the ancient hotel made of Roman cisterns. Barring snakes, bugs, scorpions and rats, the place was not too bad, and the Doctor broached some rare Sicilian wine, to help us bear the presence of the snakes, though he mildly suggested that over indulgence in wine tends rather to increase the reptiles within sight.

The whole region bordering on Numidia is full of Megalithic remains, similar to those which are to be found in many parts of the world. They are one of the most absorbing mysteries of archaeology. Who were the people who built their awe-inspiring, and often gigantic tombs on lonely plains or windswept hills, where the rise and set of the sun should light up their graves?

The people who built Stonehenge built similar wonders in Africa; Scotland and Persia, Ireland and the Carpathians, are linked in the same manner. When, how, and why, is still unknown, but if ever the Megalithic question is to be studied and solved, I believe the first clue will be found in Africa.

Often I have wondered if the menhirs, those tall, pointed, conical stones, have not something in common with the "beyles" of the Orient. They rise sometimes to a height of ten metres, and often are built in circles. These are called Cromlechs. On the hill opposite the ruins of Bulla Regia they are in long lines, and at Carnac in Brittany, the alignment stretches for nearly four kilometres, with about eight or ten metres between the stones.

They are built in the direction of the rising and the setting sun, and of the solstices and equinoxes. The Arabs of Africa hold them in superstitious awe, and they have many legends centring around them.

Roknia, in Algeria, is the greatest African field of the Dolmens, and comprises upwards of 1,500 of these strange sepulchres of a lost race. The rock rooms beneath the stones are generally one metre by one and a half or three metres, and contain the dead, with equipment for the other world; silex, stone necklaces, even beautiful objects in gold, and hatchets of jadite, sometimes of great proportions. It is thought that the first Dolmens are of the neolithic age, probably about three thousand to four thousand B.C.

Reygasse believes that the Dolmens of Africa are the tombs of the original Libyans and Berbers. I explored several great tumuli with Reygasse this year, and it made a very fine film, with the actual uncovering of the crouched skeleton, with jewellery in the form of bronze bracelets still attached to the body. The last resting places of all those strange people are invariably built in the most rugged spots, sometimes crowning the mountain tops, as they do near the old Roman city, north of Tebessa.

The tombs look sad and mysterious, especially in the mists and shadows of the giant rocks of the wild Atlas Mountains.

Funds have recently been raised to allow Reygasse to continue his digging into the mystery of these people, and I hope that next year may see an important contribution by him to the knowledge we possess of the subject. The field is large, and General Faidherbe is the only explorer who has hitherto touched the area on any large scale. Unfortunately due to the methods of exploration, little was discovered, and we must wait for the more expert and modern methods to bring us light.

Certainly the investigation must go on, for there are many things to be solved. Many of the Megalithic tombs in Africa had skulls in them that had been trepanned, and I recovered a fine specimen, but whether the trepanning was done as a surgical operation, or as a religious ceremony, it is not known. A strange corollary lies in the fact that the Aures hill-folk still practice the art of trepanning, to this day.

There it is, however, I can but present the field, and give a little indication of the immensity of the subject. The rest must be left to systematic exploration, and the protracted study of the complicated problem.

Chapter 14

THE CHOTTS

Between the land of the Troglodytes and the Matmatas, stretch the great inland lakes of Southern Algeria and Tunisia. The Lakes, called Chotts, cover an area of several hundred kilometres in length, and from sixty to seventy kilometres in width. They are really salt fields, whose surfaces reflect the sun in undiminished brilliance during the dry season. In the rainy season a little water rests for a while, and the Chotts seem to be the Lakes they once were.

Chott el Djerid, which is the greatest of the series, we crossed by motor, and, with the sun shining on the salt, and our cars reflected in the glazed surface, we appeared to be motoring across the sea. The Chott resembled nothing so much as a gigantic snow-field, the salt was finely powdered and closely packed, whistling a little under our tyres as snow whistles, when the temperature is well below zero.

A track, it is even less than that, is laid across the Chott from Kebili to Tozeur and Nefta, glorious oases whose wealth of palms is incredible. Probably the fertility of either bank of the Chott gave De Lesseps the idea, which has never been executed or entirely dismissed, of flooding this region, to bring back prosperity to the district.

It is believed that in early history the Chotts were actual lakes, and that the oases on the banks were really what the Romans called Nefta "ports of the Desert."

Legends tell of naval actions on the Chotts, and Arab historians of the middle ages record the discovery of a galley in the bed of the lake, which by that time had dried up. Chott el Djerid is identified with the lake of the Tritons described by Homer, and the legend recounted by Herodotus still persists, that it was prophesied to Jason, on behalf of the Argonauts, that a hundred Greek cities should be established in this region.

They are argonauts of different race who traverse the Chotts to-day, but the treachery of the salt is always to be remembered. Inviting as the surface appears, the invitation is only to be accepted with due care. It is best to keep to the defined trails, and doubly advisable to take a guide who knows where the trails are. Although the French have raised little mounds or towers of stone across the Chott from Kabili to Tozeur, the towers are not always visible. They have a way of sinking, or of getting some-what obliterated, and the track itself is far from permanent. The salt covers the marks of the wheels quickly. The whole surface levels out before many minutes have passed.

We raced across in high-powered cars, and were quite con-tent when we reached the other side. From the island of stones which lies in the middle of the Chott, and is called the Island of Pharaoh, a sandstorm threatened to overtake us. We were only able to keep just ahead of what looked like a solid wall of sand, coming like an express train behind us. Yet, we left a lone Arab at the Island, who seemed to care little for the treachery of the Chott, or the menace of the sandstorm.

He may have been a secret follower of Ammon, visiting the scene of the ancient cult, or have been communing there with the spirit of the past, for that Island is hoary with legend, and a lone pilgrim or two would not be entirely unexpected.

However, the surface of the Chott, where it is safe, is magnif-icent for speed. Full out, in a Farman car, we travelled at a rate that touched a hundred kilometres an hour, and the riding was easier than forty kilometres an hour on a European road. We did that, knowing we could trust our guide, and that the surface would hold. There are places where the journey would have been downwards and not along. It is recorded that on one occa-sion a caravan of a thousand camels disappeared below the surface, and in a few minutes the salt had closed in on them, obliterating all traces.

We, happily, reached Tozeur. It was nightfall when we found the oasis, rising from the inland lake, like a mystic city charmed into existence by the slaves of the ring. It seemed, from a little distance as though the trees were reflected in the sea. It was the salt playing at mirror again.

Tozeur boasts a million palm trees, and the fantastic Arabs have re-created the story of Creation. Their legend says that the oasis was originated by planting two palm trees, male and female, and now there are a million. I believe they have actually been counted.

To drive through the groves of palms is to drive through fairyland. At every turn our headlights illumined new groups of trees, through which gurgled little streams, or tiny fresh-water pools glistened. The earth was a mass of multi-coloured flowers, and, away from the oasis were the thatched palm-leaf huts, clustered together and surrounded by stockades made of palm branches and latticed with fibre, the whole surmounted by chevaux-de-frise of giant briars, sufficient to keep out any kind of marauder.

We followed the example of the natives, and pitched our camp outside the oasis, on the dunes that are threatening its very existence. Why one should sleep outside the fairyland is obvious, after the first night. The Arabs, of course, do not wish to waste an inch of the precious land by covering it with houses. The traveller soon learns that these bewitching places have an insect population which strongly resents, or welcomes effusively, the invader. And when the wind is still, there is another incentive to stay out of the oasis. One might call it "attar of Palm and stagnant water."

For our delight, it was the Moslem month of Ramdan when we arrived, the time when the Faithful fast all day and feast all night, and we found ourselves serenaded by the village merrymakers who came in full strength to our camp fire, beating their strange drums and shrilling their mysterious fifes.

A semi-circle of musicians, sitting tailor-wise, played for the dancers. Haunting syncopation urged a group of dancers to do their utmost. Their bodies postured and twisted as they trod the sand in the body-dance of the Orient, breaking now into a swaggering cake walk, and again into a wild jig.

Mr. Kellerman, of course, photographed them, and his flares added immeasurably to the unforgettable quality of the scene. The dancers seemed to be hypnotised by the sudden incandescence, and danced like madmen in the light; while, from the shrouded night, in the background of the oasis, a myriad palms bent and swayed, as though to ask what new dawn was breaking.

When dawn did break, we travelled round the settlement on the humps of camels, across the oasis, to see the efforts that are being made to fight the desert. The place is laid out in a complete system of irrigation, which fertilises the area, and the canals form a sporting ground for Arab children, who use the irrigation works as swimming holes. From the humps of our camels we could peep over the mud walls, which run along either side of the canals, into luxuriant private gardens.

The oasis, like many others we have seen, is being enlarged gradually, and at great cost. Always there is the steady fight with the desert, and the French have sunk many artesian wells, and, according to the authorities, nearly every time they bore, they find water which quickly converts the sand into fertile soil.

The warfare against the desert, however, is by no means ended. It will go on as long as the sand continues to creep in, and that will be long. In this region the dunes are at their worst. Composed of minutely pulverised sand, they are driven to a fine crest by the wind, and every breeze changes the contour. The sand dunes, when the wind blows, have the appearance of a chain of small, but active, volcanoes, or of a stormy sea, whose waves are breaking in a torrent of foam. The sand creeps on steadily, and it is not uncommon to see palm trees covered to the leaves in sand of recent accumulation. I saw a shred of vegetation sticking like coarse grass from the crest of a dune. On investigation, it proved to be a palm, completely buried.

The natives are fighting the sand incessantly, with groynes and sheds, much as snow is fought on the railways of America, in the winter.

A little below Tozeur, and still on the borders of the Chotts, is Nefta, an oasis similar to Tozeur, but having a palm-tree population of only a quarter of a million.

Nefta stands on the very edge of the Sahara, and suffers more than Tozeur from the invasion of the desert.

This oasis was actually the port of the desert for the caravans that went South across the Sahara to bring back the products of the tropics, both in the time of the Romans and of the Carthaginians. It is mentioned in the histories of the ancients that Nefta was once connected with the sea, and it is a few miles south of this oasis that, according to Tissot, the galley is reported to have been found.

It is the Nepta of the old world, and below the dunes there lies a Roman city. The sand has conquered, and a once important outpost lies several hundred feet below the surface.

Certainly the old Nepta was influenced by contact with Egypt, for rocks bearing the horns of Ammon Ra have been found here. Legend says that Athena came from Nefta, and, according to Herodotus, her worship was the religion of the city in the fifth century B.C. She may have been a Libyan goddess with a Greek name!

All round are the signs of the city's two-fold fight against her enemies, natural and human. Nefta, now no more than an oasis on the edge of the desert, and a port of the Chott, has battled without respite, and the signs of her tribulation are everywhere apparent.

The Chotts are littered with the bones of camels. Jackals from the mountains find their food here, and the bones are dragged around in every direction.

It may well be that modern science will be able to restore the prosperity of the Chotts and the country round about. There is water in plenty to be had, wells exist even in the centre of the salt lakes, and together with the signs of tribulation, are the unmistakable indications of former civilisation and trade.

Military roads used to skirt the lakes, and though Pliny calls the district "the sad place where there is no possibility of living" there are the mile-stones of the Romans still remaining, which tell their own quaint story. One is more impressed by the generalship and valour of the Romans here, than almost anywhere else, for, to prevent invasion, the natives needed only to fill up the wells on their retreat. Natural conditions would then do the rest.

The Roman mile-stones are the guide books of the ancients. Much more massive than the sign posts of to-day, they convey detailed and adequate information to the traveller. On them are still to be read distances and directions to the great cities. The distance from Carthage to Tebessa, from Carthage to Gigthis, from Carthage to the centre of the Sahara, are all there, and not only do the mile-stones give the route and distance to the next town ahead, but to towns further afield, where there are rivers, deserts, marshes, and often where "hot baths can be obtained!" Suitable caravanserai, where travellers can find accommodation for the night are also indicated, as well as the condition of roads and bridges. Usually the mile-stones are headed by a dedication to one of the Roman Emperors.

One stone, I remember, gave warning of an unprotected road, counseling care against an avalanche of stones from the heights above. Another had a "good luck" message to the traveller.

From these stones, we have learned the names of cities that were in the centre of the Sahara, even as far as the Hoggar, cities that have not yet been found, but which are a challenge to archaeologists.

Chapter 15

THE GOLDEN CITIES

Sbeitla. Archaeology and excavation would become popular indeed if all the sites were as beautiful as Sbeitla, the magic Sufetula.

It is placed with the desert cities, but the golden city of Southern Tunisia is, in fact, located on the high plateau that looks down on the Sahara.

We reached it after a journey across barren tracts, whose only vegetation was tuffa grass. Through the hazy heat-mist of the desert we could see the vague outline of hills, mauve and crimson tinted, and almost detached from them, like a mirage, dim and mysterious, a city of temples, an island floating on the horizon.

The magnificent triumphal arch bears a dedication to Diocletian, Constance and Maximian, and the monument stands as an everlasting challenge by civilisation to barbarism. But, as in many of these cities, it is colour that impresses the spectator most, for in harmony with the graceful proportions and architectural composition, time and nature have painted the monument in colours unequalled for vividness or variety.

In the midst of an arid country it appears like a bouquet of flowers. The stones are softened into old gold and saffron, draped with delicate mauve and sapphire.

Silently we passed beneath the wondrous arch, our footsteps passing among the overturned columns and stones. The old roadway still bore the marks of the chariots of the Romans, whose wheels cut deep grooves into the pavement.

To the right stands the ghostlike columns of the theatres, silhouetted against the sky like the strings of an Aeolian harp. A
silver thread of glistening water trickled around their bases,
when we saw them, for the theatre was built on the banks of a
deeply sunk African wady. As at Gigthis, palaces and paths were
built on the water's edge, and the limpid stream still reflects the
crumbling monuments.

Crossing the stage, we struck a road lined on either side by
great ruins, partly excavated by the Services des Antiquités, and
suddenly stopped, amazed. Between the columns of a great
basilica there rose before us the greatest spectacle of glorious
ruin in all Africa, and the equal of any on earth.

The Forum of Sufetula, with its triumphal monumental doors,
its fluted columns, tinged like shafts of gold, and carrying in the
central space the majestic Capitolean Temples is probably the
most perfect specimen of the work of the empire builders
remaining. There is no sensation equal to the surprise of that
dreamlike place. I felt that it was so unreal that at any moment
the vision might fade, but I reached the temple steps, treading
softly for fear of disturbing the heavy silence, and sat on an
overturned capital to take in the magic of the city.

On either side the temples stand, and under the peristyle and
between the great Corinthian columns our party collected and
gazed across the ancient plains.

From the temple steps the whole skeleton of the dead city can
be seen. In the distance, gracefully outlined, is the triumphal
arch, and beyond it lie the dying nuances of the phantom mountains.

The river lies to the left, and leading to it, from the Forum
below, the road we had just traversed. One imagines that, in the
old days, the people of fashion trod that road to the river's edge,
to enjoy the cool of the evening. It has no fashion now. No chariots or clanking legionaries cross the beautiful arched bridge
that, still intact and perfect, spans the silvery river. The incense
rises no more from the altars that once stood before the statues
of Jupiter, Minerva and Juno, only the mists rise on the horizon

that widens round this sleeping collection of stones that once was the city of gold and ivory, called Sufetula.

Timgad. As every traveller through North Africa would say, Timgad is unique. The multiplicity of statement does not diminish its truth. It is the bare fact.

It sprang, full armed, from the mind of Trajan, who conceived the city as a fit testimonial to his gallant Legion, Uplia Victrix.

There are many things that are unique in connection with Timgad. Chief among them is the fact that it stands as the ruin of the first city that was "town planned." Its streets and avenues run at right angles, and full use has been made of the site chosen. The site, incidentally is nothing, just a stretch of barren waste, which never before bore houses or buildings. The city planners needed nothing but their own ingenuity. There were no impediments to the work. Nobody to-day would think of erecting a city in such surroundings. That is, unless they were Empire Builders, and had an eye to the garrisoning of large numbers of forces in view of emergencies.

Thamugadi, as the Romans called it, is an outpost of empire on the fringe of desolation. As an outpost, it faced the four quarters of the globe, fenced round about by walls, of which now there is no sign, but squarely built, and stoutly fashioned, embellished by art that fell short of the great cities, but yet was graceful. To the city access was gained by means of four gates, and from east to west ran the military road, along whose pavement the chariots raced, and traffic gouged a rutted way through the slabs of stone.

Deserted, unfavoured by climate or surrounding, a grim testimony to the weight of the Romans, and witness to their thoroughness the ruined city stands in the midst of denuded mountains and gruff wilderness.

Perhaps it is its position that has preserved it. The sand has blown and drifted over the place. Its inaccessibility saved it from being despoiled by the ravagers who wanted stone and columns for their other cities. Now, the Services des Antiquités, following on the work of M. Joly, have uncovered that stretch of sand, nearly four hundred yards square, and are restoring the place to recognisable form.

There is much that is curious and enlightening at Timgad. It has ruins of grandeur and stateliness that remain to tell their story. The ruins are not comparable with others in Africa, but, in their collection they are every bit as significant.

The roads especially bear witness to their service. On either side is a footpath, colonnaded and porticoed, where the soldiers, and such of fashion as was to be found in the garrison town, wandered. There are buildings too, which leave room for the archaeologist to work upon, and, for the artist there is the Arch of Trajan.

The Forum is illuminating, its pavement still carrying the little gaming tables, where doubtless the soldiers and others played to beguile the dull hours. Here is the inscription, now famous, which reads VENARI LAVARI LUDERE RIDERE OCC EST VITA ("Hunting, bathing, gambling, laughing, this is life"). One wonders whether that inscription revealed the soul of the soldier, or only his boredom with the life of an outpost settlement.

The Forum, easily recognised, whose columns are especially graceful, is broad and spacious, with the shrine to Fortuna Augusta, the Rostra and the Temple with a little room nearby for the philosophers who waited for their public speeches.

The Market place, with its little stalls, evokes memories. There was trading aplenty in the garrison, and astute merchants catered to the wants of the soldiers who had only time to kill and money to spend when the Empire was not at war. The Baths are not large, but are fairly numerous, in different parts of the city.

Timgad was supervised, as was nearly every Roman settlement, by its genius. Near the Arch of Trajan lies the little temple to the "Genio Coloniae Thamug.," and the frequency with which one meets these little temples to lesser divinities recalls at least, if it does not aid in identification, the habit of the former inhabitants of the land, who had the lesser god for every fertile spot, every spring, every special enclosure. How difficult it is to say where the Baalim stopped short and the "genius" began.

The most imposing, but not the most beautiful, of the architectural possessions of Timgad is the Capitol. It is heterodox in its style and in its composition, though its constructors have tried to overcome by size what they failed to accomplish by art, and the usual Trinity of the Romans were housed in the immense structure.

Timgad boasts also a Byzantine fortress, and a monastery.

Khamissa. Khamissa we passed on the road from Timgad to Souk Ahlas, the birthplace of St. Augustine. We reached this wonderful and mysterious dead city just as the sun was setting across the wild and ragged Atlas mountains.

Here is an entirely different phase of the many sided continent, and a setting to the ruins entirely different from Timgad and Sbeitla of the valley, Gigthis of the desert, and Carthage of the sea. This is a mountain city, the ancient Thurbisicu Numidorum, first stronghold of the Numidians, then a rich city under Trajan.

Before reaching the fine ruins of Khamissa we passed the vague and grotesque, mist-enshrouded, towers of crumbling Tipasa, where ten square towers overlook the plains and the ruins they hold.

Our road mounted rapidly to the city that is the source of the great Medjerda, and Khamissa's triumphal arch suddenly came into view. Through the gate, we saw ruins on every hand, capping the panorama of the valley.

Two Berber shepherds stared at us as we passed, wondering doubtless why any sane man should want to come and see broken stone, and disturb the peace. We climbed among the ruins for an hour, amazed at the beauty of the site. The most attractive of the ruins at Khamissa are the basins, rectangular and circular, filled with limpid water. Temples are reflected in their cool depths, and we lit a fire by their majestic remains, for the weather was cold, and we were at a considerable altitude.

Africa, the land of sun and brilliant skies can be as cold as the poles when the sun goes down.

Here, at Khamissa, the ancients built a tribute to the divinities superintending the source of North Africa's greatest river, and many a festival must have taken place in honour of the Gods. The spot is beautiful enough to encourage festivals. Our party was completely fascinated by the extent of the ruins and the almost endless number of fine specimens. The theatre still stands perfect, even in its ruin. The walls of the stage are thirty feet high, and here it is possible to get an idea of what the back of a Roman theatre looked like.

The temple columns in the Forum are made of the golden Numidian marble. There are twenty-six of these gigantic columns, which, some day perhaps will be raised again.

M. Joly has already done much archaeological excavation here, with the assistance of Mr. Gsell, but more remains to be done. It is a land of wonderful possibilities, for the history of the Numidian is a long and romantic story. From these mountains came the famous horsemen of Hannibal's all conquering hosts.

From Sallust we learn that the famous library of Carthage was brought to these mountains in 146 B.C. and placed in the hands of Hiepsal.

The question that always awaits an answer is whether we shall find any traces of this great collection when the cities of this region are thoroughly excavated.

We left the land of the proud and valiant mountain kings, that had defied the Empires of Carthage and of Rome, wrapped in its mountain mists under the stars. Descending, we passed the great Byzantine fortress of Ksar el Kebir, and the ruins of baths and a Byzantine church.

One more triumphal arch, and this dead city of the mountains was gone, but memory lingers over the temple reflected with the stars in the basins where the Medjerda rises.

Bulla Regia. The city of "Royal Baal" stood on the banks of the Medjerda River, in the land of Numidia. To-day there is only a wilderness, but the wilderness blossoms with the rose of natural grandeur. The ruins here lie on the slopes of mountains that overlook the valley, and the ridges are covered with forests in which boar and wild game abound.

The game are not always peaceful, for once, camping at Bulla Regia, I witnessed a battle between black panthers. The boars are so numerous and so destructive that not infrequently crops are laid waste, and the natives organise veritable expeditions against them.

With excavation at Bulla Regia must always be associated the name of my friend Dr. Carton, who entertained the expedition at "the city of subterranean palaces." Our lodgings were unique, and I claim that the Doctor had reconstructed the oldest hotel in the world, for the walls of the ruins were at least two thousand years old. They were actually cisterns, which had been whitewashed. Such is the use modern science makes of the enterprise of the past. Each room was furnished with a table, a bed and a chair. The table, what an anachronism, was a marble capital, and the wash-basin, in my room, was an early Christian baptismal font!

The nights there can be bitterly cold, and damp fogs floated up from the marshes below the ruins, chilling us to the marrow.

Dr. Carton – the famous pioneer of archaeology, was a typical adventurer-scientist, brave and patient, fighting for his subject, and died as the result of exposure and privation consequent upon his work at Bulla Regia.

With Jules Renault, of Carthage, his name should be inscribed in the records of science and of history as a martyr to the advancement of learning.

The enormous baths of Bulla Regia can be seen for miles, looming up like the horny spine of a monster whose sightless eyes glare blindly at the world. Close to the baths are two groups of cisterns, incredibly vast, used to-day as the dwellings of the Berbers. In the centre of the city are the ruins of the sacred temple, erected to the water divinity, from which the remains of an aqueduct stretch across gorse and cactus to Souk el Arba. There are also ruins of a temple to Apollo and Augustus, where magnificent statuary was found, and a theatre, carved out of the hillside.

The chief marvels of the old Numidian city, however, are the subterranean palaces, unique in archaeological discovery. They were found only recently, and the indication of their presence arose from a strange coincidence.

A hunter was following a fox, and tracked it to its lair in a hole under the heather. Reaching the hole, and looking in, the hunter was amazed to see a vast space below, and in the dim light could just distinguish upright columns and worked walls. So the first palace was discovered and excavated. Such a find, of course, led to the continuance of exploration, and now the world is richer by the disinterment of a series of such buildings.

The palaces are named after the mosaics found in the atrium, such as "The Peacock Palace," "The Palace of the Hunting Scene," "The Palace of Venus."

Each palace has a square area open to the sky, and carpeted with mosaic, in the centre of which stands a fountain of graceful design. The walls are still full of colour. From the courtyard access is gained to the living rooms, which to-day are resplendent with moss and flowers, and trickling crystal water.

The palaces still have their upper floors, and are, with the exception of Cato's villa at Utica, the only two storey houses I have seen excavated in Africa.

It is not difficult to understand the reason for these subterranean palaces, in the heat of an African summer. The citizens of Bulla Regia lived in the cool depths of the underground rooms during the hot months and in winter they moved upstairs and enjoyed milder weather. It was a most admirable arrangement. Instead of migrating to the shore, with consequent expense and difficulties (they had their transportation difficulties even in those days) they just changed floors with the climate. There are obvious indications that we have by no means exhausted the possibilities of excavation here, and we are faced with a glorious opportunity to carry on the work started by Dr. Carton.

Next to Djerba and Utica, Bulla Regia offers the greatest archaeological opportunity, judging from results already obtained, which are not far short of being unbelievable.

Little is yet known of the history of the city, except that it enjoyed a great reputation in the days of the Numidian kings and in the time of the Romans, but around the wild places are to be found megalithic remains, and on a little hill opposite the Numidian city there are strange, prehistoric, alignments of stones.

We visited them one morning while the swirling mountain mists still hung over the place, and ourselves felt the awe they must have inspired in the hearts of primitive man.

Bulla Regia is just off the main road from Carthage to Constantine, and is within easy motoring distance of all the surrounding dead cities. From our camp there we made several visits to Dougga, Chemtou and Thurburnica.

Chemtou. Chemtou, within easy reach of Bulla Regia, is particularly interesting, and one of the weirdest of African ruins. Here, the ancient Simitthu, were situated the quarries of Numidian marble whose name has weathered man's forgetfulness as long as her stone has weathered the storms of time. The city is in the Medjerda Valley, standing by the marble mountain, near the station of Oued Meliz. A multitude of ruins wait for the pick and shovel, for the light railways excavators use, that her wonders may be made visible again.

The Forum is visible, as also is the theatre, with its orchestra paved with mosaic, and there are vast cisterns and baths. The natives call the cisterns the subterranean city (Medemit el Aud).

The aqueduct itself would be worth a lifetime of research, and here it is particularly interesting, being partly raised and partly subterranean.

The quarries are probably the most interesting feature of Chemtou, where the working of the ancient slaves are still to be seen, as well as unfinished columns half-worked, in the hillside. Both Phoenicians and Romans were taskmasters in these quarries, driving Numidian slaves to the hewing of Numidian marble, and to the north, across the mountains, lies the old road, still discernible, along which the marble was carried to the sea port of Tabarca. The huge slabs were dragged or rolled by hundreds of slaves over the mountain passes. Here is written in stone the tragedy of the underdog two thousand years ago. His lot was not easy. Life was but slightly preferable to death.

Near this place the famous inscription of the little freemen, who were not quite slaves but were compelled to give a certain amount of unpaid labour, was discovered. Carved in the stone they worked was their plea to Commodus, and their protest against the terrors of life and the malice of their masters. And in stone, too, was the reply of Commodus, their franchise, the slaves' magna charta.

But not even these mines could have been so terrible in their administration as the mines of Signs where Christian slaves worked in the cimmerian darkness of the bowels of the earth. For an adequate description of these horrors it is worth turning to Louis Bertrand's *Sanglue Martyrum*. There one lives again in the place and in the time of the terrors.

These half finished columns at Chemtou are eloquent, not only of the art and craftsmanship of the Greek sculptors, but of the agony of men not born free in the days when the only real distinction was between the bond and the free.

Cato the elder, speaking in 152 B.C. told of the wonderful "pavimenta Poenica" of the mansions of wealthy Romans, and at Utica we found the floors of one of the villas paved in this same warm-coloured Numidian marble. Carthage is full of it, and I have fished up pieces of the same stone at Sbeitla, Gigthis, off the isle of Djerba, and even encountered it on the borders of the Sahara, as well as in a dozen dead cities all over the country.

Considering all things, it is not surprising that the slaves mutinied several times, and on one occasion their mutiny assumed considerable proportions.

Thurburnica. From Chemtou, it is well to ride to the ruins of Thurburnica, a complete city of the dead, as yet untouched by archaeological research, and in a beautiful situation. Here, temples, mausoleums, palaces, baths, triumphal arches, roadways and a graceful bridge, are surrounded by a silent forest. We camped there in the ruins of a Byzantine fortress. The blaze of our fire illumined the ochre ruins, and chiseled them against the dark mass of the forest beyond. The wolves howled, outside the range of our fire, and occasionally the ghostly hoot of an owl added to the eerie atmosphere.

No human presence spoiled the ruins. All that prospered there was the riot of flowers and the mountain gorge. The old Roman arch rose from a field of violets, and the floor of the temple of Mercury was carpeted with moss, from which peeped primroses and scarlet pimpernels. A mad mountain stream dashed down by the ruins, to flow under the bridge that Augustine and Cyprian crossed on the road that went from Carthage to Hippo, by way of Thurburnica.

Spreading to the horizon is the valley of the Medjerda, leaving the enclosed and sleeping city, and in the dim distance the Algerian frontier stands, in the purple hills of Numidia. Above are the hot baths, where the ancients, as was their habit, erected a beautiful nympheum to their water divinities.

Here is vision and romance. I was sketching there one day when some Berber maidens came to bathe in the clear waters, and for once I was caught back across the span of many centuries. It seemed as they laughed and splashed, that the nymphs and satyrs had returned, that the gods were coming to earth again in an African paradise of flowered moss and shady groves. The world was far away.

It will always be far away from beautiful Thurburnica with its olives and pines, and its ivory ruins framed in the everlasting green, jeweled with the flowers of the garden of Africa.

Dougga. The ancient city of Thugga, or, as it is now called, Dougga, is the gem of the dead civilisations of Africa. There is none to approach it for beauty on the continent, and none to surpass it on the shores of the Mediterranean.

It is not a place to be "taken in" in an hour or two. It is not anxious to reveal itself to the passerby, rather it is the place wherein men must woo the muses, and quietly look on the scene of past splendour, to dream again. At night, the temple columns rise like shafts of gold outlined against a pall of velvet in the moonlight, with a myriad of stars glistening overhead.

The fortunate man sees the sunset beyond the Temple of Coelestis, Africa's most sublime ruin, when the rays of the departing sun turn the graceful marble pillars into columns of blazing fire.

Rarest thing of all, I saw the theatre of Dougga in a storm, with the lightning flashing, and thunder rolling in the crags and echoing in the distant mountains.

This is a city of gods, and of men like gods. Beauty possessed their souls, and genius was their endowment. Not in this earth is there the equal in grace and beauty of the marble temple that crowns the hill. To see Dougga is to see antiquity, to weep for an age of beauty that may not return.

In the midst of scenery fitting for the mounting of the jewel, are the theatre, the Capitol, the Temple of Coelestis, and the Punic Mausoleum.

Each is an ineffably magnificent structure, and to crown the glory of their conception, time has given a superb tone to the stones themselves. Old gold and ivory, sepia, orange, vermilion and ochre battle with shadows of purple and green against sapphire skies. Colour trembles in the air, and the mellowed ruins are caught up in touches of polychrome that have baffled the rolling centuries.

Dougga is only a few hours distant from Tunis, and the roads wind smoothly, with an enchantment of their own. The traveller passes over a bridge made from the ancient stones of Madressa, called Medyez el Bab. Near the mountains, as we approach is the dead city of Ain Tounga, the old Thignica.

This must have been a place of considerable importance in the days when the legions passed on the military road from Carthage to Theveste. In the centre of the ruins rises the Byzantine fortress, a magnificent old pile, which would be interesting to explore in detail. It is composed of capitals, inscriptions, statues, steles and stones of varying sizes and texture, hurriedly gathered together by the Byzantines in their mad haste to fortify the land.

North Africa is dotted everywhere with these Byzantine relics, the fortresses that were constructed of any material that came readily to hand, for the Byzantines were not archaeologists and regarded the past infinitely less than they tried to safeguard the present. Byzantine fortresses are actually museums, but museums made for defence, not for the advancement of science.

The fortress of Ain Tounga is typical of the hundreds of such erections, and merits inspection. It is worth while to climb over it, exploring the walls and deciphering the inscriptions.

A number of the more important sections of the fortification still stand. Chief among them are the Triumphal arch and the temple.

Probably the most important Byzantine fortress I have seen is at Haidra, the ancient Ammoedara, on the Algerian-Tunisian frontier. It is a digression, but a forgiveable one, to say a word or two about it, for it conveys a better impression of the Byzantines than any other. The walls are over two hundred yards long and rise like an enormous derelict in the desert, standing in the shadow of the mountain called the "table of Jugurtha." This, like all the other fortresses, was built, with towers and gateways and precipitous walls, to withstand the invasions of the Arabs from the desert.

From Ain Tounga, the road to Dougga frequently crosses the old Roman road, and we see the paving stones and bridges every few miles. Before Dougga is reached our way takes us through Teboursouk, an Arab village now, but once a Roman city, called Thubursicum Bure.

Climbing swiftly, we turn on the crest of the hills, and there, before us, in a blaze of sunlight, outlined against the bluest of skies, rise the graceful columns of Dougga.

Mounting the seats of the theatre, still intact, one obtains the most magnificent panorama Africa can offer, after the view from the hills of Carthage.

Falling away, before the spectator, are the empty seats of the
theatre that once held the choicest and rarest of Roman warriors
and their ladies. The tiers sweep away in a graceful semi-circle
to the mosaic floor of the orchestra and the stage, with a background of magnificent columns. The finest theatre of Africa is
before us, and, fortunately, as in the case of the theatre at Khamissa, the facade is almost intact.

For many years the Services des Antiquités of the French
authorities have been working on the restoration of this gem,
and now it stands almost as it stood for the excited crowds who
witnessed the spectacles here.

Between the columns lies an endless vista of flower strewn
fields, leading to mountains fissured by ravines that are transformed to the shadow of the imperial purple that was Rome, and
covered by the brilliant emerald foliage of olive and cypress,
with here and there a shimmering gleam of silver, as a stream
flows along its course.

On either hand is the dead city. Above us tower the columns
of the temple of Saturn, as graceful and slender as the strings of
the lyre of the Gods. There is nothing but grandeur and beauty.
These two and silence. The air is brisk, and fresh with the purity
of high windswept places. The landscape is clear, almost trans-
parent, utterly unearthly and mysterious. Everything; colour, air,
stone and imagination conspire to recreate the mystery of
ancient palaces and temples.

There is a path from the theatre, through an Arab village, to
the perfect Capitolean temple, erected in the time of Marcus
Aurelius, and dedicated to the Trinity of Jupiter, Juno, and Minerva. Crossing scores of fallen columns and capitals to the
"court yard of the winds," we are confronted by the temple that
has inspired Louis Bertrand and Gaston Boissiere to words that
will remain in living language even beyond the duration of the
temple itself. It has been described scientifically times enough
for any addition by me to be unnecessary, and in verse and prose
by masters whose diction I may not even imitate. All that I may
do is to try to talk about these ruins of Africa. It is the intensity

of colour that first assails the senses; gold and crimson, sienna and cream, with veins of amber: that is the Capitole. The winds have modelled crevices and softened the corners of the stones, while the sun has burned the hues of sunset into the walls.

The setting is matchless. To the right is a graceful little forum, with a smiling temple, whose Corinthian doorway has a soft carmine tint. Beyond is the temple to Augustus, and further distant a vague agglomeration of the ruins of roadways and palaces. Thistles and bluebells grow between the stones, and deep moss covers the base of tall columns. From the temple steps one sees, in the valley below, the famous Libyo-Phoenician mausoleum.

It stands on the slopes of an olive-clad hill, looking out across the famous battle-fields, and is the most perfect example of Punic architecture remaining in Africa. It is a massive tomb, more than twenty metres high, and dating from approximately the fourth century, B.C.

Until recently it had resisted time, weather, and the spleen of the Romans, standing there in peace against the corrosion of years and the successive invaders, who either cherished its beauty or considered it of no military importance. The old grey stones have mellowed with age, and a serenity that comes only with the centuries has softened its sharp outlines. Four-square it stands among the gnarled old olives, a memory of the past, witness to the dead, and the labour of the slaves, an immense three-tiered building, surmounted by a pyramid.

Its three floors are obviously Greek in spirit, but the pyramid is reminiscent of Egypt. Nowhere have I seen a more perfect embodiment of the best of two great conceptions.

The lower floor, supported on its foundations of steps, is decorated, as are the others, with pillars speaking of Greek art. The walls are broken gracefully by "blind" windows, and on the eastern side is the door.

The next floor is practically a duplication of the first, maintaining the square formation, though receding a little, and decorated in Ionic style. The third storey is slenderer, and more profusely decorated, with pedestals at the corners of the building carrying sculptures of horsemen. On the walls are bas-reliefs of quadriges, four-horsed chariots somewhat conventionalised.

Above the whole rises the pyramid, at whose angles are four great statues of winged female figures, possibly "Victories." Sheer into the wind, silhouetted against the sky, on the pinnacle of the pyramid, stands a lion.

The mausoleum, however, that stood its ground against Romans, Berbers, Vandals, and every scourge that whipped Carthage, suffered at the hands of over hasty science. On its face was a stone, in the two languages, Lybian and Phoenician, a great commentary and a most useful clue to the languages of which we know so little. Sir Thomas Read, then British Consul, realising its great interest and significance, obtained permission for the inscription to be sent to the British Museum.

His workmen, in attempting to secure the text, were not so careful of the superstructure as they might have been, with the consequence that columns that had rested undisturbed for twenty-four centuries were thrown out of place, and considerable damage done, which now has to be repaired. The Services des Antiquités is at work restoring the mausoleum to its original state, though the inscription still remains in the British Museum.

The incident is regrettable, for Sir Thomas Read was a great and gentle man, and though he rendered magnificent service to humanity in prevailing upon the Bey to abolish slavery throughout his dominions, this one error of overzealousness is counted against him, and has occasioned much exasperation.

Following the path through the Capitol, by a grove of olive trees whipped by the wind and gnarled with age, one comes to the Temple of Coelestis, the most perfect individual splendour among all the ruins. It is one of the world's romances in stone.

Ancient Dougga is most entrancing in moonlight, for the African moon is somehow softer and more golden than in other places, as though her beams were tempered to the ancient places and fell more gently on the ruins of days whose glory has become only a memory. Once, we built a fire by the steps of the temple, that the light might people the shadows anew. The flickering flames gave a vestige of life to the ancient place. The spectres of the past camped with us, and Dougga became real again.

Here could be enacted the whole gamut of African Mythology, all her wondrous history staged on the arena of her ruins. Possibly in the future, not too far distant, we may, on the ancient stage of the theatre, present the epic of the country it adorns.

Beyond are the plains of Zama, where Hannibal was at last ignored by destiny. Further afield is the road to Sicca Veneris, along which marched the revolted mercenaries. In the surrounding mountains fought the mighty giants of Numidia, Massinissa, Jugurtha and Juba, and in Dougga itself, Vandals and Christians (Donatists and Catholics), fought a hand-to-hand fight from house to house.

The place equals the spirit it breathes. It evokes Hannibal, Hamilcar, Salammbo, Sophonisba, Dido, Tertullian, the Kahena, Cyprian of Carthage and Augustine of Thagaste, the dancers of Hesperides guarding the golden apples, the mystery of the lost Atlantis, the Lotus Eaters, and the myths of the desert and the legends of Greece. These are the spirit of Dougga, where a lost world awaits to be resurrected.

Chapter 16

UTICA – EXCAVATION OF THE PARENT CITY

Utica lies two kilometres off the road from Tunis to Bizerta, and in early history was a peninsula closely resembling the peninsula of Carthage to-day, only not quite so large. A semi-circle of purpled hills surrounds the ruins that once looked out over the sea.

The city was one and a half miles long, and half a mile across, washed by the sea on three sides. The Medjerda River is continuing the work of silting up the land, a work begun in the third and fourth centuries A.D.

Until some thirty years ago the site of Utica was simply a stretch of marshes that were a hotbed of malaria. Recently, however, the brothers Chaban-nes-La Palice have irrigated and redeemed the land on either side of Utlea, to the sea shore, and transformed it into one of the biggest and most prosperous farms in Africa.

Counts Jean and Jacques de Chabannes are descendants of crusaders who fought and died with St. Louis, at Carthage in 1270. They bought the site of Utica for a song, just after the French occupation of Tunisia, and their farm now covers a quarter of the ancient city. This section, according to my investigations, and those of the Abbé Moulard, is entirely Roman. The more important Phoenician settlement is on the last half mile of the lower end of the Peninsula.

The old Roman cisterns and the ruins of the great edifices have been turned into farm buildings, electric light plants, garages, pig-styes and store houses. There are inscriptions embedded in the walls of some of the stables.

From the summit of the acropolis, one can see the vast results of the agricultural enterprise of these two noblemen. Thousands of acres of grain, countless herds of sheep and cattle now are raised on the land where once the fleets of Tyre and Carthage and Rome were enclosed.

On dry land, thanks to the vagaries of the Medjerda, I have walked over the place where the great naval battle between Rome and Carthage was fought in the second Punic war, just off the walls of Utica, and naturally, I wondered if we should find naval relics, were we to dig there.

The whole site of the Phoenician colony, and onetime Roman capital of Africa, is rich with priceless marbles from many an ancient quarry on the shores of the Mediterranean. No question exists, in my mind, of the artistic, archaeological and historical importance of a prolonged campaign at Utica. It should occupy at least five years.

The "Island" on which lie the great Egyptian granite columns of the Temple of Apollo, is certainly one of the most important sites of North Africa waiting for scientific excavation. This Phoenician temple to the Greek sun-god Apollo possibly corresponded with the cult of the sun-baal of the Carthaginians, Baal-Hammon. Pliny amply testifies to the gorgeous richness of the temple, and its repute spread to the ends of the earth (Pliny, Elder, xvi 216).

On this "Isle" there are also the ruins of quays pronounced by scientists to be the first probable traces of the early Tyrians in Africa. The furthermost point is covered with rich buildings, chief among which are the ruins of the elaborate hot baths of Utica. Count Chabannes pumped the water from a stagnant pond here, years ago, and for an hour or two was able to examine the magnificent mosaic floors and the summits of several exquisite fluted columns, which were still erect. The water gained on him, however, and rose to its normal level, to cover the treasures until the day comes when we can not only pump the water away, but lay down ditches in a complete system of drainage that will take care of the flood. We shall finally have to run the water off into the marshes, but that will take time and money.

The water comes from a hot sulphur spring, and it is more than probable that the spring existed in the days of Utica's glory, and that the baths in the vicinity were actually a complete spa. Throughout Africa I have found baths near the hot sulphur springs, relics of a time when the luxury of bathing was freely indulged, a condition which, I am sorry to say, has left few traces in the habits of the present occupants of the wilderness.

On the "mainland," opposite the ruins of the Temple of Apollo, are a group of Roman villas and a Phoenician necropolis of the fourth century B.C. waiting to be laid bare. In some places, the sandstone edges of the sarcophagi are actually appearing through the clay.

For convenience, we speak of the "island" and the "main-land" at Utica, but they are terms intended to indicate the geography of the place two thousand years ago. To-day, of course, as I have pointed out, there is no sea, and "isle" and "mainland" are one, wedded by the silt of the Medjerda, grain by grain, piled up during sixteen hundred years.

Below the acropolis, soundings have showed us Punic tombs, a Christian basilica, and an unidentified edifice with columns standing upright, the lower half of which is standing in water. The acropolis of Utica seems to have been searched, for treasure and building material, but Abbé Moulard uncovered forty yards of wall belonging to Phoenician times, near which, one morning, I dug up a Punic inscription so worn by the elements that Abbé ·Chabot has not succeeded yet in deciphering it. Perhaps – it is more than probable – the goddess Tanit had a sanctuary on these slopes.

The acropolis to-day has the twin Arab marabouts on its summit, and the tombs of Moslem conquerors. Below, looking towards Carthage, are the ruins of the theatre, the richness of its material suggesting that this, rather than the other theatres near the acropolis, is the one that Julius Caesar describes so vividly in the notes of his African campaigns.

Its position certainly was unique, with the sea on either side, and the great marble columns lying shrouded in the soil support Caesar's testimony to its beauty and chaste proportions.

All the region of the acropolis, and below it, is open for archaeological research. There is no real-estate problem here, as there is at Carthage, for the Count de Chabannes has placed the whole "domaine d'Utica," as it is called, at the disposal of Abbé Moulard and myself. He has also put mules and carts and rails at our service, to carry away the excavated earth, which we dump into the great marshes.

This is a wise combination of archaeology and agriculture, for the land so reclaimed is turned to good purpose. By serving science, Count de Chabannes extends his acres.

The entire region is free of houses, exactly the reverse of Carthage, and it was not used so much as a quarry, like Carthage, which helped to build Tunis, Granada, Pisa and Genoa. Utica escaped the holocaust. No Roman raised the fires of vengeance with a warcry like Cato's "Delenda est Carthago," outcome of fury and spleen. Utica was not cursed by Scipio, and so far has escaped the devouring real-estate agent. It has escaped the tourist invasion, and here we shall not hear the foolish questions of the pseudo-scientific. It is hard to credit, but it is actually true that a certain group at Carthage wanted to know why "the naughty Romans *dynamited* the city!"

The farms of the Chabannes, their chateau, and the homes of the many hundred workmen employed lessen the sense of desolation on the plain, but otherwise only the silent ruins, the dreary marshes, and the farm lands fill the landscape. But, like Carthage, Utica is a starting point for memory. Where desolation is was once a mighty people, a nation with a great history, for whom now the few stones speak. Yet, I hope that before long the glory of Utica will be apparent, and her magnificence speak for itself.

The funds for such work as has been done in the past were raised during my lecture tour of America and Canada, with private donations from Dr. W. Maloney and W. F. Kenny of New York. Count de Chabannes provided for the collaboration of Abbé Moulard, the material, and the site, while the cost of the scientific publication of Abbé Moulard came from the general fund, which amounted to Frs. 50,000. I am now trying to raise one hundred thousand francs a year for Utica, which will ensure a worthy excavation on a good scale.

Utica is practically untouched as regards excavation. In 1860 a few soundings were made by Nathan Davis, the results of which are now in the British Museum, including a few mosaics and a head found in the Temple of Apollo. Sainte Marie did a little work in 1884, and so did Davis and Herisson. In 1907 Père Delattre went over from Carthage to assist Count de Chabannes in the exploration of several tombs of the Phoenician necropolis. Unfortunately the development of the farm has caused the destruction of several important ruins, though Count Jean de Chabannes has made a little museum in the chateau, and has had several mosaics taken up and roofed.

The museum is now well arranged and catalogued by Abbé Moulard, and contains several gold treasures from the Phoenician tombs, which alone are well worth a visit.

The serious work of excavation was inaugurated in 1922, under the supervision of Abbé Moulard, and was confined to the Phoenician tombs, with the object of discovering material for the documentation of the first Phoenician colonists of North Africa.

It had long been my own ambition to open a serious excavation at Utica, and I had many times searched for the superficial indications of the great buildings that once made the marble city the envy of mankind. Nothing remains to-day that can give an adequate understanding of the majesty of the past. It is no longer a port, but has been pushed back, miles from the sea. That very change in the situation makes Utica more desirable from the point of view of the archaeologist. The marine works will proba-

bly be more easily uncovered, and reconstruction made comparatively easy.

As in other cities of the country, there are numberless small
objects which are brought to the surface by the rain, to serve as
indications of the wealth that lies below, and history serves us
well in an attempt to visualise the city, as it once rode, like a
jewel, on the sea.

Utica, in its pride, must have been a magnificent sight. An
interesting feature, proof of its ostentatious wealth, were the
three theatres and the great hippodrome. These buildings were
so situated that they commanded a view of the sea on three
sides, and I have come to the conclusion that the ancients built
their cities and their great buildings with a due sense of fitness
and of setting. From the seats of the theatres, spectators would
have a view of the great spectacles on the stage, and the immensity of the view to the horizon must have enhanced in no small
way the beauty of the presentation. Not only at Utica, but at
Carthage, Dougga, and in many other cities, the theatres were so
placed that they commanded a panorama of inspiring natural
beauty. Utica must have been unique, even among the most
magnificent of its competitors, giving the impression that it was
placed in the midst of the sea. Its Phoenician citizens must have
loved the sea, and everything that pertained to it, for sea
emblems are to be found on many of the objects we have recovered, and naval spectacles were often staged.

There were rows of seats in a semi-circle at the entrance to
the Admiralty harbour, where probably the people gathered to
welcome their returning galleys. Opposite, on the "island" stood
the mighty Admiralty buildings, between which, and the cheer-
ing crowds, the fleets manoeuvred. Even a feeble imagination
can visualise the scene, and anticipate the rush for good seats
when the fleet was signaled, or the eagerness of those who
watched to see if their loved ones were among those who had
reached home safely.

But now the site is covered, in part by the barren marshes,
and in part by the grazing lands of the Chabannes farms. At

night the owl hoots among the crumbling stones, and is answered by the jackal in the hills. Melancholy desolation rules in the stead of fashion and splendour, but the ruins speak a language of their own, more eloquent than words.

This then, was the field that was calling me, and in the five years that I have been exploring and excavating in North Africa, I have never seen a richer site, nor have results been so great as they were almost from the moment when we began to dig in earnest, during the early part of 1925.

We explored and ran trial trenches for some days, and there was a shadow of disappointment when our soundings gave no result. We knew, of course, that we could move on to other places, where we were certain of ruins, but we had begun at the place where de Chabannes had found the Punic tombs. It looked as though the tombs did not continue further, but one morning, when Abbé Moulard and I were cataloguing certain items in the museum, our foreman, de la Rocca, ran in to say that a tomb had been located.

Cataloguing could wait on discovery, so we raced the foreman back to the spot, and were overjoyed to see the corner of a great sarcophagus appearing.

The soil is hard and deep, and it took considerable time to lift the lid. We were working, I remember, for four solid hours, loading the earth into mule-trucks, to be carried away over the rails to the dump, and everything had to be sifted carefully, lest we should miss some little thing indicative of greater discoveries. The tombs themselves are, on an average, four to five metres deep, and lie East to West. They are much more massive than the tombs found at Carthage, and are made of stone quarried at Cape Bon, a greyish-red sandstone.

I visited the source of this stone several years ago, to measure the quarries, for much of the stone in and around Carthage and Utica must have been worked there, and carried to the various cities.

The workings extend over thirteen kilometres, and the face of the stone shows that slabs of incredible size were cut and transported.

Cape Bon is the ancient Cape Hermes, and the quarry was known to be in operation as far back as the seventh century before Christ (See Gsell, Vol. II, p. 145) and the slabs were shipped on barges to Carthage and Utica (see also Diodorus, XX, 6, 3. Strabo, XVII, 3, 16).

It is almost a labour of Hercules to move some of the sarcophagi to-day, and often it took eight of our men to raise even the lids, and then we had the assistance of modern jacks and winches. The rich Uticans, however, had labour as cheap as the Pharaohs in Egypt, and these tombs are witnesses of their pride.

The publication of Père Delattre (*Contes rendu. Acad. Inset.*, 1906, pp. 60, 62) places these tombs at the fifth century B.C. but M. Merlin is inclined to believe them to be earlier, due to the discovery of a little Bucchero Nero cup, which dates from the sixth or seventh century B.C.

The tombs already mentioned were the only Punic discoveries made up to the 1925 campaign (see Gsell, Vol. II, 145) and the first tomb found this year contained only traces of a skeleton, and a bronze razor.

I remember how amused the people were, who watched the opening of the tomb, when I held up the razor.

Standing around were the Countess de Prorok, Mrs. Stoever, the Abbé Chabot, Count Jean de Chabannes, and many others who, though they could not get their hands to the picks and shovels for want of space wherein to work, were urging us to redoubled efforts. Our New York *Times* correspondent mentioned that surely it must be a barber's tomb, and I explained that his guess was not improbable, for in ancient Carthage they had *sacred* barbers.

The razors were hatchet shaped, and shaving must have been rough, and many an old Phoenician must have had his skin thoroughly well scraped. Similar razors have been found at Carthage, and date from the sixth century B.C. Gsell thinks that these hatchets are symbolic talismans not rare in antiquity. The negroes of Tanganyika, near the equator, use similar razors today, and the ancient Egyptians made their instruments in the same shape. (Gsell, Vol. IV, p. 77).

The second tomb, discovered a few days later, deep in the clay, held a skeleton in a better state of preservation, and two little perfume bottles, two objects that looked like little bronze bells, and traces of rouge. The bottles were said to have come from Egypt, for the most part, but these at Utica showed unmistakably Greek influence in many of the designs. The bells were sacred emblems, and are supposed to have been used for the purpose of frightening away evil spirits.

The third tomb was discovered below a Roman cistern, and had suffered in consequence. The contents were practically rotted away. Steady infiltration had permeated the lid, and the sarcophagus was nearly full of earth and rain water. The foreman gently removed the earth, which was sifted, but we found only a few beads and traces of bones.

The fourth tomb contained several beautiful and important pieces of early Phoenician jewelry. When the heavy lid was at last thrown back and wedged into position, we saw the skeleton well outlined, and by the right hand a glitter of gold indicated that we had discovered an important tomb. Lying among the ribs we could distinguish another significant object, and there were two gold discs on either side of the skull. The position of the objects was carefully noted, and a drawing made by Mr. George Scott, of Cornell University, one of my assistants.

The preliminary sketch of the ensemble is an important detail, never now omitted.

Jewelry was worn profusely by the ancient Phoenicians. Both men and women alike adorned themselves to such an extent that their showiness became a byword among the nations.

The fifth and sixth centuries B.C. must have been great days in the history of Utica, for wonderful jewelry was found by us in nearly all these tombs. The ring found in this particular tomb was of pure gold, and covered with Egyptian hieroglyphics that the Abbé Moulard believed corresponded with the reign of Thothmes III. The ring was oval in shape, flattened on one side, and fitted easily on my fourth finger. The other object was a cornelian scarab, with a clear cut figure of a man on it, perhaps a portrait of the dead man himself. At Carthage, Père Delattre found several rings on skeleton fingers, the engraved faces corresponding exactly with the heads sculptured on the lid of the coffin.

Earrings were common to both sexes of the Phoenicians, though sometimes only one ring was worn. The earrings in this tomb were of gold, gold that had been brought from Central Africa and across the Sahara, perhaps to Gigthis and thence shipped to Utica.

It was distressing, but essential, that, during the time of excavation at Utica I was compelled to rush backwards and forwards between the work there and the work at Carthage nearly every day. The Abbé Moulard was left to supervise the work in my absence, with the successive assistance of Paul Groseille, Horton O'Neill, C. C. Wells, George Scott, William Morris and Rey de Vilette, who took turns during the three months' excavation.

Maurice Kellerman, of the "Pathe News" made a detailed film of all the excavations and the opening of the tombs. He, too, was kept racing between Carthage and Utica, to be on hand at every new discovery. The documentation of finds on an excavating expedition is a much greater task than is generally appreciated. Literally hundreds of photographs were taken by a battery of photographers at each of the sites.

Punic tombs and sanctuaries, Ceramic specimens, Roman cisterns and villas, Christian chapels and a quarry or two were being excavated at the same time, and I had only one body, to be in many places at once.

The sixth and eighth tombs at Utica were empty of everything except the skeletons. One wondered if they were patriotic citizens who had given up their gold in some national crisis. It was common in those days for the people to surrender their jewels in the time of strife and need. At Carthage the women even gave their hair to make bowstrings, which may, or may not, have been the origin of the first bobbed-hair craze.

The ninth tomb was that of the dancing girl.

The charm of archaeology palls a little, if one does the actual pick-axing and shoveling himself, but it is my firm belief that the seeker should put his hand to the manual labour from time to time, and enjoy his own actual discoveries. Probably most people think that the excavation of lost cities is done by Arabs in picturesque costumes, while the organisers sit by and look on, waiting for the great finds. At Utica and Carthage, however, it was often preferable to do the delicate work personally, and many an hour I spent in the blazing heat, digging at the tombs.

In the case of this tomb, labour brought its own reward, for it was my pick that found, at Utica, the wonderful sarcophagus. There was no special reason why I should have relieved that particular workman of his tools, I suppose he was nearest, or the least energetic at that moment, but I swung away for an hour, and then hit something – a crack, and knew it was stone. Then I carefully enlarged the hole, and gave a positive whoop as I found that I was uncovering a tomb. I had discovered a treasure house of the dead.

My own unaided progress was too slow for me, so I called in my companions, and we worked for hours shoveling away the earth. By sunset the lid was free, and the jacks and winches were brought into play.

The same impatience takes us every time. We are never educated in self-restraint, but crowd in and try to catch a glimpse of the contents of each discovery through the opening as the jacks begin to take hold. Our Arabs are the same. Before it was possible to see into the tomb, we were all lying flush with the lid, ignoring the dirt, almost flat on our faces, with the Arabs crowding behind us. Just as one of the men operating the jacks said "It is full of gold," one jack slipped, and it looked as though the lid would fall back into place, possibly taking somebody's hand or arm with it, but fortunately the second jack held, and we were all saved either injury or disappointment. The lid was slipped back and wedged with stones, and we scrambled to our feet to see if the Arab had exaggerated. It did look as though the tomb was full of gold! A thin film of dust lay over the contents, but we saw a magnificent necklace shining through the veil.

Then we had to wait again, for Mr. Kellerman to get his apparatus in position, and for other people to focus their cameras. The skeleton was quite distinct in outline, and very carefully we began to take out the earth, removing the jewelry after its position had been carefully marked. First there came a fine cameo, set in a solid gold ring. It was made for a very small finger, and we thought that we had disturbed the last resting place of a lady of quality among the ancient Phoenicians of Utica. The next article found near the fingers was a finely cut scarab, and then we removed the sand that had collected round the head.

Treasures were uncovered more rapidly. Beautiful earrings of delicately worked gold, a chain of golden stars and gold drops. There were a hundred and fifty stars around the little girl's neck.

Our specialists had read the message of the skeleton while we were gently removing the objects. All that remained of the young woman were the ornaments that had adorned her, and the bones that said she was five feet tall and yet in her teens.

Beside her were tear and perfume bottles and, finally, other things that told us more about her, the bronze cymbals which indicated a dancing girl. Her audiences must have made her a favourite, and in her last farewell covered her with jewels, to make her tomb the richest found in Africa, with the exception of the Egyptian potentates.

There is no doubt that a touch of sadness clouded our faces as the gay little dancer took her final curtain. At least she had a distinguished audience, and though her twinkling feet had long ceased to tread the mystic rhythm, surely never audience was so moved or so sympathetic.

The amphitheatres may have held senators and aristocrats, and the galleries have been crowded with the commoners of her day, but, when the cymbals were again brought to light it was in the presence of people who looked back across the centuries and sent her kindly thoughts. For the last call, her audience included the Grand Duchess Marie Pavlovna of Russia, the Duc de Clermont Tonnere, Marquis de Guise, Prince and Princess Jean de Faucigny, Baron and Baroness Rodolphe d'Erlanger, and Count Phillipe d'Estailleur.

Gently, the world who had never seen the idol of Utica clothed the bones with personality, and as gently laid her to rest again as the setting sun in a parting salute flooded her tomb with light, and we hoped for forgiveness from the merry little soul of the dancer of Utica. We had disturbed her centuries of sleep, and sighed a last tribute to the beauty that must have been.

Tomb number ten was opened in my absence, and among the bones was a bronze fish-hook. One wonders if this was a patient fisherman who, centuries ago, in view of crossing the Styx hoped to try his luck just once more. Similar objects have been found at Carthage (Gsell, Vol. IV, p. 75).

The eleventh tomb had traces of a white veil around the head, the only shreds of cloth we had seen in any of the tombs up to that moment. The dampness of the Utican marshes destroys all the materials that have been put into the tombs. Even this powdery shroud disappeared in a few moments. It had covered the head for twenty-five centuries, to vanish the moment we raised the lid of the tomb.

In one of the tombs, we discovered strange little objects, hollow, and shaped like animals, which must have been toys. Another had a string of beads, corresponding to artificial jewelry. They were made of some sort of composition, identical with those we have found in the tombs at the Sanctuary of Tanit, at Carthage. Made of paste or cement, they were glazed or varnished to give the appearance of precious stones. The beads are in the images of the gods, and bear the signs of Tanit, Isis, Osiris, Horus, Anubis and Bes, charms supposed to have prophylactic value, as well as to afford protection against disaster and the evil eye.

Here were the "sacred eye", the open hand, and a veritable menagerie of crocodiles, cats, jackals, etc. In Sardinia, as well as on the northern part of the continent of Africa, these varnished jewels are found in the oldest tombs. We have discovered hundreds of similar objects, whose composition varies from cement to alabaster and semi-precious stones. The necklaces were usually composed of amulets and jewels, and I have collected several dead pearls.

In another tomb we found a corroded metal object nearly worn away by the action of the water, which looked like a pair of scissors. Near it were some rusted pins (fibulae). Probably we were in the presence of some dead seamstress or tailor. The once busy hands were distinct, though nearly dust, and the fingers were long, as though they must have been nimble and dexterous.

The twelfth tomb was not rich, but it contained a surprise. The objects were near the motionless hands, telling their tale as plainly as though men from the past had been standing by interpreting for us. The little cubes within reach of the dead man's fingers were a pair of dice! They were made of bone, and identical in shape, size, and numbering, with those used to-day. Possibly this gentleman had lived by a combination of "come seven come 'leben" popular in Utica in his day. Certain it is that the presence of these dice made a colourful human touch, more than the age, dimensions and quality of the tomb could ever do.

As our work progressed, we penetrated into a site more fruitful than we hoped, at least in quantity. Four new tombs were discovered in one day. The first contained a gold signet ring, the stone being a cornelian beautifully engraved. It revolved in a socket, and the mechanism was as smooth when we tried it as it could have been the day it was made. The flat, inscribed portion of the jewel was next to the finger, and the rounded sculpture faced outwards. In this tomb, also, we found the "Nezems" or nose rings, reminiscent of an old habit of the Canaanites (Genesis, XXIV, 47).

One can hardly imagine anything less graceful than a ring through the nose, and yet this habit persisted for a long time in Carthage, though the Carthaginians were only led by the nose after the Roman conquest of 146 B.C. Plautus in his famous comedy dating from 190 B.C. makes a facetious character remark that the slaves of Hanno surely had no fingers, since they wore rings through their noses.

The last tomb contained two perfume bottles, six inches high. The perfume was gone, but the significance remained. It recalled the lavish use of perfume by the Carthaginians. This tomb also contained a little lead box, somewhat resembling one I had seen in the Bardo museum. It was divided into two compartments, and was certainly designed for cosmetics (cf. Delattre, and Gsell, Vol. IV, p. 81).

So were the habits and customs of the people of the past revealed by our excavation of the tombs of the dead. It is very probable that the tombs of Utica will teach us more concerning the history and manners of the city than anything else we can discover. Little by little, and year by year, we can delve into the mystery surrounding the lives of this once great people, and make the dead speak.

Here lies the true romance of archaeology. It is now only the years that separate us from the lives of the little dancing girl, the gambler, the fisherman, the seamstress, the soldiers and wealthy citizens. Even the years are bridged as they talk of the days gone by.

A few points of interest in connection with the whole question of Punic tombs may well be incorporated here. They help us to reach conclusions and may serve as a guide to those who wish, for one purpose or another, to arrive at a viewpoint in respect to this era.

Often, our indications of tombs come from a row of beautiful amphores standing above the tomb, and once we found six such vases, five feet high, all in a row. Professor Washington of the Carnegie Foundation, took specimens of the contents. It is thought that they once contained food for the journey to the next world, a custom common among the ancients.

The bodies must have been wrapped in shrouds, for we have frequently found bronze pins, which were used to hold the coverings in place. The pins are usually found near the right shoulder (see Delattre). The only time we have found actual traces of the shroud itself is recorded earlier in this chapter.

Many of the tombs, too, contained sulphur and bitumen, probably placed there for sanitary and prophylactic reasons.

Occasionally, also, we found traces of wood, which showed that a wooden coffin was placed in the stone sarcophagus. Identical evidences were found by Père Delattre, at Carthage.

The Phoenician name for the grave was "the eternal abode." It is said that the tombs were sunk so deep (sometimes nearly thirty metres at Carthage) that the spirit could not return, but it is much more probable that they were placed deep for safety's sake, and as a protection against thieves, for the tombs contained gold and ivory from the Sahara, amber and coral from distant seas, the emeralds of the Garamantes, and garnets, carbuncles and escarbouches of the Nasamons and Masoesyles. (Strabo, XVII, 3, 11: Pliny, XXXVII, 104.)

Chapter 17

THE KILNS OF UTICA AND ROMAN VILLAS

Count Jean de Chabannes put at our disposal this year a little house large enough to accommodate the members of our Utica staff. It lies near the homes of the farm workers, and it was while taking a meal with the men that I met the officers of Wrangel's "White army" who were stranded in Tunisia several years ago. Count de Chabannes employs ex-noblemen, admirals, captains and nearly all other ranks on his great estate. Many of the victims of the revolution are highly educated, university men, who take a great interest in the excavations when off duty.

It was a great day when the Grand Duchess Marie of Russia came over as the guest of Baron d'Erlanger to see the opening of the Punic tombs. The old uniforms were taken out again and refurbished, and the men lined up and saluted the car as it came into the gardens of the chateau. It was a scene whose emotion can be imagined when the exiles were presented to the Grand Duchess, and kissed her hand, while tears streamed down their faces, and hers; the reunion of people loyal to the country that is no longer theirs, and suffering in spirit and estate.

Utica had already seen the exiled Marius, but it was tragic to see the meeting of refugees from the late cataclysm, with the Punic tombs for background.

We had much of interest to show our visitors, for the first pottery kiln had been discovered a few days after our arrival, while we searched for something else. We had actually been trying to locate the old Punic fortification when we came across the

circular walls of a kiln. Our great question was whether it was a
Roman or Punic ruin we had come across, and it was with a feeling of sudden wealth that we watched our foreman unearth a
piece of pottery with an unmistakably Phoenician trade mark on
it.

The date of our discovery was March 4th, 1925. That is an
important date, since it meant that we had turned another page in
the history of Phoenician Africa. Thereafter, hardly a day went
by, but we found something useful and informative. The tombs
told us a great tale, peculiar to themselves, but the pottery told us
more.

Magnificent pottery has been found in the necropolis of
Carthage, and in Malta and Sardinia, but it fell to our lot to discover a whole quarter of Utica, where the pottery of the early
Phoenicians was made. The kilns discovered are five in number,
and we have been able to preserve them intact as they were
found, with the pottery, ashes and fuel in place.

The kilns are built of rough red bricks, the furnace being
elliptical in shape and deep in the earth, covered by a light roof,
with sustaining pillars in the centre. The entrances are narrow,
and lead into the circle where the pottery was fired.

Above there is the cylindrical funnel, which communicated
by pipes to the hearth. This is covered by a cupola. The air holes
are still undamaged, as well as the adjoining laboratory, where
the pottery was classified and deposited.

My joy was very great when I was able to take the Franco-
American committee through the kilns, and it was not without
its humour to see the sedate savants crawling on hands and
knees, in single file, round the kiln, with one solitary candle for
illumination. The participants in that scene were Professor
Kelsey, Professor Washington, the Abbé Chabot, the Abbé
Moulard, Mr. Stoever, Mr. George Swain, Count de Chabannes,
and half a dozen students trailed behind. But we have done more
uncomfortable things for the pure delight of academic satisfaction.

The appearance of the party as it came out again through the manhole was disastrous. Fragments of Punic pottery, dust, and ashes, were extracted from white beards on the journey back to Tunis.

Maurice Kellerman, indefatigable as ever, made a detailed film of the kilns, and of how they were used twenty-five centuries ago, as well as photographing the excavation in full swing, with the trucks, mules, Arabs, and scientists working *at a great pace* to bring up dozens of objects in five minutes. I sincerely hope that the people who see the films do not really imagine that specimens are recovered in so few seconds, or vainly imagine that our Arabs are so speedy. Simply the physical limitations of a certain number of feet of film, and the patience of spectators in far off countries determined the "reconstruction" of many scenes, that they might be true to the spirit, and not monotonous, as I fear actual excavation frequently can be.

Mr. Kellerman is something of a genius in his use of material (and personnel). When the light was bad in interiors, he contrived huge reflectors, which every available member held, to turn the sunlight on to the object being photographed. He even used the lids of biscuit tins. Other people profited by his ingenuity, and there were often wonderful opportunities at Utica. The "still" photographers would line up, and their cameras click in succession, like a machine gun firing a clip. I have heard ten click, rapid fire, many a time. Vilette, Swain, Streit, Kellerman, Stoever, Abbé Moulard, Morris, O'Neill, d'Estailleur and Scott, would "shoot" like a platoon at drill. It was amusing, but good for documentation.

Near the kilns we found thousands of broken pieces of Punic pottery, pottery that had "missed" and was thrown aside. There were also many fine specimens absolutely without blemish.

Close to one of these heaps we found the little savings bank, with the coins still inside. Its young owner had gone. Where, no one knows. He may have followed the long procession to the fires of Moloch, or he may have profited by his lesson in thrift.

Here, however, was his bank, made of pottery, with a slit in the side for coins, and when we shook the box the coins still jingled.

The Phoenicians made their money-boxes with a view to the difficulty of extracting savings, for it took us a long time to bring out the treasure. In the days when "poor Richard" amassed his childish hoard the coins would have counted for little, but they gave us a strangely pathetic light on the past.

The bank now lies in America, telling its story to modern boys. It also tells a little of the great financial genius of the Phoenicians, who are supposed to have been the original bankers. We are used to the various instruments of commerce, but it is worth while giving a thought, once in a while, to the ingenuity of the brains that conceived them. It is attributed to the Phoenicians that they first used paper, or leather, cheques and bills of exchange (Aristotle, *Politique*, V, 10.4). Certainly they were the greatest traders of antiquity, and their ships sailed over all the seas to enrich the two cities that once were the wonders of Africa, and now are plains and muddy marshes.

Utica was known by the ancient historians to have had ship-building companies (Gsell, Vol. IV, p. 110), and had a bitter rivalry with the shipbuilders of Carthage. The enterprises were financed by bankers who also lent money for far distant cruises, and doubtless exacted usury in consideration of their participation. Incidentally, it is known that contracts were made in duplicate.

The pottery money-box, six inches high, brought to mind the business activities of these trader-citizens more than any object I have found.

Not far from this site we found traces of what might well have been an arsenal, for we unearthed considerable quantities of sling-stones made of pottery. These sling-stones are of various sizes, mostly about an inch in diameter, and are of different shapes, oval and round, and made of *"terra cotta."* At Carthage we found sling-stones, but they came from a different munition factory, being made of lead, and most of them bore the sign of Tanit. Occasionally, too, as I have said, they are engraved with maledictions and imprecations. We compared these small-arms of the past with the Mills bombs of the present day. One modern shell would have razed a considerable section of old Utica.

Other discoveries near the kilns included a series of grotesques, which must have been children's toys. There were conventionalised figures of horses and goats, sheep, cocks, and most of the domestic animals with which we ourselves are familiar.

The most human of all objects, however, of which we discovered many examples, were babies' milk bottles. They are small jugs about six inches high, with the top covered over, and a tiny little hole, through which the jug is filled. The nipple was part of the jug, shaped to roughly represent a diminutive breast. Sometimes eyes, and a laughing mouth are painted on these pathetic relics.

Excavation has its sad side, even though history may value the additional verification of certain theories. I have discovered similar milk bottles among the sacrificial urns at the Temple of Tanit, in Carthage, and Père Delattre has found them in the tombs of little children in his own excavations there. They date from about the fifth century B.C. (Gsell).

It is long since those children were carried through the streets of the city to the beaches at Utica, but one imagines that they were little different from children in our own homes.

During all the excavations of the kilns, pottery was being classified, actually in hundreds of examples, so that we might recognise the Phoenician "trade marks" on the handles. Some of the seals were as clear as though they had been done yesterday, and were of real artistic value. Most beautiful of all was the mark of the factory that used the dolphin sign, of whose product we found at least twenty magnificent vases.

Some stamps bore only one or two punic characters, rarely more, and a few were marked in Greek. Perhaps the olive oil and wine merchants ordered them, with their own house signs sealed into the vases before they were sent to distant lands.

Abbé Chabot made a detailed study of eighty different "trade marks" found at Utica. Many are contributions to the Phoenician nomenclature and script.

A Punic lamp was found near one of the kilns, dating from the very foundation of Carthage, 800 B.C.

In one of the kilns we found a skeleton. It might well have been that of the potter. The crumbling bones lay among the débris of the amphores, pots, plates, Punic and "Corinthian" lamps, vases, perfume burners, and little molds for making cakes. It looked as though there had been many a bull in the china shop, in light of the hills of broken pieces we dug out.

But the pieces tell a tale. The long still hands that made the pots speak through their art of how they lived in those days, and one sherd of pottery may link up civilisations thousands of miles apart, or place the date of a city.

The excavation of the kilns, and indeed of the whole quarter, is unfinished. There are more kilns, and more pottery, to be dug out. In one spot we were bringing to light a whole series of partly destroyed statuettes when reluctantly we had to close down excavation for the season.

The third major excavation of Utica was the section between the Isle of the Temple of Apollo and the Punic necropolis. We had a light railway for our trucks, leading to the marshes west of the dead city.

Our first discovery in this vicinity was the "bone and ivory" factory, one of the most amusing and unusual discoveries yet recorded in the history of excavation. From the number of hair-pins recovered in the first two days, the site was soon nicknamed the "hairpin factory." That this ruin was such a workshop, I have no doubt whatever, for not only did we find several hundred hairpins and bone needles, but found also the raw material from which they had been modelled.

Here were spoons, pins, combs, needles, musical instru-ments, buttons, a clasp, pens, rings, and various other objects hard to classify, all of which we recovered in ten days. Our haul was quite enough to start a museum. The objects were lying jumbled up in the earth mixed with the débris of mosaics, pottery, stone, glass, etc. It is a little difficult to determine the period, as the earth had been disturbed, and we were not quite sure of our strata. The close proximity of the Phoenician business quarter, and the similarity of the objects found to those discovered by Père Delattre at Carthage seem to indicate the probable Punic origin of these bone and ivory specimens.

The hairpins were of great interest to the visitors, who came over daily from Tunis to see such a humorous discovery. From the purely artistic point of view many of the pins were worth examination. They were beautifully carved and of varying lengths, from three to six inches. Most of the pins have a round button at one end, though many are adorned by carvings of female heads, and some, now in the Lavigerie museum, have women's names inscribed on them. Some of the pins were in ivory, as were two little boxes we found close to the pins, and which undoubtedly were designed for my lady's cosmetics.

The ivory came from the elephants of North Africa and the Sahara, and the excavations of Carthage and Utica have revealed many things of great artistic value, especially a beautiful ivory fan and comb, carved with Phoenician and Egyptian symbols. These are in the Lavigerie museum, for the enjoyment of the public.

A spoon, found at Utica, is well worked, and Père Delattre believes it to have been used for incense. Two other carved pieces this savant identified as handles for mirrors or knives. They were five inches in length and an inch across, engraved with parallel lines.

The buttons and pens were added to the Lavigerie museum, also.

A word of description of the pens may be worth while. They are long, slender shafts, flattened at one end and pointed at the other. The pointed end is slit, and pared down in a fashion not dissimilar from the quill to which we are accustomed, while the flattened end looks as though it might have been used as a desk knife or for erasures.

The objects which we suppose are musical instruments we have sent to Baron d'Erlanger for study. He has made an exhaustive study of ancient instruments and music, and is at the same time an ardent archaeologist. Several Punic tombs at Carthage were excavated by him in 1894.

Shortly we hope to complete this curious excavation. It proves, more than ever, that our novelties are quite ancient, that there is "nothing new under the sun."

From the hairpin factory, our work extended to the exploration of three Roman villas. The largest of these which has three floors still remaining to be examined, has been called "Cato's Villa" for many generations. There is no historic reason we can discover to identify this ruin with the villa where the great republican patriot prepared himself for suicide by reading philosophy. Tradition alone has located the site, and identified the villa with Cato. It is a habit of the country, I suppose. At Carthage "the baths of Dido" and the "house of Hannibal" are indicated in the same manner, but it seems to us that the association is unsupported, and purely conjectural.

One fact is certain regarding "Cato's Villa." It is among the richest so far discovered in Africa, for the glorious mosaic floors taken up by Count de Chabannes and housed in a special pavilion attest its magnificence. A singular item about the villa is that the mosaic floors were made in successive layers. There are actually six mosaics, one on top of the other. It seems as though the rich old Uticans changed their floors as we change the pictures on our walls.

It is the same with frescoes. Here again we could see different layers and designs. One can imagine a lady of Utica saying to her husband at spring-cleaning time, "let's have the walls done in a blue colour scheme, and put a fishing scene on the floor, in place of the old Bacchus design!"

The frescoes uncovered by us at Utica this year were very rare (see Audollent, pp. 638-40), so rare indeed that the "Services des Antiquités" had them removed to the National Museum two days after we had uncovered them. They were found in a series of rooms in a second villa, near to "Cato's." They depicted graceful Cupids, in different colours and postures, and were framed in vivid borders of mural painting imitating marble.

The general effect of these villas is very Pompeiian, and in due time we shall have a typical Roman section in this part of Utica, with mosaic floors, frescoes, statues, bronzes and other objects identical with those of the great city in the shadow of Vesuvius.

The "household" specimens recovered from these villas include many beautiful lamps of the first period, pieces of many kinds of pottery, a bronze lamp and pedestal, several terra cotta statuettes, and several hundred Roman coins.

Most interest, however, lies so far in the mosaic floors. Those we have uncovered in the villas are all perfect in preservation and design. With the exception of one or two, they are all geometrical, with prophylactic symbols (see Audollent, *Carthage Romaine,* p. 660) and date from the first years of the Roman occupation of Africa.

Below the third villa, nearest the Punic necropolis, we discovered several small terra cotta pipes, precisely similar to those found by Dr. Carton at Sousse (Hadrumet) in Roman tombs of the first century A.D. They bring up the picture of some old captain of industry sitting at his desk, transacting his business, with one of these pipes in his mouth and one of the bone pens in his hand.

So it runs. Tombs, kilns, buildings and objects from the daily life of Utica, and a thrill every day. It is hard to imagine a richer site in all the field of archaeological research. Certainly the result of our excavation cannot be equaled for human interest.

Chapter 18

THE CIVILISATIONS OF THE SAHARA

Excavation and exploration in North Africa seemed to demand a completion by reference to the great hinterland of the desert. Many signs, which have already been recorded, led us to believe that there was something to be discovered in the Sahara which would throw a useful light not only upon the commerce of the ancient cities of the coast but also, perhaps, upon the very origin of man and the beginnings of Libyo-Phoenician civilisation.

Certain members of the Franco-American committee decided that it would be advisable to undertake the journey to the Hoggar mountains, and an expedition was therefore organised. It is easily said "an expedition was organised." The countless details however took many months, and the last few weeks before we started were particularly harassing.

Long in advance of the expedition, camel caravans had to be dispatched along our route, to lay down supplies of oil, gasoline, water, and food, and full allowance had to be made for the inevitable loss by evaporation and damage en route. We counted on a thirty percent loss, but that was found to be entirely inadequate. The stores must have received a greater amount of damage than usual, for there were times when we found our entire reserve vanished.

Though explorers may travel now by motor, across the desert, they yet rely on the earlier method of camel caravan for supplies. The cars themselves have improved considerably since the first traverse was made, and the Franco-American expedition was equipped with three powerful Renault cars, twin six-wheelers, which have been tested and thoroughly proven. They sometimes made extraordinary speed across the sand, though, as would be expected, there were times when considerable ingenuity had to be exercised in the negotiation of the most difficult sections of the route.

To ride in them, across the dunes that rise many feet high and then suddenly drop (on the lee side) in precipices that are almost sheer, was to experience both the reliability of the transport and the strange nausea that cannot always be avoided.

After the usual delays, half-expected or totally unforeseen, our fleet was drawn up in Paris, and Madame Rouvier, wife of the late Premier of France, poured a libation over them that they might be well and truly started on their journey. Our cars had names, appropriate to the desert: "Sandy," "Hot Dog," and "Lucky Strike." For our own purposes we called them the "Renaultosauri."

To break them in, the three cars, with the chauffeurs who drove them throughout the trip, were sent over the road to Marseilles and thence shipped to Africa.

Immediately our troubles began. Transport to Africa was difficult, and we are indebted to the French government for the use of the space allotted to Government stores on the transports, the only means of getting them across.

The members of the expedition not already in Africa followed after by train to Marseilles and then to Djemila, for the great fête in the ancient theatre there, where the company of the Comedie Francaise gave a performance of *Polyphemus* on the reconstructed stage. We were entertained by Governor Violette of Algeria, who gracefully complimented the Franco-American committee on the work that had already been accomplished under its direction, at Carthage and Utica, and wished us the best of good luck on our impending journey.

The Comedie Francaise surely had never played to a more picturesque audience, or under such impressive circumstances. For the first time for many centuries the grey walls of the old

Roman theatre echoed the voices of performers, while from the banks of seats on the hillside a crowd of spectators applauded both drama and occasion.

On the hills overlooking the theatre, white robed figures added a touch of the grotesque. The Arab population of the neighbourhood was en fête, and when the blare of trumpets announced the end of the play, these spectators gave their own idea of applause.

As we left, a score of Arab sheiks, with their gorgeous ceremonial saddles polished up for the occasion, rode round us at full gallop, their brilliant robes flying in the wind, a medley of gold and purple and scarlet. And, since they take every opportunity for making a gladsome noise, they fired a continuous salute in our honour.

Then, we were on our way, fully conscious that exploration is vastly different under modern conditions from what it was for Barth, Rohlfs and Duveyrier, those men who blazed trails with great labour and whose equipment was incredibly inadequate. The French Government had given us the protection of their desert forces, and it was unlikely that we should be faced by those contingencies that have proved insurmountable to so many previous expeditions. The Tuaregs are for the most part peaceful, now, and not antagonistic to the French administration, though they have in the past put a sudden stop to exploration, and compelled the abandonment of commercial enterprise through their territory.

For our individual protection against raiding Arabs, we were equipped with small arms and rifles, and the leading car was fitted with a machine gun.

However, we hoped to overcome most, if not all, of the difficulties, and to make a reasonably close survey of the area through which we passed.

The expedition was representative of many sides of life, and we were in a position to document any finds made, so that our discoveries may be followed up by other explorers, and the amount of verified knowledge of the Sahara extended.

Our party was composed of M. Maurice Reygasse, Captain Chapuis, Alonzo Pond, of the Logan Museum, Beloit, W. Bradley Tyrrell, big game hunter, of Chicago, and a friend of the Franco-American Committee, Mr. Denny of the New York *Times,* our special correspondent, Mr. Barth, our motion picture operator – a great name in exploration, by the way, which augured well for us – Caid Belaid, our interpreter, two native guides and a native chef, and our mechanics. In all, we were seventeen strong, a respectable company in case of emergency, with varied interests and personalities sufficient to overcome the possible ennui of long stretches of uninteresting country, a cheery crowd around the fires at night. Some members of the original expedition were unfortunately unable to join us, and we missed Baron D'Erlanger, who had to abandon his intention of journeying through the desert with recording instruments to preserve the native music. Ill health robbed us of his presence.

Other members who had made all plans for the journey had to withdraw at the last moment, and it was Mr. W. F. Kenny of New York who saved us from a threatened abandonment of the whole expedition.

Thanks to him no abandonment was permitted, and we were able to go forward with our project. Our purpose was many-sided. In the first place we hoped to learn much more about the ancient trade routes, which were the sources of Carthaginian produce, and also we expected with the assistance of M. Reygasse to examine the traces of prehistoric man in the desert. This particular study is of considerable importance, as traces of early man may have some bearing on the great subject of the desiccation of the Sahara. Incidentally, there were rumours and legends to be sifted, especially in the Hoggar region, where we were told, on authority that is not so assured as it perhaps might be, that there are buried cities and strange races. It is a land of myth and mystery.

The preliminary stage of our journey ended on the sixteenth of October, when we reached Touggourt. We were a little behind schedule time, due to the unexpected happenings of the road. We had been two days in the desert and probably had crossed as difficult places as were likely to confront us before we reached the Hoggar.

Personally, I was glad to renew my acquaintance with the road south, for the whole area is full of archaeological enticement, as well as of unexpected beauty and charm. To the traveller and the merchant it offers barriers and difficulties, to the explorer it presents a field for work. There are ruins to be uncovered, quaint civilisations to be catalogued, and customs to be traced to their roots. It is enough for one man's lifetime to classify all the lore, enough for an army to attack the research.

We entered the desert over the old Roman Bridge at El Kantara, which is the pass through the Atlas range, so cleanly cut that the Greeks deemed it worthy of a myth. Here they located a feat of Hercules, who is reputed to have ground the pass clear with his heel. On either side the mountains rise in majestic splendour, and the road, now well paved, runs through scenery that is very reminiscent of the Rockies.

But, as we passed over the bridge we left behind the orange groves and continuous vegetation. From now on we only hoped for occasional green spots, with here and there a small settlement and a friendly greeting, or unfriendly.

The oases we passed lured us a little, and timidly tempted us. My mind went back to a piece of work I should like to do, sometime; to go slowly through this region, where the Libyan gods had Greek names and often Egyptian characteristics. But we might, en route, have learned a little of the infiltration of other civilisations into Libyo-Phoenicia.

Our minor adventures began before we reached Biskra. My own began at Tunis, where the unusually heavy rains had washed away the dyke, and we were confronted by a raging torrent, which stalled our motors, and we found ourselves aswim. It looked rather like a bad omen for the moment, but, like most things, it was no worse than it seemed, and we came through.

Travelling down to Touggourt from Biskra, we were checked by the consequences of the same torrential downpour. Rivers that ought to be little else than dry beds had become raging streams, careering along unchecked, and carrying away the native huts with them. Instead of sand, we had to deal with mud; and not only ourselves but the motor that makes communication between the two centres found the going hard. In fact, we came across the "stage" well wedged and stalled, unable to move one way or the other, and it became evident that we had done wisely in fitting one of the cars with a windlass. That windlass was put to the test at once, and there was a certain satisfaction in seeing the appliance do its work, for the coach was hauled to a level keel and set free to travel again.

Then we were mired. It was plain mud for us, and not a case for the windlass. We had to get down and use shovels, so that we might move at all. We had camped under the stars, and it looked fairly safe for a comfortable night, and we were all in excellent spirits, but the rain came, and simply washed us deep into the desert. Even that did not end the trials of the Renaultosauri. They were called upon to make a risky fording of swollen rivers, and came through famously.

Our stay at Biskra was timed to coincide with the celebration of Cardinal Lavigerie's centenary. The members of the expedition laid a wreath on the great monument, so exquisitely modelled and interpretative of the man. We owe much to Cardinal Lavigerie, in Africa, and from time to time on our journey we saw the mystic print of the order he established, the White Fathers, whose members go throughout the desert places on their Christian duty. As they walk they leave the sign of the Cross, a welcome thing in the lonely places, a sign which tells the traveller that there is a companionable soul not so very far away.

Robert Hichens met us at Biskra, considerably interested in our mission. Biskra is, of course, very grateful to Hichens for having written the famous novel that has made the town a popular winter resort. He is held in reverence, if not in awe, and the reverence closely approaches religion. When he dies, which I hope will not be for long long years yet, the Arabs will surely make a marabout of him, and Biskra will be his shrine. At least, it would if I had my way.

Louis Chapuis, browsing about the outskirts of the town, found prehistoric traces, and that of course delighted M. Reygasse, Africa's greatest authority on prehistoric man.

We were all elated that such a discovery had been made, and argued over the flints as though they were the emeralds of the Garamantes. Reygasse has led me on several expeditions to the haunts of prehistoric man, which sometime will be recounted in full, and he was the chief of the scientific side of the expedition.

From Biskra our route took us through the Chotts, where most things, save the ingenuity of man, give way to the dry hunger of the sand. Imported religions, successive emperors and empires, all have gone. The sand remains. The sand and man's determination; what the desert gains on one front the French administration is gaining on another, by sinking deep wells and creating new oases.

Touggourt gave us a royal welcome, and we enjoyed for the last time for two months the hospitality of real beds and modern comforts. While we halted, our mechanics overhauled our cars, and filled them to the last ounce with gasoline, oil and water. They carried enough for five hundred miles.

From here we began the long plunge of a thousand miles of desert to the Hoggar, in whose valleys are white people of magnificent physique and classic features, whose origin is a mystery, and on which they themselves have steadfastly refused to give any information.

In one sense the Hoggar is unknown. There had been expeditions before us, some of which had done remarkable work, particularly in the field of geology. There were other men who had done much in the Hoggar, living there long enough to know the people and their customs. Our own interpreter had lived in the Hoggar most of his life, and entertained us each evening by reciting the poems of the people and translating them for us into pleasant French. Just enough is known of the Hoggar to make its mystery more fascinating. Our particular advantage, in this expedition, over our forerunners, was that we had a modern caravan, economical of time, and we had with us experts in the special fields of archaeology, paleontology, and anthropology. We were as free as is humanly possible of the difficulties incidental to travel, and were able to concentrate on the main point of research.

Some little success has been mentioned in the discoveries by Louis Chapuis of flints at Biskra. These have been classified now, and belong to the Upper Mousterian and Lower Aurignacian periods, dating back roughly a hundred thousand years.

The Hoggar was our principal hope. Here in what is often described as a veritable Garden of Eden, are the mysterious people, tall, straight and slender, who regard themselves as the greatest of all races. Many writers have commented on their similarity to the Egyptians as represented on the ancient tombs of the Pharaohs. The men are veiled, considering it shameful for a woman to see their faces. The women however, are unveiled. Perhaps their domain has been too eloquently described. The traditional picture of the region is one of great loveliness, telling of valleys lying at the bottom of fantastic gorges, blooming with roses and mimosa and acacia, and dotted with lakes teeming with fish and harbouring venerable crocodiles.

The Tuaregs are a strange people. Their moral code is unorthodox, but strict. They are shepherds, poets and warriors, but the outside world regards them as marauders, and their impetuosity in attack has made them dreaded throughout the Sahara. For long years they have kept their sheep and tended their flocks, trading as far as Timbuctoo and reaping the harvest of honest toil. But their most profitable occupation has been raiding caravans. Apart from that, they are an honest people. A Tuareg despises petty theft, though he regards an armed raid as perfectly justifiable and a man's job.

There is every reason to believe, however, that the days of murder and pillage are over, for the French have put the whole region under military control, and banditry has been kept down.

It was not so for the expedition under Colonel Flatters who led an expedition of sixty French soldiers in 1881, and was permitted to penetrate far into the Tuareg region, without molestation, only to be presented with poisoned dates as a gift from the natives. The poison was one which causes insanity, and when Flatters' men became hysterical, and ran out into the desert in a mania of laughter, they were cut down by the waiting Tuaregs, who closed in with spears and knives, and made the massacre complete.

With all their hardihood, the Tuaregs have a unique culture of their own. Poetry is the national pastime, and they have their own version of the "salon." Their social assembly is usually held at the tent of a woman famous for her beauty and intelligence, and Tuareg braves have been known to travel a hundred miles to attend. Before the assembly the young men and maidens talk of love all in verse.

Naturally, the Tuaregs are rich in legend. In the centre of their country, the region of Kel-Ahaggar is a high mountain which men never climb. The Tuareg women say that the plateau at the summit is haunted by supernatural women, and tell how two young men once climbed up, far enough to encounter them. One was taken by the spirit women, they say, and was seen no more. The other escaped from the embrace of the goddess who had elected him to be her consort, and fled down the mountain to his own mortal beloved. Since then no man has attempted the ascent.

Without doubt, this is the legend which furnished Pierre Benoit with the central idea of his famous "Atlantide." Those who have read the novel will remember the supernatural beauty of Queen Antinea, descendant of Cleopatra and Marc Antony, who reigned in the palace of the Hoggar, and for amusement loved and killed explorers.

We hoped to climb the mountain, but were assured that there was neither goddesses nor Red Marble Hall, with its niches filled with the embalmed bodies of Queen Antinea's victims.

Forgetting romance, and romances, for the moment, there were many incitements to consider the legend of the lost continent of Atlantis. Plato told of a great continent, with a magnificent civilisation, ruled by kings descended from Poseidon. In a day it was engulfed by the sea, and other continents were raised from the floor of the ocean, making the world as we know it now. According to Plato, however, before the catastrophe, priests from Atlantis had gone to the Nile valley, and so, according to the story, the civilisations of the ancient world were the offspring of Atlantis.

Atlantis is located everywhere, and is a pleasant legend, but there is a theory held in many places that the Canary Islands, the Atlas mountains, and the Hoggar have remained as the high places of the lost Atlantis, and archaeological, geographical and biological evidence at least bears a considerable influence on their unity. We dismissed the legend, but, in the craters of the extinct volcanoes which we visited in the centre of Africa, there were old dolmens, tombs, and monuments of an unknown age, about which we cannot even guess. And, in the rocks of the Hoggar are carved inscriptions which the Tuaregs can read, but whose meaning they cannot decipher.

Without taking too great notice of legend, one of the things we hoped to do in the Hoggar was to investigate how there came to be this race at once so high and yet so primitive in the valleys of the district. If they did not originate in the desert, it must have been under terrific impulse that they crossed it to their present home. Père de Foucauld, the "Hermit of the Sahara" decided after long study of them that they were closely allied to the Egyptians and other very ancient peoples. Emile Gautier, one of the most notable explorers of the Hoggar, believes that they are the last survivors of the Libyans, and there is another theory which identifies them with the Berbers, a race with traces of distinguished lineage, who were driven from the Atlas Mountains into the desert by invading Arabs.

We reached Ouargla after a wonderful day's run of nearly two hundred kilometers. The morning was passed in a steady rain which chilled us through.

Something happened to the Saharan weather for we alternated between hot winds and chilling rains. Cold nights we expected, but cold days are unusual. We took to fur coats for the occasion.

When we left Touggourt, the whole population seemed to turn out to see us off, and two red robed Caids led the procession out of the city. Everyone wished us well, and as a parting gesture the authorities invested me with a decoration that is reserved for explorers of the desert, and then, to shouts of "Ar saret" (au revoir) and "In chalak" (God will it that we see each other again) we were gone into the dawn.

The last Koubbas were passed, and the wind whistled round our ears across the Sebkas, where the only signs of life were a few little Bedouin tents, from which the inmates gazed out in wonder, and crept back again. Probably they regarded us as the legendary djinns, going out to seek the occult in the heart of the sands.

The dunes proved difficult of negotiation in the rain, and one of the cars missed its hold, and was sandlocked, but the others hauled it free, with the entire personnel of the expedition lending a hand to the work.

Our arrival at Temassin was announced by a single horseman, a solitary Arab, who stood outlined for a moment against the rose-tinted sky, and then whisked his horse around and sped to the village, where we followed, to take coffee with the Caid, and talk politics.

Time pressed, however, and we pushed on very quickly, into the growing day. Temassin looked wonderfully prosperous when we left it; the palm trees silhouetted against the horizon like magic lacework. Even the drinn, that tufted coarse vegetation of the Sahara, seemed less useless.

Our immediate objective was Ouargla, where it was intended to make as close an examination as possible for signs of prehistoric man. We made a good run, keeping an average of nearly 35 kilometres an hour, and fortunately after five hours rain the sun shone, and the air was clear.

We were thoroughly caked in sand when we arrived, however, and the welcome was both magnificent and cordial. Descending from the cars, we were surrounded by the officers and Caids, and in the midst of a lot of filming and photography we told of the journey. The inhabitants were very interested in the names of the cars, which we found very hard to translate. Our mascots, especially "Bonzo" and the "Parrot" received nearly as much attention as we did, and how they brought back Paris! The machine gun was of less importance to them than our ice machine, which we had to demonstrate, but the ice was put to good use!

Nothing can express our gratitude to the Commander and officers for the way in which we were received, and Ouargla itself must stand as the monument to the French administration who are doing a work in the Sahara as stupendous as anything ever attempted by the Romans in Africa. The desert is steadily being conquered, and the frontiers of civilisation are constantly being pushed forward by the new company of Empire Builders.

The evening we spent at the Cercle Militaire, where we learned more of the desert in two hours than could be absorbed in a year's reading. We were lodged in the fortress, to which we went across a stretch of sand and palms, with the stars shining brilliantly above us, and an Arab flute playing plaintively in the oasis near by.

Such fertility as there is at Ouargla depends on the subterranean river Oued Mya. Artesian wells now provide water for innumerable date palms, and there is a population of nearly four thousand people within the fortified village and some three thousand others outside the walls.

Right of the Oued Mya, Colonel Flatters reported a find of neolithic implements, so we had some indication that investigations here would not be useless. To cover the ground quickly, we divided operations. Mr. Pond of the Logan Museum, Beloit College, and Captain Chapuis explored the flat summit of Gara Krima, a great rock that dominates literally hundreds of miles of desert. It is an old stronghold of the pirates of the Sahara, from whence they scanned the desert, sweeping down whenever a caravan was signaled, and raiding the country far and wide.

Here were found traces of prehistoric man, and an old well, over eighty metres deep, of pre-islamic origin. Early man had left his signs, in the form of a well hearth, and we also found some early Berber pottery, belonging to about the ninth and tenth centuries.

This old rock has been called "the Earth Sister of the Rainbow," a name not at all hard to accept, as one sees its many tones and colours, accentuated by every change in the light of the sky.

The remainder of the party followed the dried water-course, and was successful in making discoveries that may lead to an addition to the knowledge of prehistoric periods of the Sahara. A neolithic site was located, and Barth, our operator, after crossing six miles of sand dunes on foot, found a perfect stone axe of the acheulian period. In the course of the day a great prehistoric foyer was located, where successive fires had been burned for endless years on the same spot, making a field of ashes nearly two hundred yards by one hundred and fifty yards in width. We recovered nearly a hundred neolithic flints. In the river bed we found considerable quantities of snail and cockle shells, which tend to support the theory that the Sahara was once far less of a desert than it now is, if not, indeed, a veritable ocean at some remote period.

Our discoveries also strengthen the belief held by the scientific members of the expedition that Africa was the scene of human activities in prehistoric periods. The axe, which was identified by both M. Reygasse and Mr. Pond as belonging to the oldest but one of the stone ages, antedates by perhaps a hundred thousand years the work of the Cro-Magnons of Southern France.

When we had finished our explorations, dusk had fallen and night came rapidly, though we were miles away from the cars, so hidden in the monotonous dunes that we could not see our way out. Then I felt, for the first time, the horror of being lost in the desert. Hills and dales of sand, terribly uniform, surrounded us. I thought of the great Dr. Barth, dying of thirst, and biting through his own veins, to drink his blood. Lieut. Bruce, who accompanied us told us of a soldier who had died in these same dunes only a year ago, from thirst. We were only twelve miles from Ouargla, the same distance as the soldier, but he had lost his company, and died wandering about in the dunes. Modern equipment helped us. In the distance we saw a light revolving, and made for the bright spot, through the darkness. Our mechanicians had guessed that we were lost in the dunes, and had started signaling. In two hours we had all gathered round the beacon, like moths, glad enough that we were not to be compelled to spend the night in the desert cold.

Returning, however, we found the disquieting news that nearly two thirds of our gasoline deposited along the route by camel caravan, had evaporated, due to damage to the cans. The French authorities, however, came to our rescue, and wirelessed orders to the military posts along the way to the Hoggar to supply us with gasoline, even to the extent of all their stores. They also placed army food at our disposal, against emergency.

To raise our spirits, perhaps, Commandant Belaudon, Chief of the Sahara forces, and the officers of the post, entertained us, and our talk turned to Scott and Amundsen, and not without reason, for it was cold under the stars. When we turned our headlights on to the sand it might well have been the frozen north, the illusion was so complete.

The sand dunes growl and grumble under the changing temperatures, as the millions of particles contract and expand, and set up friction. One heard the desert speak, as it has spoken to many an explorer not so well situated as we were. It is difficult to describe the many voiced sands. The Tuaregs say it is the call of the evil spirits, or the moan of lost souls wandering over this earthly hell.

The rocks speak, also, from the same cause. The ancients used the natural phenomena to produce their oracles, and to impress the superstitious with awe of their divinities. There are supposed to be stones of that type in the Hoggar, which may give us a little sidelight on certain traditions and legends that come from that region.

We left Ouargla, oriental and many coloured, with shadows mixing with half lights, and the colours fading into the sands, to press on to Hassi Inifel, where the tombs of the massacred White Fathers lie side by side. The Arabs call them the "marabouts of the Sahara," the saints of the desert, but it is sometimes dangerous to be a Christian in this neighbourhood. Then we went along the great Ergs to In-Salah.

We were five days late at In-Salah, for two reasons. One that the going was a little hard in places, and the other that we made discoveries that would have merited a much longer stop. On our way down, we found many new and interesting inscriptions and relics of the Libyan people. In the most desolate spot imaginable, on a barren brownstone cliff, overlooking the desert, we located a connecting link between the Libyans and the mysterious white people of the Hoggar. Above the bed of the Aolgui river, we found scores of inscriptions in Tifinar, the language of the Hoggar, which is closely related to Libyan.

The great cliff might well be called the mountain of love, for, deeply cut in the floors of the caves were inscriptions indicating that the place had been used as a tribal trysting place centuries ago. Here, the young men and maidens of the original inhabitants left their messages of devotion, their proposals of marriage, and their rejection. Belaid, our interpreter, translated the messages for us. Some are signed in masculine names, others in feminine names. They are human, terse, and to the point.

One woman said "I Beltaim proclaim my love for Lili," and another, evidently despairing, message, to an unsuccessful lover read "I surely have said all I can to you."

Near to these love messages in stone were found peculiar sculptures, crude but distinguishable, depicting feet, in pairs. On the sheer edge of the chasm, a man's foot and a woman's were outlined in the rock. Evidently they were a sign of betrothal, for not infrequently names are inscribed in the spaces enclosed.

Maurice Reygasse was of the opinion that they are formal notices of betrothal, having their origin in a tribal custom. When a maiden was pursued by her suitors, she ran to the edge of the cliff, and poised there in a pretence of throwing herself over. The favoured suitor caught her, and embraced her, etching the outlines of their feet, to inform the tribe he had won her.

These inscriptions, which bear every evidence of great age, were covered by a deep layer of crumbled rock, and though we are at present unable to make an accurate estimate of their period, it is believed by the scientists with us that they date from the earliest years of the Christian era.

The important point in connection with their discovery, apart from their human interest, lay in the fact that they are three hundred miles further north than any Tifinar writings hitherto discovered. They also stand as a mute testimony to a life that had place for romance, in a region now utterly barren and forbidding. The geologists are inclined to weigh this evidence as being in favour of the belief that the desert was not always the desolate stretch we had just crossed.

Three miles away from the trysting mountain, we found caves on whose walls were rock sculptures of camels and gazelles.

This discovery of inscriptions and cave pictures was the climax of the thousand miles of exploration which lay behind us at that point. Along the route were found many prehistoric sites, confirming our hope that in the inner reaches of Africa the deserts will show much light on the nursery of humanity. At nearly every halt we gathered specimens of neolithic weapons and implements, and sometimes we found ornaments of fossilised ostrich shells.

En route we had minor difficulties and major pleasures. Everywhere the tribes were cordial, and the Caids gave us lavish hospitality. The trails were by no means easy to follow, even with compasses, for the desert plays tricks, and it was easy to travel in a circle if observations were suspended for only a little while. Trying to make up time and to reach In-Salah before nightfall, we passed through a little crossroad oasis, the meeting point of indistinct trails, and we lost our way. The drifting sand had completely obliterated the route, and we took a course by compass, but it was only after many hours of wandering in the desert that the French garrison saw our beacon flashing, and sent out an escort which guided us to the fortress wall, through the unending dunes of a country without relief and without landmark.

After In-Salah we were out of touch with civilisation which perhaps served us well, under the circumstances, for when we reached Tamanrasset we were greeted with a solicitude that was more than a welcome. We had got away from In-Salah too early to receive messages that had been relayed to us advising us of the possible presence of an armed force of raiders nearly two hundred strong. We had missed them, however, and our journey had been undisturbed by the thought of impending attack.

The message which awaited us told of five hundred rebel raiders moving on the Hoggar from Southern Morocco, the strongest armed force loose in the desert since the war, and that their probable route would cross the trail of our expedition before we reached Tamanrasset, at a considerable distance from an outpost.

The French authorities regarded the raiders as a manifestation against the administration, and purely military in character, its object being to steal cattle and camels from the region south of Tamanrasset. It is known, however, that a considerable body of banditti were with the raiders, and the French had dispatched, before our arrival, a well disciplined body of loyal Tuaregs, to intercept the foragers.

Meanwhile, we had been exploring parts of the Tanezrouft areas, to study ancient Tifinar inscriptions, and to follow up reports of ruined cities. We collected certain evidences which need close investigation and comparison before they permit any definite statement, but it was possible to say that, at least, we had found clues that indicate the possible influence of Carthaginian civilisation even so far south as this.

The Tanezroufts are actually deserts within the desert, vast and pitiless. One passed through them as quickly as might be, with stars and compass as sole pathfinders.

Here rises the dread simoun, "the curse of the Sahara," that has buried many a caravan in the cloud-mountain of sand that moves forward at an incredible pace. To go forward under such circumstances is impossible, and the expedition was encamped against the natural enemy as it would have been drawn up against a raid by hostile forces. The sand, driven forward, irresistibly lashed the exposed parts of our bodies, and drew blood on the hands of the camera man. The cars take only a few moments to be half buried.

South of Ouallen, Algeria, the Tanezrouft is about five hundred kilometres in length, while, south of the Hoggar, beginning near the Oued Tafaraset, a similar area of unexplored and desolate land is persistently indicated by the Tuaregs as the site of a great ruined city. We were interested to discover whether the indications had any shred of foundation, and to what period and civilisation the city belongs.

The run from In-Salah to Tamanrasset was, as we had anticipated, the most difficult stretch of our journey, but we had not entirely foreseen the difficulties, with the result that for several days we found ourselves under the necessity of careful rationing, both of food and water. Well after well was dry, and water was scarce. Our food supplies and gasoline were missing, and the trail impossible to follow. It was hardly possible to call it a trail, but that is the vaguest word we have to express that vaguer thing that is only a vanishing track through shifting sand.

This is still the greatest of the dangers of the Sahara. The raiders we should not have minded so much, even had we known they were liable to attack us, for we were prepared against that emergency.

Water is different, for many expeditions have perished from salt poisoning and impure wells. The temptation is to drink the first water that comes to hand. We ourselves found it difficult to refrain until the water was tested, yet a quick drink can mean a quick death. Some of the water is so chemically active that it burns linen, and inflates those who drink it. General Laperrine records having found one well so saturated with saltpeter that they who drank it vomited blood, and Barth has left the most graphic account of the tortures of thirst in his story of exploration in the Fezzar. The Tuaregs call the Tanezrouft "bled el khouf" – the land of fear.

We held out fairly easily, however, and reached the place we had designed for our camp, the village of Arrem In Amegel, whose population belonged to the black Tuaregs. Here there was tumult which became panic as our headlights cut a broad beam through the darkness and lit up the encampment. Gongs clattered and drums boomed, and the braves ran madly through the street of the village, doubtless wondering what had befallen them.

Since we intended to stay the night, however, they had to be propitiated. We were, naturally, carrying novelties as presents to the chief men, and the gift of an automatic torch, that makes its own light, does wonders in the Sahara. When the alarmed natives were reassured, their braves began a ceremonial dance of praise and welcome. The welcome and the dance were long, continuing for some hours. While the festivities were in progress other members of the community brought us offerings, which included a bullock, goats, and chickens. The chief brought his six wives to keep us company, and they sat around, curiously and solemnly watching the members of the expedition eat. When the meal was over, the women took up the dance, which would have continued all night, had not our interpreter diplomatically persuaded them to leave us in peace.

Just short of the Hoggar we passed through the gorge of Arak, which the Tuaregs believe is haunted by evil spirits. Actually, the place was for many years the stronghold of brigands.

We found neither spirits nor brigands, but we did find the trail nearly impassable, with fallen rocks and uprooted trees covering it in many places, and making it necessary for us to build a new road as we advanced.

We hoped to reach Tamanrasset early in the day, but dusk was falling as we entered, and our searchlight caused another flutter among the natives, this time not one of alarm, for the fort was prepared for our arrival. The roll of drums here was one of welcome, and the whole village gathered round the cars, to shake hands with us, everyone individually, and at the gate of the French fortress our party was received formally by the two officers who were stationed there, while a guard of honour drawn from the Tuaregs presented arms.

The morning after our arrival, with M. Reygasse, and assisted by the Chiefs and the French Commandant, I placed the bronze wreath of the expedition on the tomb of Père de Foucauld and General Laperrine, those two men who did so much for exploration and the pacification of the Sahara. Père de Foucauld was murdered in 1916 by "anti-Allies." It is better to say it so. The tribes came from the east to remove the influence of a great man who was doing a steady and successful work in the consolidation of peace and loyalty to the French administration. General Laperrine, to whom the peaceful government of the territory is largely due, died after years of self sacrifice, the victim of an accident.

The scene was impressive, both in its colour and its significance, for these two men are now of the saints of the Sahara, according to the natives. They have been elevated to the local calendar of the "marabouts."

All the Tuareg chiefs of the vicinity were present, headed by Amenokal Akhamouk, the king of all the Hoggar. With them were the French forces, headed by Commandant Count Beaumont, and a detail of veiled Tuaregs saluted the graves.

At this point our expedition divided. M. Reygasse and Sir Alonzo M. Pond went north, to accomplish a long planned study in detail of the mysterious veiled Tuaregs, both on the ethnographical and historical side, and King Amenokal was with them.

With a few other members of the party, my road lay south. A body of twenty Tuaregs was detailed to accompany us, and our objective was the full investigation of a vast pyramidical mound located in the southern stretch of the range, among peaks seven thousand feet high. As each of the four sides of the pyramid is twenty feet high, it was a matter of considerable difficulty to remove the quarried stones, but they have been placed there, on a terrace over a yard high. The structure is probably the tomb of an early Libyan ruler. Fragments of ancient pottery in the neighbourhood point to a similarity to the relics of the Carthaginian empire which we have already discovered in our five years' excavation at Carthage.

Unfortunately, though we had made preparations for a longish stay in Tamanrasset, we found that our stores had not arrived, and we were compelled to subsist on the scanty stores of the military post, and native supplies.

Before we left for the pyramid our couriers had not returned, so we were somewhat in doubt, not only as regards our supplies, but also as regards the armed force from Southern Morocco. The raiders are an elusive people, for they travel on mehari, those thoroughbreds of the desert, camels that can travel a hundred miles at a stretch without undue effort. That is the strength of the brigands; they are so mobile that they may be reported a hundred miles away, yet with the dawn they will make their swoop, and be away again, lost in the sands to pursuers but safely on their own way. Their day is rapidly passing however, for the Tuaregs as a whole are unwavering in their loyalty, and the French are thoroughly capable of maintaining peace.

Chapter 19

THE ANCIENT TOMBS OF THE SAHARA

The work with the Tuaregs and on the tomb of Tamanrasset terminated, our next great objective was the finding of the tomb of Queen Tin Hinan said to lie on the road to the Sudan.

During our stay in the mysterious Hoggar Land I had enquired into the legend of Tin Hinan from the Tuaregs and they were unanimous in declaring that the great monument at Abelessa was the tomb of the "mother of all the Tuaregs," Queen Tin Hinan.

The finding of the Tomb took several days, for the Tuaregs were suspicious of our intent. The negroes, however, on being asked where was the great tomb answered by a pointing of the hand in the direction South. This was the way we found the location of the vast mound. How many people have asked me, "How did you know where to go to dig?" "A few legends, a few records of travellers and six-wheel cars that can travel 200 miles a day, and a lot of luck and there you are!" I announced.

The distance from Tamanrasset to Abelessa is about 80 kilometers – due south east. We passed through a wild volcanic region before reaching the river Tit. The Tomb is on a small hill at the confluent of two rivers and is backed by the stupendous panorama of the Hoggar Massive.

It was not unduly easy to get away from Tamanrasset, for the natives were gradually evidencing their trading instincts, and looking around for the little plunder that alone remains to them after the lessons in pacifism taught by the French. We found the same characteristics, however, they will drive what they con-

sider a shrewd bargain, and will barter to the very point of dis-
honesty, and then – be fairly honest. Just as the warrior Tuaregs
will not leave a raided caravan without some means of subsis-
tence, however slender, so they left us with a possible satisfaction of not having been entirely overcome in bargaining. I have
said previously that the Tuaregs, in their simple and direct code
of what is ethical, and what is not, do not descend to petty thiev-
ing, but consider an armed foray as part of their virile existence.
One thing I omitted to say is that when they have launched a
successful raid they do not strip the victim of his last bidon of
water nor his last morsel of food. It is not necessarily murder
they are after, it is plunder, legitimate plunder in accordance
with their heritage; confiscation, it might be called, were the
objective an aeroplane in difficulties on alien territory. So,
unless it seems strategic or essential to do otherwise, the victim's
life is spared and with it enough food and water for him to reach
a source of supply, by exercising due caution and conservatism.

That is gone, for the moment, but they practiced the same
rudimentary tactics on us. When they thought we were escaping
them – they seemed to believe that we should never go away
again, at first – they brought around their matting, their basket
work, and their worn out pipes and knives, their peculiar combination locks and wailing flutes, rings of brass and silver, their
armlets, even rawhide powder boxes and their purses, made
from the undressed and untrimmed skin of domestic animals.
We had to fight a little for the crude silver ornaments they wore,
for the metal is rare in the country, and emblematic of position
and beauty, and though the face of the ornament was often
roughly but painstakingly chiseled we found that the backs were
eked out by the lids of beef and other tins discarded by the military authorities. Impeding our progress were piles of bags, and
pouches, saddles, old flint locks and assegais, wooden spoons,
daggers, with native handles and blades made in Sheffield,
camel manicure sets – peculiar these, that resembled a combination knife and fork more than anything else, and which are used
to trim the pads of the camels and to extract flints and thorns

from the feet – even the domestic pillow cases, emptied of their grass stuffing.

One had to be watchful, just the same, in the midst of the bargaining, for the Tuareg positively refuses to barter. We had gone prepared to trade, but goods for goods did not appeal, they wanted, and they finally got, cash for goods. Their position was justified, for we had not the slightest intention of carrying back the items of trade, and they found their way gratis into the possession of the chiefs.

Our cartridges were especially surveyed. We lost a few. . .the Tuareg knows better than to steal a gun, but cartridges have a moral. To steal them and to hide them means that so many fewer shots can be fired at the natives should there ever be any breach in the existing peaceful condition, and the Tuareg has his own variation of the proverb "a stitch in time."

The trading took place near the well in the patio, and we were compelled at last to start the motors before the bargainers would cease. All the time, in wide eyed amazement a tame gazelle stood by, watching us and occasionally sniffing at the items for sale. He sniffed once, only, and took a rest, for which no one could blame him, but curiosity brought him back again.

At the risk of running down one or two of the traders, we moved off, and within a few yards we had lost sight of Tamanrasset; it simply faded into the sand, only to be distinguished by the slender masts supporting the wireless aerial.

The town, save the word, consists of a settlement which, if it rained, would disappear, leaving the five hundred inhabitants homeless, but it doesn't rain. Everything, including Fort Laperrine, and the officers' quarters is of mud; low lying hutments, the best of which have a rough framework of twisted tree-trunks, and all baked to the colour of the sand. As a settlement, the post covers about two hundred and the fort about two acres of ground. Yet here men are assuredly weaving the network of civilisation, are laying foundation for a forward march that needs only imagination to be carried to great advantage. There is water at Tamanrasset, lots of water, and with time and organisation that part of the desert could, and probably will, blossom in abundance.

Our objective was Abelessa on the Oued Tit, where rumour, founded on practical observation, located a giant tomb. We had had much conversation concerning this tomb, which fitted in with the legends of the neighbourhood in a manner that left us no alternative but to take the hundred mile journey to confirm or otherwise all we had heard.

On account of the supply caravans being late, we were short of provisions of all kinds, food, oil, equipment and gasoline, so we had drained all the cars to give one car a chance to get through, the others to follow with stores as soon as the caravan reached Tamanrasset. Progress was not fast, and it took us some two hours to reach Tit, a scattered group of grass huts in the midst of the normal Oued vegetation, which is coarse grass, with an occasional scrubby tree very much resembling an Australian pine. We had no time for the cordial greeting of the natives, some six or eight of whom we saw, as time was precious. All we could do, and it seemed to be much, looking back on it, was to hand them our empty sardine tins, which they licked with a relish that was almost unbelievable.

Tit is a tiny little cultivated spot, the natives raising meagre crops of vegetables, and one or two scrubby chickens, but it has an advantage far excelling most of the fertile spots in the region. It has a minute stream, flowing in the open, which is something like a foot wide and about eight inches deep, carefully cleaned out and cherished. It has also a unique irrigation system, the like of which I have not seen elsewhere. It is primitive, but entirely pragmatic. There is a well there, which is in constant operation. An old native pesters the life out of a docile steer, whose daily lot it is to walk along a straight track, and back again, hour after hour, day after day, and when he dies as some day he will from sheer boredom if from nothing else, there will be another to take his place. But he performs useful work while he lives, for he hauls up a skinful of water every journey, and the ingenious natives have dispensed with the boy at the well who should tip up the skin into the trough. A crude projection catches the lip of the skin, and tips the water into the trough, whence it runs through the ditches. The old negro who drives the steer, knowing to a pace the length of his stretch, promptly turns the beast around, and lets the skin drop back to be hauled up again and the same performance repeated.

From Tit we drove north for two or three kilometres and took a course south-west on the Sudan road toward Abelessa, but, as only we knew the road and were expecting the other cars to follow, it was essential that we make our own sign posts along the way. This we did by building a cairn of stones, with a note containing instructions wedged down on the top.

Night fell with considerable abruptness, and with night-fall the flies deserted us. Throughout the day flies were with us interminably, they were persuasive, insinuating, tame things with an intimate approach beyond anything I know in the insect world. Confiding too, for they could be killed in hordes, but it was futile to kill, there were millions more. But, if the sun went down at five forty-five, at five forty-six the flies had gone, where, no one knows, but they were gone, and we were able to camp, cook, and sleep without disturbance.

We camped having made about sixty kilometres, and for the site chose the only tree stump within a radius of three or four miles. That tree stump will serve no other expedition, but it made a good fire.

Martini, our chauffeur, as spirited as his namesake, and as good a precursor to a meal, cooked a magnificent repast; lentils in the frying pan, with plenty of water, which gave us lentil soup, and then lentils. He sliced tomatoes, which he dropped into the frying pan with some olive oil, then broke eggs in it, making a toothsome dish. Bread (soggy) and red wine with water were supplemented by coffee. The coffee was unroasted; it always is in this country, and has to be prepared for each meal. Martini roasted the beans on a shovel, over a fire in the sand, dried it on his ground cloth, which was an old tent drop, and ground it by pounding it with the handle of a hammer in a mortar which was his own tin cup. All the same, it tasted like coffee.

We made our camp against the wind, which was coming from the southwest, but before nine-thirty it had changed completely, and we were compelled to remake camp. We had already crossed the Tropic of Cancer, but that night was the coldest we had experienced. Our elevation was somewhere about 5,000 feet. The wind was chilling, it was necessary for us to cover up completely against it. I think we did manage to keep our noses out but that was about all.

With dawn we were up, and drank the warmed over coffee, then Chapuis went ahead searching for game. We caught him about eight o'clock, empty handed, but an hour or two later he sighted gazelle and got one.

We passed the fringe of Abelessa and from the scattered huts, made of rushes lashed together with still more rushes, one or two natives watched us, but not for long. They refused to pay much attention to us, for that was the day they were working on their community gardens, little stretches of land, as yet not planted, but being prepared for irrigation.

Here we crossed the Oued, and went directly south to the tomb, under the direction of Chapuis, who had scouted in this neighborhood in the time of General Laperrine.

Between Abelessa and Silet, we reached our objective on the Oued Tit which here is a very wide sandy bottom, whose sides are well screened by ragged bush, gnarled and brittle, yet green with scanty needle-like foliage. There is no water apparent here, but the natives have dug deep holes, about two metres long by a metre wide, and two or three metres deep, in a broken chain across the Oued. The water is warm, a foot or two deep, and moving sluggishly, which leads to the conclusion that it is a well defined, subterranean river, capable of supporting a considerable amount of vegetation. In fact, I believe that an oasis of some magnitude might be created here.

The tomb stood on the north side of the Oued, the stream at that point flowing west. From the more definitely marked course of the stream, stretching back for most of a quarter of a mile was a level patch of sandy earth, which corresponds well with the customary wash of a large river, and thinly covered by a tall, stiff, hard, fibrous vegetation not unlike bunch grass, heavily knuckled. The grass has a source of nourishment, for though it is dry enough to serve as kindling for fires, it still has green shoots at the tips. Moving through the grass, which we did on foot, we came to a low range of hillocks which seemed imposing by contrast with the flat area we had just left. From the flat to the site of the temple-tomb was perhaps a hundred and fifty feet high, but exceedingly difficult of approach on account of the jagged and slippery formation of the hillside. To give a picture of the approach, perhaps it will suffice to say that the slopes seemed to have been covered by a multitude of small boulders, tightly packed, and baked black. So far the agglomeration was obviously of natural formation, and not the work of man. But surmounting this rocky approach, in majesty hard to describe, was one tremendous aggregation of huge blocks of sombre stone, which, for how many centuries has withstood the attacks of the storms of the Tanezrouft, the disintegrating forces of great changes of temperature, averaging fifty degrees fahrenheit from noon to midnight day by day, as well as the spasmodic ravages of predatory nomads.

Without destroying, all these forces had helped to ruin the original exactitude of design, without detracting either from its imposing grandeur or diminishing the testimony to the patient and skilled labour of what must have been a great people.

After our first awe, close examination revealed that the temple-tomb rested on a flat base, which looked to have been constructed for the purpose, although there remained, so far as we could see, few, if any, evidences of paving.

Rising sheer from the base, though littered by the débris of centuries was a gigantic principal tomb surrounded irregularly by sixteen smaller tombs. The architecture and design of all the tombs, greater and smaller, bore striking resemblance to the

"Tombeau de la Chretienne," which was, roughly in the form of the old straw beehive.

The tombs were composed of stones laid in a kind of Flemish bond, but no traces of cement or mortar were then discerned.

On the north side, the principal tomb had suffered the least damage and it was possible to recognize the skilled craftsmanship of the builders. This wall, relatively intact, rose some twenty to twenty-five feet from the base, but what was the type of the superstructure, or how much higher it carried, it is not possible to say, for the roof had at some time caved in, and the whole area was littered by a great mass of loose rocks, hewn boulders, and sand. The outer walls of the tomb must have covered an area of sixty by ninety feet, and later we discovered that the walls themselves were about three feet thick at the highest remaining point. The walls of the smaller tombs were from eighteen inches to two feet thick.

It must be carried in mind, however, that when we first attacked the tomb, as a scouting party, none of this was evident, save the one North wall, which was of comparatively easy access. What we first came upon was a great pile of rocks, into which has filtered the sand of the Tanezroufts and the accumulation of ages whose extent we do not know, as yet.

We got the lead, however, that first day, almost on the first flush of the day, and promptly dispatched a messenger to the Caid. Nothing could be attempted without his co-operation, and while we were making our preliminary examination he arrived. He was by no means the picturesque figure of the type of the northern Caids, but a swarthy black, with a very keen eye to the main chance. We informed him that we needed workers, at once, and he delegated a runner to round up a score of men for us, whom we engaged at the usual rate of pay. One is almost afraid to mention the rate, for it might precipitate international labour troubles, but we paid what was demanded, and it seemed to be a most highly satisfactory sum. It was actually less than one cent per day per man, and it is impossible to work more cheaply than that.

We had the men at work before we made our temporary camp, and by mid-afternoon the dust of ages was pouring out of the ruin, like smoke from a volcano. But that was the first day. We had our subsequent troubles, not unknown in the region of solid labour.

Then, we dressed Chapuis' gazelle, and hung the strips of venison on the bushes to cure in the sunlight.

The tomb of Tin Hinan, reputed to be the burial place of the legendary ancestress and goddess of the Kings of the Hoggar, was not the first ancient tomb we had excavated. It is, however, without doubt the most outstanding discovery made by the expedition, and may lead to a documentation of Saharan civilization which up to the present has been lacking, and the full contribution to be made must have influence in solving many problems, ethnographical and even geographical.

The expedition has, at least, accumulated evidence which largely assures us in the belief that we have established the trade routes of the Phoenicians, and that Carthaginian influence extended into the very heart of the Hoggar many centuries before Christ.

The first tomb we had excavated, before reaching our objective at Abalessa, was a smaller mound of rough stonework, similar in type, but less imposing, to that of Tin Hinan. This tomb we found in the Oued Tadent, some fifteen kilometres east of Tamanrasset, in territory not yet mapped. It was composed of a mass of loose stones piled to a height of about three and a half metres, and with a perimeter of a hundred and twenty metres, obviously of human construction, the stones being unlike any found in the immediate vicinity.

All that remains is a gigantic mass of loose rocks which on a proportionate estimate numbered one hundred and fifty to two hundred thousand separate pieces. This estimate was arrived at by the careful count of the contents of a cubic metre and the survey of the full dimensions of the tombs. The very collection and placement of the stones must have occupied considerable time and a large body of men, and we are inclined to believe that the tomb is that of an exalted personage dating from the earliest Tuaregs, or more probably before their association with the district.

For the excavation of the pile, we engaged a number of natives, who began to work on the tomb on the fifth of November. It took us three days of heavy and painstaking work to strike a six foot trench straight through the mass to the centre at ground level.

From the centre of the tomb we succeeded in recovering objects which are now being considered by the French scientific authorities. The body and objects were found in a roughly made sepulchre about two feet above ground level, and we took away a skull and earrings, and what may possibly be a nose ring.

Some rough effort had been made, it seemed, to erect a burial chamber of larger stones before the great mass of boulders was deposited.

For us, however, the experience of the burial mound was invaluable. In the first place it gave us an idea of the great labour that was necessary to reach our objectives, and at the same time it told us something of the rough architecture of the builders.

Therefore, when we came to the tomb at Abelessa we were not entirely unprepared.

Not entirely unprepared, it is true, but there are times when preparations go astray. We had reached the end of our outward journey, and we had seen the tomb, but the background was not very hopeful. As I have said even to get one car, with the four members of the expedition already mentioned, to the place, we had had to take every drop of gasoline and every drop of oil we had. The other two cars were useless at Tamanrasset, and our supply caravan was three weeks behind schedule.

At Abelessa we had for stores the remnants of our beans which were running low, and a few eggs that we were able to get from the natives. Our coffee and sugar were gone, and for two days we were on very short rations. A camel load of provisions was sent out from Tamanrasset two days later, but either the camel was a weak one, or we were very hungry men, for provisions ran down again, and it was ultimately decided that while M. Chapuis and I stayed to superintend the work Mr. Tyrrell and the chauffeur should drive in to the fort and see if our supplies had arrived. For five days our supplies had been gazelle and beans, but gazelle only lasts three days (in the desert).

Those five days were not without their excitement, however, for we worked ourselves literally to a standstill alternating between hope and doubt, a hope that ultimately justified itself in the most spectacular manner.

Just as at the sepulchre in Oued Tadent, our first task was the removal of the mass of stones from the top of the tomb, that we might make an entry into the chambers. There were many indications which told that the mound at Abelessa covered more than one tomb, and we took rough sondages to give us a lead for concentrated work, and laid bare the walls of a chamber on the south-west corner. Here the walls were well marked and of regular formation, and enclosed a room slightly more than five by four metres and two metres deep.

As soon as we reached regular masonry, sieving had to begin, lest small, but important, objects be lost. Our sieves were few in number, so we fell back on the mesh coverings we had used for the protection of our food against the flies. As a practical point, I might say that the meat covers served exceedingly well.

During the whole of the operations a strong hot wind blew, which played with the fine dust so that before work was far ahead it was almost impossible to distinguish between us and the native helpers we had rounded up. When work was finished we washed but the natives, probably philosophically, simply rubbed the dust off, believing doubtless that there would be as much more on the morrow, and of course they were right. The dust was incredibly fine, so pulverised that it rolled away on the wind in a fog that actually served as a guide to our reinforcements, who could clearly distinguish our cloud from a distance of four kilometres.

In this room, then, by slow degrees, we discovered the last resting place of a personage of considerable importance. The bones were later identified by Dr. Gabrielle Nicolle (Aide-Major) at In-Salah as being those of a woman, an opinion supported by his colleague at Ouargla. We ourselves were not in a position to make such identification, but the natives were extremely excited, convinced that we were disturbing Tin Hinan herself, their ancestress and legendary goddess.

Their superstitions and fears seemed to be on the point of realisation, for they were driven into an angry panic by a thunderstorm that broke with dramatic suddenness; the flashing lightning and intermittent splashes of rain drove the negroes to shelter. Storms are rare, and according to Tuareg mythology the dead are under the protection of demi-gods, djinns who live in fire, control thunder and lightning and once made the mountains flame. When the black labourers saw the lightning curling around Mount Ilaman they flatly refused to continue, and one ran excitedly among his companions screaming that the djinn were avenging the sacrilege of the tomb of Tin Hinan. But the storm quickly passed, and the negroes, finding themselves whole, returned to their homes in a calmer state of mind.

The floor of the room was of rough stones and clay, resting on large slabs of stone, nine in number and of varying size and thickness, the largest being 1.70 metres long by .75 metres wide and .20 metres thick. On removing some of the smaller slabs we were able to reach the actual burial place, which, however, was completely filled by sand and clay. When measured the tomb was found to be 2.30 metres long by 1.40 wide and 1.50 metres high. Along the partition was matting to the height of about a metre, and in the centre of the enclosure was the bier.

The body lay face upwards, the head slightly raised, supported by a piece of sculptured wood, looking towards the east. The legs were folded back and slightly crossed, and the arms folded on the breast.

A leather shroud, which crumbled on the slightest touch, was thrown over the skeleton, and a large quantity of jewelry of a design which spoke of considerable culture was still in position.

Whoever the personage was, whether Tin Hinan or one of her peers, she had been given the utmost honour in her death. Her jewelry was indicative of her rank, and in the antechamber of her tomb lay her clothing neatly piled, and ready for her use beyond the shadows. Here were garments of leather, painted red and yellow, as well as clothing of cotton and other fabrics, in various colours, ornamented by intricate fringes. No weapons were found, but food for her journey was by her, dates dried to the thinnest film of skin on the stone, and a store of what looked to have been grapes, together with jars of grain.

As we worked, two scorpions, the last guardians of the royal mausoleum, scurried away out of the ancient dust at our feet and fled through the cracks in the walls.

Careful examination of the mould that covered the body revealed scores of cornelian and turquoise beads and the golden stars of a necklace that was composed of a hundred or more items; mixed with these were beads in amazonite, garnet, gold and silver, and two of glass, painted in the semblance of a trinity of eyes. From these last beads we obtained the first suggestion of a probable date of the tomb. They are identical with the amulets of the third and fourth centuries B.C. discovered in the excavations we have made at Carthage at the sanctuary of Tanit, when Greek bead making there was declining.

Proceeding carefully, we uncovered the most striking sight of all. Each arm was freighted with massive bracelets, decorated with beads and circles. In all, fifteen bracelets were worn, seven on the left arm and eight on the right.

The metals we have not yet been able to identify. It may be that some are of an alloy of silver and others of an alloy of gold. They have not quite the correct colour or ring, however, and I am inclined to believe that they are alloyed with antimony, for we know that the Carthaginians made much use of antimony, cunningly combining it with gold to increase its bulk and hardness. They obtained antimony from a secret source in central Africa, carrying it to Carthage on caravans of humped, horned oxen, possibly passing over the trail we ourselves had taken, down the Oued Tit, past Tin Hinan's tomb to the Sudan.

If metallurgists support my idea that the bracelets of Tin Hinan contain antimony, we have one of the most important links between the civilisations of the North with the Southern Sahara that can be found. Certainly there is little room for doubt that we have worked over the route by which the Carthaginians brought their ivory, gold, gems and slaves from Central Africa, and along which merchants went to exchange beads and jewelry for the gold dust in the possession of the natives.

It may have been in such trading that the personage we have exhumed obtained the wealth of Carthaginian objects found.

As M. Chapuis removed the bracelets, and began disengaging the bones it was found that the weight of jewelry and of years had broken several of the ribs of the skeleton, but the bones came out in excellent condition, and further work revealed the remains of the bier.

This was an elaborately carved wooden couch, much decayed, and crumbling, but it was possible to reconstruct the pomp of the day it was placed there. The fauteuil had been heavily decorated, painted red and yellow and silver, and the head and foot were curved, and of a latticed motive, topped by moulding of good workmanship closely resembling the ornamentation still used by the Tuaregs on their scabbards.

The wood, however, was in such a fragile condition that it was not possible to remove it intact, and all that could be done was to collect the pieces still holding together, in the hope of partial reconstruction.

There still remain many rooms to be explored, probably seven or eight, and we are led to believe that the central room will contain an even more remarkable documentation of the civilisation of the Hoggar region, since so far as we can see it is the principal chamber of the temple tomb. The contents of the one room completed urge the final and thorough excavation of the whole.

All the objects found are now being considered by the scientists of France, and a considered judgment will be forthcoming shortly.

One discovery, which is almost unique in archaeological research was the small, crudely carved statuette, which had been called the "Libyan Venus." This was in the antechamber above the tomb, and must antedate the sepulchre considerably. It is a worked stone, about the size of the flat of the hand, roughly conforming to the human, female form, grossly distorted and disproportionate, with a clothes-peg head and stump arms outstretched. Almost lacking in trunk, but with crudely marked breast, the statuette accentuated the hips, which form the base of an inverted triangle, almost equilateral, the legs being represented by the slightest possible division of the apex of the triangle.

This statuette may be aurignacian, it certainly is influenced by the aurignacian period, and may date as far back as a hundred thousand years before Christ. The tomb is unquestionably very considerably later, and the statuette cannot be considered as an indication of the period of Hoggar civilisation. What is possible, however, is that the "venus" has been a family heirloom, handed down from generation to generation, finally to be lodged in this tomb, perhaps embodying occult powers in the mind of the inhabitants.

If the expedition had discovered nothing more than this small object, from a scientific standpoint the whole enterprise would have been justified. So far as I am aware there are only two others of its nature in existence, and neither is of so advanced an art. Here we have the very beginnings of the craving of human nature for sculptured representation of life, and I believe that with the facts now discovered we can go much further forward in the scientific documentation of the least known of the great fields of the world.

We had to leave much work to be done, for the schedule of our tour was considerably overreached, and the rest must remain for a later expedition.

The natives resented our disturbance of the tomb, and the black chief of Abelessa arrived one day, just as we were finishing off, to protest that we had removed large quantities of treasure. He arrived as some of us were cleaning the bracelets, but, to avert possible trouble, we told him that the bracelets were of brass and iron, and he went off. The dislike shown by the blacks is due more to the fear that we have come in, and discovered a treasure that has lain in their territory for countless years, rather than for any reverence for the dead. The blacks in this region are entirely different from the white nobles of the Tuaregs, and the sepulchre has had no significance whatever for them.

That is, it had none, until they knew it was a tomb and the thunderstorm came.

Our three-weeks late caravan arrived finally, and we stocked up, and began our homeward journey. Further excavation is only deferred, for it is probable that other bodies, possibly those of Queen Tin Hinan's nobles, lie under the same mound of stones, circled by the volcanic peaks of the Hoggar in the heart of the great Sahara.

Printed in the United Kingdom
by Lightning Source UK Ltd.
9806800001B/80